D0197519

Bliss and Blessings

the DIVINE ALCHEMY
OF THE
STAR FLOWER AND GEMSTONE ESSENCES

Star Riparetti

Laughing Star Press

Bliss = Perfect Joy. Gladness
Blessing = Good Fortune

Bliss and Blessings to everyone who reads these words.

Please Note:
Star Essences mainly address consciousness and evolution. We do not make any medical claims. If you have a physical healing while taking the essences (and it happens all the time) we won't take any responsibility.

© Star Riparetti 2003
First Printing 3/2003

All rights reserved. Please share this book. If you reprint parts of it, please ask. I'm sure we will say yes.

Computer formatting and wizardry
by Linda Trujillo and Lou de Bourbon
Proofreading genius by Jem Robinson
Book cover design by Linda Trujillo
and Star Riparetti.
Many editors listed in acknowledgements
Printing by A & G Graphics Moorpark, CA

Published by Laughing Star Press
312 W. Yanonali St.
Santa Barbara, California 93101

Library of Congress
Control Number 2003091352
ISBN 1 892457-08-3

www.staressence.com

Dedicated to
Roger Valencia,
St. Martin, Master Kuthumi

Who well could be all one and the same…

Acknowledgements

A tidal wave of Love- in fact, **a Tsunami of Love and Infinite Appreciation**- from me, goes out to:
Pam Oslie, Aanjelae Rhoads, Debra Farris, Linda Taylor and Jeanette- 11:11, Marjorie Shepherdson, Renee Sundarum, Brenda Montgomery, Joleth Lindsey, Angel Eileen Kianna, Shamballa who casually left me a message once with the words Bliss and Blessings in it. I have adopted it - scooped them up and made them a mantra. Michael Bromley, Cerena for having classes. Everyone who has ever given or lent me money or helped me to borrow it, (the list is vast)- thank you. Alison Stone for giving me money once that I kept for a long time in the drawer. Knowing it was there helped my mental health, knowing I wasn't completely broke. Flo Free, Russel Bayly and anonymous friends- Thank you for the loans. Noraleigh (Diane Alison) for giving me $500 so I could buy stamps and envelopes for my Christmas mailing in 1995, at a time when she was living in her van with her 10-year-old daughter. Many others along the way… Ros Segal for always coming in for a big order right when I need the money the most and for continuously being an inspiration. (and for supplying me with an awesome cabin to do some of the writing of this book in…) Thank you for your generosity to the world. Shilea and Zandriel, initial encouragement and setting the business up as Light in the beginning. Jeanne Housebrook, Mira El- angelic presence- and co-creator of the Angel meetings for 2½ years. Dr. Bach of course, Saint Germain, Carmel Denton, Ken Kalb, Paula Vigneault, SuRay Raycraft, Lou de Bourbon and Linda Trujillo for their stellar graphic acuity formatting this book, Barbara Queen, Esta Stough, Roland Reed, Robert Tennyson Stevens, Larry Lopez who was the Angel that was there at closing time nearly every night that I worked and closed late at Riparetti's for 8 years. Lilac, Magic Heart kitty. Ruby, Peggy Lane, Sandra Marshall, Phil and Barbara Olsen, Kathryne Alexis, John Steele for his contributions to the world especially of flowers, Aluna Joy Yaxkin, Dan Cummings, Mer Cailliet, Randy Ridder, Matthew Morgan, Thad and Lynn Snyder, Mark Richman, Nicky Phillips, Michelle Fulton, Becca Ellis, Rick French- in his own way, Sofia Van Surksum and Calvin Cooke who traded me a Volvo (which was SO perfect at the time) for flower essences.

Prosperity comes in many fabulous ways. Susan Winter Ward, Dianne Summers Pendergras and our favorite Apricot tree that kept all our secrets, Dr. Jesshill Love, Great name…James T. McClintock, M.D. for allowing and for encouraging out-of-the-box behavior- thus making all of my years at the Cancer Foundation fun and fulfilling. Diamond- One time when I was beginning to get tired- this guy- Marty Varble, who worked on oil rigs in Alaska and was also a body alignment practitioner, came to my class for a 2nd time. After the class he called and asked if he could help me out. That took me quite off guard. I kept saying no, I didn't need any help, and he persisted. I really didn't even know what kind of help to ask for. I was used to doing everything myself. I told him I was taking the essences to a little holistic fair they were having at a place called the Green Dragon. He offered to help. He asked if he could come help me load the car- and I said no, just meet me there. (The joke about that is that I really did need help - and for the next 2 years he carried everything.) I didn't think he would show up. Well, guess what- He was there before me and had already gotten logistics taken care of and had done all the parts that I don't like to do. Then he helped set everything up. We had a lot of fun that day- and a spark was ignited. Marty became Diamond on the day his mother left the earth plane- a name she channeled in to him, through me. I was there at the moment she passed over. Diamond was my boyfriend, constant companion, true friend and absolutely dedicated to the Goddess, to me, and to the flowers. He was responsible for getting the essences to a next level at the time. They are so grateful- and I am, too. Angels, Leah McGregor- inspiration- youthing is possible, Katherine Grace, John Cannon, Dale Sundell, Daniel Pry, My uncle Dr. P. Paul (Rip) Riparetti for having such a good reputation, that just by virtue of having that name, doors opened. (And Amelia and Pauline and the rest of the Riparetti's, too.) Each of you who have told friends about the essences and everyone who has attended any classes. Thank you for teaching me. Lea Parker, Ryan Evans, Dr. Clark Gardner, Joy Bondy, Lynn McLaren, Rad Schreiber, Kjerstina Agne, Elisabet Sahtouris, Roger Seamans, Floyd Boyle, Dan Smith, John Eddows, Arvildo, Pamela Stumbaugh, for attuning me to the masters, Mary Staton for her light, Lucky (support from all levels and astrological expertise).

Jem Robinson for proofreading, impeccable eagle eye editing, running the Star Essence business, being nice to everyone- and for dedication. Glorianna and Tim Buynak and Namaste Santuario, Dawn and Dusk those magical times - those Harry Arthur times. Victoria Axton, Gary Mason for starting the Flower Essence Pharmacy and Kathy Kinniard for taking it to the next level and getting flower essences out there, Wynn Garber, Kizuwanda West, Yona Bachrach, Peter Johnson, LaDonna Roles, Danny Posniak, Jess Posniak, Merlin Boone, Kathy Doore for coming and helping us build the labyrinth in Peru, everyone who ever worked for Star Essence, Star Flower Essences and Star Alchemy, Dave Cosmo for creating a one word database so we could function like a real business. It took me years to realize the value and complexity and precision of what he created for me. He made it look so easy- and made it so even I could make it work. Jean Marie Seaton, marvelous marbling teacher, Maria Watkins- for abounding enthusiasm, Morning Flower, for being there at important times, Cara for being my favorite daughter and for helping me for the first couple of years in the office- to get the business going. Bob Peace for always doing electrical magic and other boy stuff around the house and office, my granddaughters Kelsea and Krista for being good reminders of what it's all about (Joy, Bliss, Fun, Play). Danielle Sato for anchoring a peace pole here (and for all the planetary work she consistently does), Wistancia, Azuriel, Anka El, Eric Ederer, Shamara, Gwendolyn Kilfoyle, Lily Bromberg, Virendra and Sia and Miriam, Lesley Myburgh, Puma, Maximo, Joel Mills, Jeda Dolan, Vee and Marvin Banaski, Shawn Tuttle, Genevieve and shining Estella, Rica and Brad, Suki Rayne, Oceanna, John the beloved, Jesus the Christ, Mary the Mother, Bill and Delora Risser for opening up the water store. We use what we consider the best water available. In the very beginning I was willing to drive 60 miles to get it. I am SO grateful to have it right here. (In addition to knowing your essence maker- it is nice to know who is distilling your water.) To my students of course, my greatest teachers who always show up- and often knowing more than I do. Brian Choppin, Nirmoha, my good friend Dr. Margarita Carman for keeping my channels open and clear. A toast to the Devas, and the Overlighting Devas, Pan, Nature, the Flowers, the Giant River

Otters, the Gemstones and YOU. Peter Hurley, Darlene Gary, Sha Ra Na, Vicki Porter-Fink, Caren Abdela, Lynn McClaren, Deb Dobbin, Tim Howell, Norma Howell (thank you for helping me get my first computer), Terry Howell, Archangel Michael, Rad Howell, Tracy and Ganga my first Yoga (and much more) teachers, Jeff Shelton for helping me with the building department, Hank Worrell (who I love working with in construction. I tell him what I want- and he always goes farther and makes it better than I could imagine. He reads my mind better than I do. Makes it so much FUN.) Mom, Dad, Marisa Bean- angelic being of light, Dina Martinez. Loren Lockman, David Wolfe, Jinjee and Storm, for the raw food exposure and making it make sense. Cyndie Jansen, Roger Valencia for everything, Don Dennis, Eduardo Grecco, Tim Tupper- my hero, Linda Snook, all of the Star Essence users who have been super-supportive and anyone who I have forgotten to mention.

I am SO very very Grateful to all of you People who make my heart smile!

....Each of you who have told friends about the essences and everyone who has attended any classes, and everyone who has gone with me to Peru.

Everything about making these essences has been a blissful mission. Many people have shared the bliss with me- and I thank you all for your support. Your notes, e-mails, and phone calls extolling your praise for the Essences are great fuel for this project and continue to shower me with tremendous, wonderful energy.

I Am So Grateful

I Am So Grateful

I Am SO Grateful!

TABLE OF CONTENTS

Part Five ☆ Reference

PREFACE

LET THE FUNSHINE IN

*—And those who were seen dancing were thought to be insane by those who could not hear the music...*Frederick Nietsche

Star Flower Essences expand our capacities to hold the frequency of ecstasy. What that means is that with the help of Nature in the form of vibrational essences, we get to experience more bliss! They move us gently into the higher frequencies that are occurring all around us by feeding our Light Bodies. (Yes, they've been hungry for this vibrational soul food!) Flower essences assist us in going to the next step in our planetary evolution. The one that has been prophesied by nearly every religion and culture and by indigenous people all over the world.

PEACE COMMANDERS ♥ DEPLOY ANGELS

Frequencies of anything less than peace cannot exist in the presence of higher frequencies. It is my opinion that the essences, by raising our frequencies, will help WIN PEACE.

In this book there are several sections. There are stories scattered throughout.

I am writing the first section of the book because I want you to know who is making the Star Essences. I believe in Alchemy and I feel it is important and beneficial to know your Essence maker, as they are part of the alchemical equation of the essence. If you already intuitively resonate, reading this section is not necessary.

IF YOU WANT TO ASK THE QUESTIONS: "HOW DID YOU GET INTO THIS? HOW DID YOU GET STARTED?"

—**THIS** IS THE **LONG ANSWER.** You can fast forward through it- and if you get curious you can come back. Or start from the back. Or read it all. Whatever intrigues you. We all have a different perfect way to evolve. We each add our own spin. I share what has value for me, and trust some parts will resonate with you, and you will spin things to an even higher level...

LOVE LOVE LOVE LOVE LOVE LOVE LOVE, STAR 

Introduction

LOVING SIGNS

When I was first starting the business - I had plenty of doubts and questions. One time I was exhausted after a day of having a booth at a gigantic Whole Life Expo in Los Angeles. I was doing it all by myself. I was in the tub that night and I told Spirit that if I didn't start the next day out with **JOY** - then I would know I was in the wrong business. It was starting to feel like it was hard. The first thing the next morning, my friend Ken Kalb called and made me laugh and invited me for some fresh orange juice. Fresh orange juice always brings me **JOY**, and laughing is good. I was beginning to feel better. Then - the first person that came to my booth said that she stayed an extra day just to come back and get some more essences. She said a million nice things about the essences. (That brought me a LOT of **JOY**!) I told her what I had said to Spirit. She said- "Oh, my name is **JOY**." I didn't even get it, I was so wrapped up in what she was telling me about the essences. That night, driving home, I got it - Her name was **JOY** and I started the day out with her. Oh what fun. Then there was the time my friend LaDonna suggested that I take the essences to a Solar Heart gathering in Jekyll Island, Georgia. She was renting a condo with a friend of hers. LaDonna said we could stay on the floor of the condo she and her friend were renting, for free. The problem was that her friend decided at the last minute not to stay there. The organizers of the gathering would fill the space with someone we didn't know. We did a three-way phone call meditation to call in the right person who wouldn't mind if we stayed there for free. I began the drive across the country with my friend Noralea and I was wondering if it was really such a good idea. It was a long way to go - and money was not my strong suit at the time. About that time we ran out of gas - out in the desert around Blythe, California. Not such a good sign. We coasted 16 miles. That was pretty amazing. We made it to an exit and the car finally came to a stop - right across the street from a gas station. I walked over to get the gas, and coming back I saw a billboard on the freeway that was facing the direction that we weren't going, so this was the only way I would have seen it. The sign said, "Wake up and Smell the Orchids." Yes. A billboard. Now there is a SIGN! When we got to Jekyll Island we met Ros, the renter of the other room in the condo, and asked her how she felt about us sleeping on the floor for free. She said that was just fine, and, she had an extra bed if we wanted that! Ros has become a dear friend. I share these stories to let you know how guided and blessed that I feel. Star Essence has grown. It began with the name Star Essence, and then I changed it to Star Flower Essences, so people wouldn't think I made STAR essences. Right after that I made a Star essence. With the coming of the gemstone essences, I changed the name to Star Flower and Gemstone Essences. That felt too long and cumbersome (plus we have Otter and Star essences). I went back to the original. Star Essence. I also had a retail store downtown for a while, called Star Alchemy. It was a great remodeling project, and it came out beautifully. I sold the essences and Stargaritas and other things. It was too much diversification for me - and I let that go. The essences are my true love. The mission now is to continue to get them out into the world. We have shipped them to over 50 countries (in small quantities up until now) and and now we are taking quantum leaps.

Billboard "sign."

The most recent activity is purchasing 20 acres of gorgeous agricultural land. This has come about through my desire to grow fabulous light-filled food. I know there is big magic afoot and I think it has to do with essences and agriculture. New stuff is emerging every moment. Oh how very exciting!!!

Labyrinth at Chaska Norte

PART ONE

Meet Your (essence) Maker

Star Riparetti
Natal Chart
Feb 8 1945
10:07 am PWT +7:00
Santa Barbara
34°N25'24" 119° W42'12''
Geocentric
Tropical
Placidus
True Node

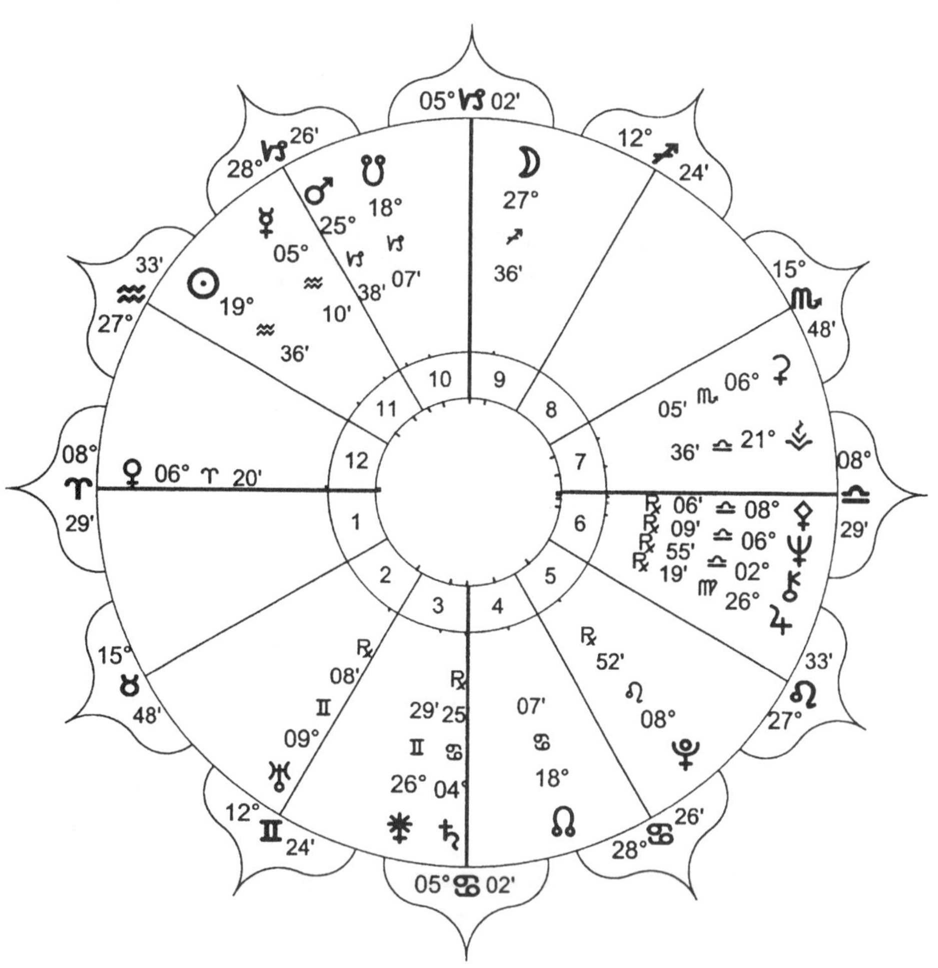

Chart compliments of Lucky Sweeney

Celebrate!

"Birthdays are good to have. The more you have, the longer you live"…-Anonymous

I like what this says, because I always think my birthday is very important.

"On the day which is the anniversary of the embodiment of the Spirit, the Holy Christ Self releases a new pulsation of Light and Life. The period immediately following one's birthday is usually the most opulent in spiritual unfoldment and inner well-being. When an individual becomes a student of the Masters (by choosing to be chosen) and under the direction of the Ascended Host, he or she receives such a Cosmic outpouring on that one's birthday as makes it the Holiest Day of the year! On your birthday, your lifestream is played upon by all the Cosmic Friends in the Kingdom of Eternal Freedom. The richness, the opulence, the Spiritual Illumination which They will give to you will remain a part of your eternal identity for all time. Avail yourselves when this Holy Day comes, and bathe in the effulgence of he Presence of the Godly."

Beloved Kuthumi, *from Wisdom of the Ages*

Happy Birthday **TO YOU!**

MEET YOUR (ESSENCE) MAKER...

STAR OF THE HEART ♥ HEART OF THE STAR

HOW THE FLOWERS HAVE CHOREOGRAPHED MY LIFE IN THE BEGINNING WAS . . .

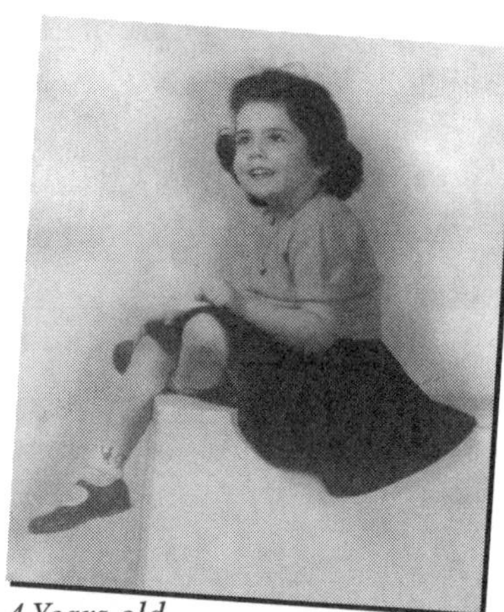

4 Years old

One of my first great manifestations was to be born in Santa Barbara, California, USA on February 8, 1945. (I've even included my astrology chart for those of you who might be interested, or curious. You could know more about me than I do, if you are an astrologer.) In my opinion, I was blessed to be born in the most beautiful place in the whole world. When I was growing up in Santa Barbara, I thought every city was this beautiful; defined by ocean on one side and outlined by mountains on the other side. I thought that's how you knew where your city borders were. Now that I have traveled to many parts of this country and the world, and found out it wasn't true, it is easy for me to hold the vision of Heaven on Earth here in Santa Barbara, because I get to see it and live it.

A first question that I am often asked is, where did the name Star come from? The name given to me at birth was Georgia Anne Riparetti.

My mother was from Tennessee and she pioneered her way to California around 1943, through the State of Georgia. Her family stayed close to home and were lawyers and politicians. My mother was very adventurous and decided to head West. She had briefly been a teacher and also a cigarette girl in a club. She used to joke about being one of those girls who carried around a tray saying "cigars, cigarettes, cigarillos." Between the teaching job and the cigarette job, guess which job paid better?

The Name Thing

Mom and Dad

When my mother got to Santa Barbara, California, she met my father, Julio Riparetti. He called her "Georgia" because she had just come from there, and because of her southern accent. Out west, she was always called "Georgia," even though her birth name was, get this: "Panthea Page Prince." (I will tell you more on that name later.) So when I was born, my father deemed that I be called "Georgia." My mother got to pick the middle name, so they called me Georgia Anne. My name felt incongruous for the short, skinny little dark-haired Italian girl that I was. I got my father's olive complexion and brown eyes. I could never relate to my name. Around the time I entered college, and for years after that, I was called "Rip," derived from my last name, "Riparetti." I liked that better than Georgia. Rip Riparetti was on my driver's license and all my paperwork. When I was married to Dan, I was "Rip Cummings." Later, when I was married to Thad, I became "Rip Snyder." Does that sound like the name of a prize-fighter, or what? After my divorce from Thad around 1980, I changed back to Rip Riparetti and decided I wouldn't change the Riparetti part ever again, even if I did remarry. So, you might ask, where does the name Star come from?

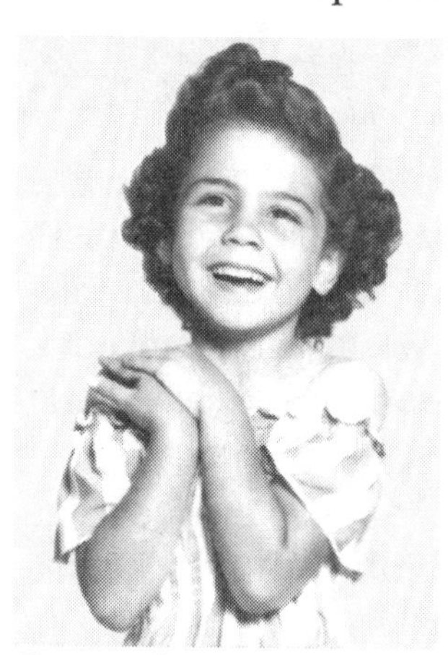
Georgia Anne

Well, the name Rip Riparetti was becoming more and more difficult for me. Every time I introduced myself to anyone, my name became a conversation. Also, my friend's grandmothers didn't seem to like calling me "Rip." I tried renaming myself, and couldn't come up with the right name.

Then, in 1992, there was a big **11:11** event. In numerology, my life number is an eleven, and I love that number. I also love the color purple, and all of the **11:11** flyers were printed in purple. Still, I ignored the flyer. I had seen Solara, the angelic organizer of the **11:11** event, and her group, and at the time, the halos and sparkles were all a bit much for me. (Anyone who knows me now can laugh with me, because now I LOVE sparkles, and halos—and even angel wings!)

During that time, I got a call from my brother Terry's ex-girlfriend Jeanette in Hawaii, saying to "find an **11:11** group;" she was going to be here in Santa Barbara and she wanted to go. I might still have ignored the whole event until my friend Linda Taylor walked into an essential oils class we were having and said, "There is an **11:11** group meeting. You should go." OK, OK, I said to myself. Enough messages, already. I'll go.

I walked into the room where the **11:11** meeting was held, and there were all these beautiful people of every age (early 20's to 80's) and they all seemed to have beautiful names. Azuriel, Mira El, Valorial, Oceanna, Anka El…and then there was me, "Rip" (clunk). I asked them who gave them their names.

They said, "Oh, it's simple. Just meditate and ask your Golden Solar Angel to come forward. Ask them their name, and then merge with them."

Oh yeah, easy for you to do, I thought.

I went home and did it, and was ever so surprised when the name "Starlina" came. Oh, no! No way! I can't go from "Rip" to "Starlina." It sounds like "Tinkerbell" or something! The next day I was doing Tai Chi and this mantra started going through my head. Starlina Santara San Ra. It was only later (otherwise, I would have for sure thought that I made it up!) that I found out that Solara's angel name was "Solara Antara Ma Ra."

The **11:11** event was very potent for me. It was a pivotal event that changed my life. I moved into a new octave overnight. I found spiritual family, which was VERY exciting and nurturing. People all over the world were meeting in groups and performing particular mudras and decrees and movements to open portals to allow more light to come into the World. **11:11** is a trigger, a code. (That is my very condensed description of **11:11**. If you'd like

Cara, Kelsea, Bob and Krista Peace.

to find out more, see the Bibliography.)

Later, around 1994, to make it an easy name for my granddaughters, I officially changed my name from "Starlina" to "Star." I love and relate to this name. Ironically, I realized I had been using the Star symbol for many years. I had named my Yoga/Tai Chi studio in the 80's "Laughing Star." As a proud grandmother, I will mention here that my wonderful granddaughters are Kelsea Rose Peace and Krista Skyler Peace. They are the children of my extraordinary daughter, Cara Page Cummings Peace, and her husband and super father Bob Peace. Of course I love, admire, respect and adore all of them. They are precious. Now imagine when these granddaughters have children, those kids can say their grandmother was Peace, and great-great-grandmother was Prince. PRINCE OF PEACE. Plus their great-grandmother (me) was a star in the middle. Hmmmmm.

In the realm of interesting names, a lady who was like "my other mother" was named - yes, her true birth name -*Fairy*. Fairy Holland. She was my angel during my childhood. With her help, I manifested nearly everything I really desired in my early life. I appreciate her teaching me that I could have anything I wanted. I remember once I told my older sister Darlene that I had seen an awesome piece of property on Coyote Road and that I really wanted it. She said, "I'm sure you'll get it then, you always get everything you want." I took that as a positive statement affirming my ability to manifest, and I got the property!

Pan Connection

So - I was raised by Panthea and *Fairy*. In fact, my mother's nickname was Pan as she was growing up. Once I was asking a question of God/Goddess, Source, Nature, Spirit: whether I really was connected to Pan (a.k.a. the CEO of Nature). I had been doing a lot of work with the essences and feeling Pan's presence so strongly, and I just wanted a bit of confirmation. That day I went to Ojai (a town near Santa Barbara) and was introduced to a guy who looked just like Pan. I laughed when I met him and told him I had been looking for something concrete that would confirm my connection to Pan. He then brought out a concrete statue of Pan (I love Spirit's sense of humor). In a meditation that night, I was reminded of my mother's name, Panthea. Thea means "of God" - Pan of God. I am the daughter of Pan of God. O.K., that works for me. I honor Pan and I do feel a strong, glorious connection. Right after that, I opened up a book called Accessing the Akashic Records, by Gary Bonnell, and flipped to a page that says that if Pan is behind you in what you do, it's a sure winner. I love the affirmation.

Concrete statue of Pan.

As a Kid

In recent years, I have thought back about my childhood, and I have wondered if I would have been one of those kids they gave Ritalin to, or some other drug. I felt hyper inside my body. I wasn't (too) disruptive. I could mostly sit through a whole class and look attentive, and yet not hear much of anything. Public school probably wasn't my best use of time, had there been another option. I did OK in school, not great. I was often distracted or daydreaming. I recently came across my 2nd grade report card, which said, "Georgia Anne is such a nice little girl. She is so enthusiastic over all of our second grade work. She has

Maximo, a Peruvian plant medicine man, and me.

such a good little mind but sometimes it's hard for her to settle down." (Sometimes that's still true.) I wasn't too interested in a lot of what they taught us, especially history, and it was hard to keep my attention on it. My thoughts now are that my guides didn't even want my head to be filled with a lot of the stuff they teach, so they distracted me. It is time to give up our ancestor worship - the preoccupation with and focus on history (which is usually HIS story- and usually war-based). It's time to write a new future (HERstory). Maximo, an 86-year-old Quechua plant medicine man and my friend, asks, "why is it they teach so much the history of war and so little about the history of love?" Yeah! I love changing that!

ADD and ADHD issues are close to my heart.

I have always wanted to help find some alternatives to Ritalin and the heavy drugs passed out to our children. I have made an essence combination directed at that: the Attention Formula, which I talk about later in the book.

My father left the earth plane via a cerebral aneurysm when I was 4 years old. My mother and *Fairy* told me I could talk to him, so when I was young I assumed it to be true that he was accessible telepathically. My mother left this plane when I was 20, via a car wreck, three months after I was married. I loved her so much. I was devastated. By then, I had forgotten that I could communicate.

Interestingly enough, my mother had called me about a week before her death to tell me that her employer had just given employees a life insurance policy, and she had put it in my name. She said it was enough for a funeral (indeed, it was just enough). She also asked me to take care of the kids, whom she adored, if anything happened to her (my sisters and brothers were ages 16, 10, 7 and 6). Somehow, it seems like at some level, people know when they are going to die, even when it is an "accident." She was very tired, and was having a very difficult time supporting my younger brothers and sisters.

My 16-year-old sister Cheryl died from falling out of the back of a pick-up truck three months after my mother died. My new husband of three months, Dan, was heroic about taking care of the details. I was a wreck. I was so sad. I wished so badly that I had something to believe in. I wanted something to help me cope with such pain and loss. I had no religion: choosing one religion over another didn't make sense to me. In my heart I knew there was something for me to find.

That was when I began my search. I didn't have any idea what I was searching for. I grew up going to a Methodist church mostly, well wholly, for social reasons. I didn't really like to see Jesus the way he is often depicted in church, bleeding (and I still don't). I love seeing Jesus in more serene settings. It helps me hold that vision of Peace. Now, I am SO grateful that I have a grand array of spiritual techniques to help with situations like that, including the Essences, and a close connection to Jesus, St. Germain and many of the other Ascended Masters.

I grew up with an alcoholic, not-too-crazy family. (We never would have called it alcoholic back then.) Rad, my stepfather, was an eccentric inventor and writer who was impeccably honest, a gambler, generous on any day he had money, and obnoxious when he was drunk. One of his alcoholic adventures was to go around to the neighborhood stores in his boxer shorts with a squirt gun, robbing stores of their bubble gum. So there it was in the local newspaper, "The Bubble Gum Bandit Strikes Again," when I was in 3rd or 4th grade. I was embarrassed about it for a long time. I used to long to be "normal." Later I found out that our weirdness was minimal compared to that of other people. They just hid it better.

I have an older sister named Darlene who has the same father that I have, and a different mother. I have two brothers, Terry and

Timmy Howell, and a sister Deb Dobbin (a fabulous Yogini), who have the same mother that I have, and a different father. Their father is my stepfather Rad Howell. I have another stepfather named Hank, who I have been very close to. He has taught me a lot, especially in the realm of construction.

★★★

On September 24, **1965**, I married Dan Cummings, after meeting him in June of that year. He was probably the brightest (and most tormented) man I have ever known. I love him dearly and know that ever since he left the earth plane in 1986 (alcoholism-age 42), he has been a close guide for me. Later, I was also married to Thad Snyder. (I believe that some day Thad will come out of hiding and reveal his true cosmic nature.)

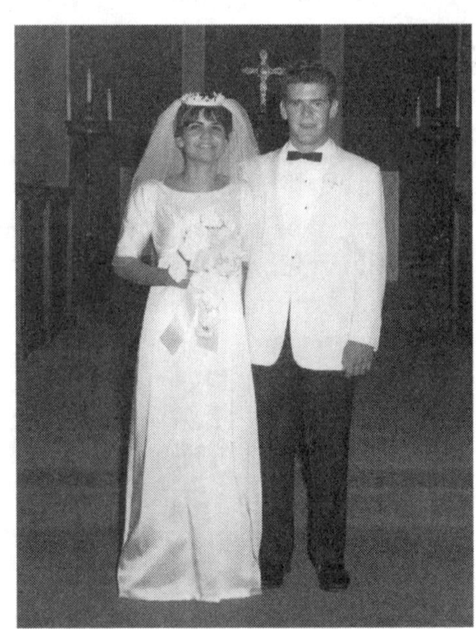

Sept. 24, 1965 marriage to Dan Cummings

There have been a number of men that have contributed greatly in my life. For a while, I had a lot of 2-3 year relationships. It was tough for me to end them, and I remember that I used to have to think of them as bad guys to end the partnership. My friend Pam Oslie (Psychic and author of the books, *Life Colors* and *Make Your Dreams Come True*) gave me some sage advice that has helped me SO much! She said, "You don't have to make them wrong to get out of the relationship." Applying that advice made ending relationships much sweeter.

Nuclear Medicine

My life seems magical as I look back at it now. Even getting my job at the Cancer Foundation in 1966 or 1967 was cosmic. My husband, Dan, was going to UCSB, while I had a job as a bookkeeper. (Yes- me, a bookkeeper. Yikes!) I didn't have any experience in Nuclear Medicine or Nuclear ANYTHING. I just knew that I wanted to be a technician of some sort, and not work in an office. That word "technician" was some kind of a trigger for me. When I saw an ad in the newspaper for a technician and I went to apply at the employment agency, they wanted to send me on a bookkeeping interview. I didn't really have the skills they wanted for a Technician. Since I already had a bookkeeping job, I just said no, never mind, so they sent me anyway to the Isotope Technician interview, without any experience. (I had to go look up the word "isotope" before I went to the interview.) Through some divine magic I got the job! That job became the foundation of my life for the next 14 years. Eventually I became the Chief Technologist and the Director of the School of Nuclear Medicine at the Cancer Foundation of Santa Barbara (also called the Radiation Center). We ran all of the Nuclear Medicine Labs for all of the hospitals in Santa Barbara and Goleta, and were based at Cottage Hospital, the largest hospital in the area.

I totally loved my job there. I remember driving to work every day and feeling how happy I was to have such a great job, and good pay. It was a lot of fun, and my colleagues were my friends and that gave me a lot of satisfaction. Our department was like a family. We worked very hard and efficiently, and we played together very hard. (Hey- do you remember the 60's and 70's?) We were each other's best friends. I got to travel around and have a nice title and feel important.

I felt like we were doing a really good thing, saving people from surgery. We could see what was going on inside them without opening them up. You just give someone this tiny quantity of (seemingly innocuous) energy frequencies or radioactive material, without having to cut them open. For example, iodine goes to the thyroid, so you give someone radioactive iodine to drink and it will collect in their thyroid, and because it is radioactive, it can be traced, counted and photographed… Or you can inject them with different radioactive materials made specific for different organs so you can do all manner of diagnostic testing. Hallelujah! Advanced technology! Guess what- I recently heard of a study that was done proving the acupuncture meridians exist. They injected a radioactive tracer into the meridian system of some animals and when scanned, the tracer had moved along the meridians. When injected into a spot that wasn't a meridian, the tracer just sat there (this is exactly the kind of thing I did with patients in Nuclear Medicine- except with organs, via the bloodstream). It is fun that they are finally proving "scientifically," with isotopes, what the Chinese and others have known for centuries. All of this with minute substances that you can't see or touch or taste or smell or hear, radioactive substances.

Our department was unique, in that we painted it bright colors and put things on the ceiling for the patients to look at. We really cared about our patients. They would be with us for a couple of hours so we did everything we could to make them feel comfortable. Dr. McClintock, the awesome man that I worked for, was unlike not only most doctors, but unlike most PEOPLE. I adored him. He wore the badge that we gave him:

James T. McClintock, M.D.
Fearless Leader
Department of Unclear Medicine

Very few folks noticed that it said "Unclear" instead of "Nuclear." The modality of Nuclear Medicine was notoriously unclear. Quite subjective when it comes to reading scans. "Fearless" used to say quite often, "If you're gonna be in this business at all, you've gotta have a high tolerance for uncertainty."

The tests we did simply weren't black and white, positive or negative. There were many shades of gray- yet at some point the doctor had to make a choice of how to call it. I learned a lot from that- especially in terms of giving your power to one person. I will say that I believe second opinions (and even third and fourth) are a good thing for important situations.

We had a back door from our department that led directly into the hospital. On the door we had a sign that said,

"YOU ARE NOW LEAVING THE MAGIC KINGDOM.
OUT BEYOND THIS DOOR LIES THE REAL WORLD."

We had T-shirts made, back before everyone was having

T-shirts made, that had rainbows on them and said

**"NUCLEAR MEDICINE-
ATOMS FOR PEACE."**

Because we got such good feedback from our patients, the administration left us alone. We were always smiling and laughing with each other and with our patients. Our department was considered the lunatic fringe - thinking outside the box.

Nuclear Medicine is like an inside-out X-Ray. You give the patient some radioactive material that is specific for a particular organ, and then trace where it goes. You can count it and scan it and photograph it. On the scanner, the signal is amplified so that it can be seen, with - get this - CRYSTALS! So I was working with huge (man-made) crystals even back then…

June 1973- Steven Rehfeld, Star (with the pigtails) and Alison Stone. Photo taken right before we went to the International Society of Nuclear Medicine meeting in Florida to present our paper on tagging sulfur colloid with Technetium 99m for liver scanning. (NOTE PEACE MOBILE)

In retrospect, it is so obvious how those years (and everything else I have done in my life) were preparing me for what I am doing now (the Essences). Nuclear Medicine is working with things that we can't hear or see or touch or taste or smell. We could listen to a presentation about Isotopes, about their frequencies, wavelengths, their spectrums, and we could apply the same concepts to flower essences, or color therapy. I was listening to a tape one time and couldn't tell for quite some time if I was hearing about color or radiation. Both can be therapies. One heals. One kills stuff. Radiation and Flower Essences; they are both frequencies. They are just at opposite ends of the spectrum. They are both effective. One is a sledgehammer and one is a feather.

Yes- I have been working with energy medicine for a long time. Now I work with energies that are subtle, magical, powerful and safe. We co-create with Nature to use them, make them and understand them. Their frequency is so high that in the past, the machines themselves were too dense to measure them. The new technology is here.

Leaving "Orthodox" Medicine

I quit Nuclear Medicine around **1980**. People couldn't believe that I would quit such a good job, especially for a woman, they sometimes added. By the time I left, I had initiated a plan where all of the technologists in our department got 2 months off every year. I had convinced the bureaucracy that it would be beneficial to them- and it wouldn't cost them any money. It didn't cost us as techs much either, when you factored taxes.

Having that extra time off made for a very interesting group to work with. We were all doing really exotic vacations, and I felt like I had created a perfect job. Well, almost. Then I initiated job-sharing, because once I had two months off, I realized how wonderful it was to be unexposed to radiation, and out of the medical environment. I preferred just the wonderful rays of our great central sun.

There I was sharing one job. I was working half time and having 2 months off. I had always loved my job. I loved it every day up until a point when I realized that I was enjoying the time off more than the time on.

One night I was walking through the halls of the hospital, and a doctor from the Cancer Foundation saw me and asked why I was hanging around so late. I told him I was going to an acupuncture lecture. He told me not to waste my time. I will always thank him for that comment. It began to put things into perspective for me.

Something had begun to bother me about the hospital and the doctors. As I began to explore other vibrational modes, I found it frustrating that they were not willing (at that time- around 1979) to look at ANYTHING slightly alternative. They laughed at me when I went to a chiropractor because my back hurt, yet all they could offer me was Valium or surgery. When the Chiropractic treatment was successful, they told me my pain would have gone away on its own. I decided that doctors didn't know everything. For awhile I wanted hospitals to disappear. I have grown since then, and I know that there are good things that happen in them, and I am happy to have them there. I am happy to see the merging and converging as they become more suited for healing, and as they encompass other methodologies.

While I was working only half-time, I decided that I needed to do something else with the other half of my time. While I was at the Cancer Foundation I participated in many building projects, including building a spectacularly beautiful house in the Montecito foothills in Santa Barbara. Both of my husbands were contractors. (I love guys who can build things. They were also both geologists.)

I had also done some fixer-upper projects with a girlfriend named Randy. We were business partners for fun. In fact, on our business cards we had a line from a Bruce Springsteen song that said, "We're not here for business, We're only here for fun." (I still subscribe to that!) We called ourselves "R and R Investments" - for Rip Riparetti and Randy Ridder. (Interesting names for two straight women!)

We celebrated anything and everything that seemed fun. We celebrated Chinese New Year, Palm Sunday, you name it! We celebrated 7-7-77 and 8-8-88 together. I have a big thing for double numbers and triple numbers… That must have been the beginning of my number thing, and I didn't even know it.

We figured that the R's stood for Raspberry so that was our color. A little pig was our logo. We figured if it's worth doing, it's worth overdoing, especially in the realm of fun!

Riparetti's (A Bar)

Randy was bored. We decided to buy a business. She had money. I had a little. We opened the newspaper, and that night, under "Businesses For Sale," was a bar. We called and found out where it was. It was on the lower east side of town. It would be the bad part of town, if Santa Barbara were to have such a thing. The neighborhood is less rich and more ethnic than other parts. Randy and my blond 6' 5" boyfriend Tom and I went into the bar that night. There was a woman there named Valie, who looked just like

Riparetti's Bar

a cigar store Indian. We joked and said that if she came with the bar, we would take it. Then we noticed a bottle of whiskey called R & R on the counter: the name of our business! Boy, now there was a sign. (I have been following signs for a long time.) Valie came with the bar, so we decided to buy it.

The day we were going in to sign papers for purchase, Randy called and said she just couldn't do it. She was afraid that her Dad would flip out. He was a wealthy newspaper owner. He would not like for her to own a primarily Spanish-speaking neighborhood "dive" bar. I called my boyfriend Tom and told him the situation, and said that I thought I was going to see if I could buy it anyway, alone. He told me he was 100% against it. In the bar he stood at least a foot higher than anyone else, and he was blond and he looked very out of place. I, on the other hand, look very Mexican (or Indian or Cuban or Peruvian - I blend in in those dark-eyed countries). I am half Italian. Riparetti, I like to say, rhymes with spaghetti. The other half - the Panthea Page Prince side, from Tennessee - is English and Irish.

I met with the owner and he was willing to work with me so that I could buy it. Suddenly, there I was with a Mexican/Italian neighborhood bar, with 3 pool tables and a jukebox. I served mostly beer and a little wine. I named it Riparetti's.

Just for reference, I've never actually drunk a whole beer. I have never much liked any alcohol. Even though I drink occasionally, I don't like beer. I didn't like bars since my childhood. What was I doing as the owner of a bar? This had to be some karmic thing. My mother's best friend owned a bar and my mother hung out there. Guys came into my bar that were pallbearers at my mother's funeral, 15 years earlier. This was a crazy place for me to end up. After having the bar for just a short time and working half there and half at the Cancer Foundation, I realized that I liked the freedom from stress, of not having to worry about what you served someone. If you made a mistake and gave them the wrong kind of beer, you just gave it to them for free and you were suddenly a hero. If you spilled a drink it was not an "incident." The same is not true for Nuclear Medicine, as you can well imagine. It was time to give up the Nuclear Medicine job and relax.

The bar was fun for a while. There, I was serving alcoholic cocktails instead of atomic cocktails. (Now I prefer to serve Stargaritas… I'll give you that recipe later.) Crazy things happened in the bar every single day. I had a variety of very interesting regular clientele. There was the lady from the Orchestra who used to come hock her violin to me for a couple of beers (I provided safe storage for it). I had the resident hooker, who was married to a reputable jeweler. There was Dr. John, a gringo with two M.D.s and a Ph.D. He spoke great Spanish and loved to come and hide out there. There was the guy living down the street in the trailer park who had come to Santa Barbara to study Sanskrit. He taught me new vocabulary all the time. One favorite word I remember is "conundrum" (a puzzle or a riddle without an answer).

Valie, the beautiful cigar-store-Indian-looking lady (named Valie because she was born on Valentine's day) was the only one in the bar with a positive tab. (Usually tabs are for when people owe you money). Folks would buy her drinks, often more than she could drink, so I would keep track. Shortly after I bought the bar she never had to pay for another beer, and she was there every day, regularly, until she died. When she passed on, a couple of her family members came in and gave me $100 to buy beers for all her friends. They said we were her family, and that was her funeral. Riparetti's was a little bar with a big heart. For many it was their living room.

It was fun to choose the music for the jukebox and fun to dance on the bar sometimes. I could because I owned the place. It was a safe, easy and interesting way to learn how to run a business. I say safe because it was such a small investment, not much to lose. In fact, it always made money. In retrospect, I can see how all those lessons and experiences have proven to be extremely valuable for the essences to help me on this blissed and blessed path that I am on. It was fun not to take life at the bar too seriously. I often sprayed the Bach Rescue Remedy around the bar (now I would use Balance and Stability from my system of essences). Life as a bar owner was O.K. most of the time, and when it wasn't, I had someone else run it. The good thing was that it supported me financially while I pursued all manner of things.

Those things were Tai Chi, yoga, Reiki, mandalas, breathwork, cranio-sacral manipulation, color therapy, crystal therapy, hiking in the mountains, and even taking my first couple of trips to Peru.

Flower Lover

I was learning about edible flowers, taking classes and reading lots of books about them. I was in the Santa Barbara Little Gardens Club. This is the time when I was learning to love flowers more and more. I was taking more wildflower walks. And flower arranging… All of this was on the other side of the world from the bar.

My love for flowers and Art and design led me in many directions before I met with flower essences. I took flower arranging classes from a brilliant teacher named Esta Stough (who has since passed over). She was in her 80's then, and a master at flower arranging. She had huge amounts of zip and spirit. She LOVED flowers! For instance, if you didn't treat them kindly - cutting and conditioning them properly - and making sure they always were in water - you could just leave her class, thank you very much. She didn't like it one bit. She said she could feel their pain. A normally very sweet person, she would get very cranky if you mistreated the flowers. She said she liked flowers at least as much as she liked people. From Esta, I learned to respect flowers on a new level. I have also taken numerous courses and read extensively and practiced with and taught about herbs and aromatherapy.

Quantum Leap: Flowers for Healing

Ah- it was when I saw this tiny little classified ad that said "Flowers for Healing" that my heart skipped a beat and I felt a sureness about something I didn't even know. It struck a chord. It was as if I had found what I didn't know that I was looking for. They didn't say herbs, they said FLOWERS. I didn't think they meant eating them as medicine. They were talking about something I had been looking for, and I knew it. I met Marjorie Shepherdson, the person who placed the ad. She charged $50.00 for a session (back in 1985). I didn't want a session. I wanted to find out what Bach Flower Essences even were, and how to find out everything I could. Marjorie did a session with me, and she gave me the information I was craving. As she was interviewing me in the session, I couldn't think of anything wrong in my life, except that I was having some sort of minor attacks of fear and I didn't even know what I was afraid of. She gave me the Bach essence Aspen (good for vague fears), and I took it and I never had those feelings again. It took me a while to realize that the essence had worked. That is how essences work sometimes. They can be very subtle. You feel good, but feeling good is normal, so why shouldn't you feel good? I think I have always just known in my heart that they worked. No one has had to prove it to me, and I am still in awe when I hear miraculous story after miraculous story of essence magic…

The flower essences felt like love at first sight. My quest began. I ordered all the books there were on flower essences, which was only about 3 at the time, and I took the six-month Bach Essence Practitioner Course. I got all of the academic basics, which was perfect for where I was. I feel like I received an attunement to Dr. Bach, who is credited with bringing flower essences into our consciousness in the 1930's. I do feel sometimes that I am a "recovering Bach essence practitioner," as they were so steadfast in their teachings that Dr. Bach was the only one who could make flower essences. That seems pretty silly because Dr. Bach taught folks how to make them, and wrote down the process as well. In order to remain a Bach Essence Practitioner back then, you had to sign in blood (just kidding- no blood) that you wouldn't use any other essences. I couldn't do it. Maybe their philosophy has shifted since then. There are now several wonderful folks that make the same essences that Dr. Bach made. I know he is one of my guides who is cheering me on for this adventure. Perhaps it is Dr. Bach who is guiding all of us essence makers at some level. Wherever and however, I love you, Dr. Bach. Thank you for being such a grand pioneer. I am eternally grateful to you.

Right after my Bach training, I studied with the wondrous Richard Katz and Patricia Kaminsky of FES (Flower Essence Services) in Nevada City, California. They took everything I had just learned from the Bach Society, on to the next level. We were actually out in the field with flowers. We connected with the Devas, the Nature Spirits, the heart, the soul, the land. I appreciate Richard and Patricia SO much. They have been dedicated to the flowers for a long, long time, and are great teachers and essence producers.

Funeral Magic

1986 was another big event. I was always very close to my first husband Dan. We were best friends – and I couldn't live with him. I could count on him, and he adored Cara, our daughter. That year, he chose to leave the planet. He felt Cara didn't need him any more. He had done a good job, teaching her everything he could. She was very self-sufficient. We got him into the hospital one day, because he was so ill from his alcohol intake. They gave him medication that helped and told him that if he didn't stop drinking, he would die. This made him very peaceful. He checked himself out of the hospital. None of his friends would pick him up because the doctors didn't want him to leave, so he took a cab. He doubled his alcohol intake. He got himself and his boat to Mexico, fulfilling a lifelong dream. Cara and I spent 10 magnificent days with him there. He called Cara from Mexico on her 17th birthday (Dec.2) and came home a couple of days later. We had a great dinner with him, and the next day he died at his friend Scott Morgan's house. He took his last breath laughing with his friends. They never did really find a cause of death.

His mother and brother were coming from Maine, and we had to figure out a funeral. This all had to happen very quickly. I called my friend Pam Oslie, who is a certified minister, and asked her if she would preside. She said yes. Since she had never met Dan, she asked me to come and tell her something about him. I was pretty shook up, and I was ready to drive over to her house anyway when she called and said, never mind, Dan had already come to her so she knew who he was. We did the funeral at Hammond's Meadow.

It is a gorgeous bluff overlooking the ocean. When Pam arrived she had two questions. First she asked me if Dan had a sense of humor. I said yes, in fact, he was super-smart and would devise very clever things to trick his friends. (Dan's friend Bob, who is now my son-in-law, told me he was certain when he came for the funeral that it was all going to be a joke that Dan had concocted.) Second, Pam said Dan wanted her to channel him in the first person and wondered if that was all right. I said, "Go for it." There were all kinds of folks there, some who would find it very strange. Oh, well, it appeared that Dan was in charge of his own funeral. In addition to giving very poignant and special messages to many members of his family, he said, "I picked the day I died on purpose. You know how much I liked harbors. Besides that, I was always bombed. I just thought I would leave you with that little Pearl." Dan died on Dec. 7 (You know, Pearl Harbor Day). His friends and family spoke. His old friend Phil got up and said, "Today the moon is out AND the sun is out. (You could see them both.) I taught Dan navigation. I know he knows where he is going." Dan choreographed the day perfectly.

The moment Dan died I could feel his presence. He was even more accessible than before. He felt so relieved. His deteriorating body no longer held him back. Dan was a guide for me while he was alive, and is now a much stronger one since he left the earth plane.

★★★

Then came the Harmonic Convergence in 1987.

It was another one of those pivotal times. I met with groups who were meditating and having sacred ceremonies. It was great to be involved in things that were spiritual, yet not religious. There was a lot of Native American ceremony and ritual, which I was exposed to for the first time. I was also introduced to crystal bowls, which really enamored me, and they still do. The Harmonic Convergence "zenith" was at 4 a.m. on some night in August. I slept outside because I wanted to watch the stars, and I was going to wake up and psychically join with everyone in meditation. I was physically going to a sunrise ceremony later. My daughter and Bob (her then boyfriend, now husband) asked me if I was really going to be awake at 4 a.m. I said yes, of course. I was putting out my stones and creating a landing strip for any E.T.'s that wanted to come visit. (This was for fun as much as anything. I was hoping…but I didn't much believe anything would happen.)

I was awakened at 4 a.m. (Something hit me.) It was pitch black and I heard this sound - like a spaceship - and then I saw flashing lights in the trees, darting around. It was just too stereotypical! I couldn't believe it - or could I ? There was a little spaceship, just like you would see in the movies. Watching my astonishment, Bob and Cara nearly fell out of the tree laughing. They had a little plastic spaceship with bells and whistles that they had gotten in Mexico, and they had been waiting for this moment. They even had to throw things at me to wake me up. Spaceships and humor and laughing included, harmonically converged I was, from that event. And a big shift took place on the planet.

Owning that little dive bar afforded me the time to pursue everything I could about flowers and other spiritual practices. I also love to travel, and it gave me time to do that. In 1988, I took my first trip to Peru. I hiked the Inca Trail to **Machu Picchu**. Sometime during that hike, I heard someone talking about an Andean Orchid that we would see on the trail. I thought the name had such a pretty ring to it. Andean Orchid. I thought there was only one, and wouldn't it be nice to make a flower essence of it? Then I thought, no, it would have to be made by a Peruvian.

1990

In May of 1990, I went to Peru again. As with my previous visit, I was in a group that my friend Carol led. On the last night of the journey, in a hotel in Lima at 4 a.m., I woke up with the complete idea of a new game in my head. I wrote down what ended up being the entire outline, and all of the symbols, for what is now called the Star Pocket Oracle. I was totally excited.

I spent the next three years researching and collecting information on the symbols and the universal laws that went with them. This was a process for me as well, as I worked with each symbol. It accelerated my growth tremendously. I had hand-drawn the game pieces and cut them out of cardboard. I knew the real pieces were to be made in Peru. Hand-carved gourds, I thought. We ended up using ceramic, hand-painted in Pisac.

It was an interesting time around **JUNE 1990**. My beloved favorite daughter (I can say that because she is my only daughter, only kid for that matter) got married, and my lease was up on my bar business. My car was stolen and I was hurried into buying a VW van. The stolen car showed up right after I got the van, as if telling me that I was supposed to have the van. I had the option, so I just went ahead and kept the insurance money, and let them have my nice Toyota Cressida. It seemed that I had the van so I could travel around and decide what to do next in my life. At least I thought that was the plan. I drove around the U.S. for two months. Every day I never wanted to figure out what to do, I just wanted to BE on the trip. I was having too much fun to figure out the future.

I got home without any idea what I was going to do next with my life. I managed to get a loan (I seem to be the Queen of Loans) and bought the run-down, tiny house next door to my house to fix up and sell. I did just that. I love building projects. It turned out beautifully, and sold during the first open house, for the full asking price with two back-up offers. While it was in escrow, the whole Kuwait War thing happened and the economy stopped suddenly and the house fell out of escrow.

My plan had been to take the money and buy a house in Oregon and be able to retire. That didn't happen. The house didn't sell and didn't sell, and I borrowed more and more money. The gift was that I didn't leave Santa Barbara. This is where I resonate best, and I am so grateful I was deterred from moving. I have learned to look at everything in terms of its gifts.

Let me now move to **1992**. Remember that **11:11** event I mentioned earlier, the one where I found out my Angel name? Well, I joined that group of folks with the cool names (Azuriel, Mira El, etc.) who wore flowing angelic clothes. We practiced the mudras and made decrees and sang angel songs and when the date came, January 11th of 1992, we wore white beautiful clothes and did these moves all day and all night, 11a.m. to 11p.m. and beyond. People all over the world were doing the same thing. Some had prepared

Angels with I Am Joyous T-shirts.

(consciously) for years: for me it had only been a few weeks (who knows how long on the inner). It was the highest day of my life up to that moment. I can't explain it. There isn't anything specific I can say- and, my life was changed. It was like an initiation. I was with spiritual family. I would never have guessed by looking at them on the street, how "out there" they were. Everyone looked quite "normal"- whatever that may mean. They were mostly older than me- with a few younger ones and some considerably older. Many had been doing their spiritual practices for a long time (like 30, 40, 50 and 60 years). After that, I read the flyer about what this was all about- and I read all of Solara's books. I had a huge sudden thirst for information. **11:11** was an encodement, a signal that we gave ourselves. A doorway that opened.

And after that very special day, I wanted to know what to do next. I couldn't just go back to life as it was. I knew I had shifted, and life had a new purpose (even though I didn't know what exactly it was). Then I read that the next thing to do was to build "islands of light." Yes! That really resonated. I wanted to build an island of light! (I love building).

Then I remembered: I had an island of light already built. I just wasn't living in it at the time. In 1975 and 1976, my second husband, Thad, and I designed and built a beautiful home in the Santa Barbara foothills. It was all redwood, inside and out, with decks and ocean views. I always called it my island. In the divorce

Angel House

I had kept it and its huge mortgage, and Thad got everything else. I had it all rented out to lots of folks to pay for itself. Suddenly I decided that I had to move back in. This was the end of January.

I figured it would be June or July before the transition would happen. I wanted all of the tenants to have time to find places- and there was one guy with a son going to school, and he for sure didn't want to leave until school was out mid-June. I began to pray that everyone would find his or her perfect place. By the end of MARCH everything worked out for everyone moving out (the guy with the son even found a free place to live), and on April 1st I moved in. The best part was that lots of my Angel friends wanted new places to live, too, so I got to rent rooms to several of them. I hadn't any idea how it would all happen, and it happened so beautifully. It was divinely choreographed, again. There we all were in this beautiful home that we fondly referred to as the ANGEL HOUSE. Its real name was **KRISTAKUMARA** and we referred to it as the Angel House. We proceeded to have Angel meetings there every Sunday for the next 2½ years, with Mira El being the main anchor of light.

I learned so many things. Everything in my whole life started making sense. We did multitudes of meditations and became initiated into our Light Bodies. We had Angel parties with fabulous impromptu music and great vegetarian food. Once a week, at our place, we had an underground vegetarian restaurant. We had fun.

Hundreds of people enjoyed the space during that time. I like to call these times the Light Nights of the Soul…

Everything is bright - each moment a de-light…

St. Germain painted by Gonzalo Medina

I became friends with the Ascended Masters, especially **SAINT GERMAIN**. Then I understood my affinity for purple (for instance, I had 2 cars painted purple). **ST. GERMAIN** is surrounded by lots of purple and teaches about the Violet Flame of transmutation. We affectionately call him the big purple guy sometimes.

A Friend For All Time

By Mira El

Pronounce the name of Saint Germain! Within the tones that the ear hears is the vibration of this Great Being of Light! He has been known by many names throughout the history of this planet. Some are: Paracelsus, Francis Bacon, William Shakespeare, Christopher Columbus, Merlin of Camelot, and of course, the Count Rakowsky of Transylvania. The later lifetime gave rise to many accounts and legends regarding his incredible abilities and talents, one of which was his alchemical 'Elixir of Life' which was reported to create a state of eternal youth. He was known as the Wonderman of Europe during the time surrounding the French Revolution and was reputed to have lived for at least two hundred years. This was the last known actual human embodiment and at the close of that lifetime it was said that he left this plane through the ascension experience. Actually, Saint Germain was an Ascended Being hundreds of thousands of years ago and was instrumental in ushering in the great Golden Age of Enlightenment in Central and South America. He was part of the creation of a culture that far excels anything that we know of today. It predated the civilizations of the Mayans, Toltecs and Aztecs as they were part of the decline of that era. He helped establish a vibration and energetic focus in that part of the world that still holds the Key to the radiant future that dwells in the mind and will of the Divine One that we call God. Now is the time when this Great Being is making his Presence felt again. Through the ages he has lent his energies to assist mankind's evolutionary journey. For the most part, he has done this within the space of Sacred Silence. Most of us have been unaware of his existence. As Jesus of Nazareth opened the door for the Sixth Dispensation bringing humanity into an awareness of Love and Peace; so too does Saint Germain usher in the energies of the Seventh Dispensation. This is the time of unlimited possibilities for a giant leap of consciousness. Within the magnificent radiance of Saint Germain lies the matrix for the outpicturing of Divine fulfillment that is destined to be the Way of Life on Earth. One of the transformational tools that he shares with us is the Violet Consuming Flame. When you invoke the Violet Flame, it releases energies that are stuck in the density of the past and moves them out into Light. It allows for the fertile possibilities of unlimited potential. The Violet Flame is a part of Saint Germain as he is One with it. It is his gift to Life. To experience the energy that is Saint Germain, it is only necessary to turn the attention to Him. Invoke His Presence into your life and he will begin to reveal to you the magic and wonder that is this Great Soul. Your life can take on the refinement and grace that is a prelude to the ascended state. The more you come to know him, the more you become aware of the great Love, Humor, and Assistance that he will share with you. There is no separation between ascended and unascended. All are One. The Savior of this world is the combined energies of all Beings of Light who endeavor to fulfill the Divine Plan. Saint Germain holds the door open as we step into the future. He will walk with you along The Way. He will touch your shoulder and whisper in your ear. He is your friend from before Time. He is your friend and brother for all Time. He is what you are becoming. If you decide to know him, he will make Your Way interesting and reveal your heart's desires to you. For it is within the Heart of Saint Germain that he holds us forever in the Light!

The Violet Flame...

–Patricia Cota Robles

Aquarius and the 7th Solar Aspect of Deity will be the predominant influences in this dawning New Age. The 7th Solar Aspect of Deity is the Violet Flame which pulsates with the Divine Qualities of Freedom, Justice, Liberty, Victory, Mercy, Compassion, Forgiveness, Transmutation, Invocation, Divine Ceremony, Opportunity, Limitless Physical Perfection and many other gifts from God. The violet transmuting flame is a key ingredient in our personal and planetary transformation.

Machu Picchu and the crystal cloud ship
painted by Gonzalo Medina

On my birthday in **1993**, I was in the hot tub and someone said to me, "I hear Adam is leaving." Adam lived at the house and had been my boyfriend briefly, and then became a very good friend; he did a lot around the house. He was very strong and handy (as well as getting his massage license and doing most of his practice hours on… lucky me!) I had just gotten some insurance money from the guy across the street, whose car had rolled into a fire hydrant and flooded our new landscaping, and Adam and I were going to do a building project at the house with the money. I choked, because I didn't have any idea he was leaving. He had wanted to wait until after my birthday to tell me. Suddenly my life was about to change again. Around midnight that night, I went up to my large, beautiful room with my huge window overlooking the city and the harbor, and I opened a gift that my friend Carol had given me. It was a little leather pouch with a note that said, "to carry your stones in when you come with me to Peru." Decision made. I was going to Peru again.

Instead of the building project, I would use the money to go back to Peru, for the 3rd time. This seemed sort of crazy, as there are plenty of other places on the planet to visit, so why go back to the same place three times? All I can say is, the energy was very strong again for me to go back to Peru. The why's I couldn't answer. The trip was leaving in one month. This time I would travel again with Carol in the beginning, and then I would be very brave and stay another two weeks and travel on my own.

Preparation for Peru

As I always do, I began doing things to prepare. I like to be as prepared as possible to let in the maximum amount of light and Peru energy. I took more Reiki classes and some other energy work called La Ho Chi, and had many other energy sessions with gifted friends. I got acupuncture, and I went to see my friend and Network chiropractor Tim Tupper. Tim has a great deal: if you go to his talk about Network Chiropractic, you receive four free sessions. So I went, and had the first four sessions, and figured that was that. Tim then asked me if I was going to sign up for a month's worth of sessions. I said I didn't think so. I was leaving in two weeks for Peru and I was pretty busy. He offered that I could do two weeks now and two weeks when I got back. I was still hesitating. Then he asked, "What do you want to get out of it?"

I still don't know where my immediate answer came from, because I didn't even think I had an answer. I said, "Well, I can talk to the flowers, and I want to be able to HEAR the flowers." Tim said, "You better come twice a day." (He has another great deal- for one price you can come as many times as you want.) That conversation stayed in my mind. I went ahead and did the two weeks of sessions.

PERU 1993
THE 1ST MAGICAL MEETING WITH ROGER

Suddenly, there I was in Peru, and my roommate, whom I had just met, was Lesley Myburgh from South Africa. We immediately felt like sisters. And, she also wanted to travel for two weeks on her own after the trip with Carol. We both wanted to go to Bolivia. Now I had a travel partner. Oh how perfect, again.

One of the first nights of the trip, we were in the Sacred Valley, in the lobby of our lovely hotel. There was a group of Israeli tour guides there, and their Peruvian guide had invited our group to watch his slide show that night. I had seen him earlier, and didn't have any thoughts about him. He walked up and Carol introduced him, and when he shook my hand, my life changed. I fell absolutely in love with Roger Valencia in that moment…whatever that meant. Lesley and I invited him for a drink and he joined us. We were both mesmerized.

We watched his slide show, and asked him to talk with us some more. We sat and talked for several more hours. At one point, I remember saying something about it being late and then said, "Oh, well, there's no time anyway." (I was being metaphysical.) Roger began to explain concepts about time, with physics. Ho hum, I'm thinking, maybe this guy isn't who I thought he was. This is boring. Then, surprisingly, through explaining how there was time, he got to how there could be "no time." I concluded that the guy was brilliant. Our transformational conversation started at ground level and ended up in the stars!

Later, we played my "game," THE ORACLE, which still needed editing. It needed more distillation, because there was still way too much information. It needed "purification," as Roger called it. Anyway, we played it and he liked it. Finally, we had to call it a night. Lesley and I went to our room, and we both felt like our hearts would burst and our bodies would explode with excitement. We both jumped up and down, and had a laugh attack like the kids that we are, and were super-happy and both totally in love with the spirit of Roger.

Our group and Roger's group were off on separate routes the next day. Lesley and I told Carol that we wanted to get Roger as our guide for the next part of our journey. She said to forget it, because first of all, he was an adventure guide, and we wanted a spiritual guide, and besides that, he was one of the most respected guides in Peru, and was always busy. Ah- but we were obsessed. We probably drove our group a little nuts, because we talked about him A LOT. We tried calling him from any place we could. We left numerous messages. Since we couldn't get him by phone, we began to send him messages telepathically. Carol even joined in to try and help us. She said we would have a party when we got back to Cusco and invite him. She said Peruvians would always come to a party. Well, we had the party and he didn't show up. We had a nice time at the party and tried not to be disappointed.

Elation at Last

Our group left and we still had not made contact. Undaunted, we continued to telepath. Finally, it was time to leave Cusco. We had another guide lined up, and we were ready to check out of our hotel. Lesley suddenly left our room and went to the desk (she still doesn't remember why she went). As she stood there at the desk, the phone rang. The girl was saying "No, no esta aqui." Lesley started saying, "Yes, yes! I think that is for me!" She somehow got the phone and it was Roger. He was saying, "But they just said you weren't there," and Lesley said, "We are here!" Within 20 minutes he was at the hotel.

He said that he had been hiking in the Urubamba Mountains, came down early and was going to stay in Urubamba, when he just jumped on a bus and headed into Cusco. When he got home, he found the volume of messages we had left and called us immediately (and just in time). As it worked out, the 8 days that he had available were the 8 days that we wanted! We were blessed! We were elated!

He went off to get our tickets to fly to Bolivia and the Lake Titicaca area. He came back and said there were no tickets for that day. We could wait and fly the next day. The only other option was the local bus that left at 4:00 that afternoon and drove all night on a bumpy road. It was a no-brainer. Of course, we wanted to go on the bus. Fourteen hours? Local, overcrowded bus? No problem. Lesley and I grinned at each other for the full 14 hours. We didn't want Roger out of our sight, or out of our energy field. He felt like a master in embodiment, or at least the closest thing that I have ever felt.

We had an ecstatic and magical eight days weaving light and working with the ley lines (the seques), the energetic lines that surround the planet and connect sacred places. The energy was building every day and culminated at Copa Cabana. We thought we were hiking to a church, and we ended up at this very special spot called the "Joyous Fountain." Roger took us there to celebrate the Lightwork that we had done. This was our "adventure guide." And he is. He has set records climbing mountains in Argentina, and is an outstanding climbing guide. He is everything else as well, including the spiritual part which just comes naturally. As I watch him in action, I am always in awe. He helps everyone. He can interact with anyone, and he can do it fluently in five languages. We were SO happy and **SO GRATEFUL**.

We continued to play with the ORACLE, and Roger said that he would be willing to come to the U.S. to help edit it…sometime.

IT KEEPS GETTING BETTER

I went home high as a kite, or higher. I went back to Tim Tupper, for Network chiropractic, twice a day, 4 days a week for 8 months. Tim is someone that I highly respect. In addition to being a chiropractor, he is an acupuncturist, healer, a master herbalist, and an Ayurvedic doctor, and he knows more about flower essences (and every other form of complementary/alternative medicine) than anyone I know. Tim has worked with essences since the 60's, when he worked with Gurudas (r.i.p.), who started Pegasus, an essence company - and Richard Katz and Patricia Kaminsky of FES (Flower Essence Services).

I was blessed with time to work on myself all of that next year. I didn't know when Roger would get here, and I knew that he would be coming. Remember, this was before e-mail. We did do faxes now and then. He had a copy of the ORACLE that wanted editing.

It took almost a year, and he came, at of course the perfect time, my birthday! I had requested that he bring a slide show of Peru to share, which he did. We had a big party for my birthday and showed the slides. At the end Roger said, "I had Alberto (his son) put some slides of Orchids in at the last minute. Would you like to see them?"

I looked at him in astonishment and asked, "What do you know about Orchids?"

Roger, this brilliant guy, said, "They're my hobby."

As I mentioned earlier, I had heard **"ANDEAN ORCHID FLOWER ESSENCE"** since 1988, and since then it had become like a mantra in the back of my mind. Andean Orchid Flower Essence. As he spoke, it immediately went across my brain that I was going back to Peru for the "Andean Orchid Flower Essence" (singular, thinking there would be only one).

★★★

While Roger was visiting Santa Barbara, we worked on the ORACLE together. Magic happened during every session. For instance, when we were working on the hummingbird symbol, a hummingbird came to the window. Then I handed Roger a crystal, and the next card that he turned over was a crystal. Once, we "felt" a rainbow and walked outside and there it was. We got very high working on it. It was obvious we were having a lot of "help."

Orchids Orchids Everywhere

And then there were the Orchid "signs." The "coincidences" were totally amusing. We went on a wildflower class up San Marcos Pass. There was one flower Peggy Lane wasn't sure of because it wasn't in bloom. She thought it might be a wild Orchid. Roger scratched around the earth and confirmed that it was. We went to Cold Spring Tavern and there were Orchids on the table. An Angel friend (who knew nothing about my Orchid thing) gave me a birthday card that she said she picked out especially for me. It had an Orchid on it. She said, "I think it is the flower of Ascension." The Orchid thing went on and on. On the night before Roger was to leave, he wanted to go to a Thai restaurant. Someone recommended a restaurant on De La Vina Street. They didn't know the name of it, just the location. We went and as we sat down, I noticed the beautiful Orchid on the front of the menu. Then we noticed the name of the restaurant was Thai Orchid. All right, all right, I get it. I really am going to Peru to make these essences.

The Great Roger/Roger the Great

Roger is very instrumental in making the Orchid Essences. I swear he can spot them at 500 paces (however far that is). We were in the train once and he pointed to something up on the hill. I couldn't see a thing that looked remotely like an Orchid. He then showed me in the binoculars. I could see what he was talking about, and I could barely tell it was a flower with binoculars, and he could tell it was an Orchid without the binocs. He jumped out of the train and ran up the hill just to prove it to himself, and he was correct.

They do come out to say hello to him. And he has taught me to remember to say hello back.

Roger talking to Orchid

Roger became interested in Orchids in the mid-seventies after meeting a professor at the University of Cusco who was working with the Orchids of the coastal region. Roger was taking a general Botany class and was studying the course of Monocots. Roger says, "I was just called to Orchids." He started liking them, studying them, and collecting them for Professor Vargas. It became a hobby. He loved to visit them in the mountains, and talk to them. He has a tremendous love and affection for Orchids. He has written a book describing them and their habits.

Roger says, *"I think all flowers have healing energies. We work with Orchids for many reasons. Orchids have always been surrounded with a very interesting aura. They are sophisticated. They are quite evolved. What we know about Orchids is that they are the latest of the flowering plants to have evolved. There are many challenges in classifying them- because of their structure. The fact that they are the latest means that in the whole world's evolution, within their cellular structure- within their DNA, they will be carrying the long history of the whole plant world. They will be carrying the whole history of life and because they carry such a long knowledge of the Earth, they are also considered to be the latest of the works of the master intelligence- of the supreme intelligence. If they are the latest of the works of the supreme intelligence, then they encompass all the other works together- so I think the Orchid Flower Essences are for healing- and not only do they help those who are sick, they will help the people who are very healthy to reach new levels of health previously unimagined.*

"When people look at the Orchid flower, they are mesmerized. The Orchid communicates a high level of recognition through the physical body and even more strongly, through the spiritual body, and that is what calls us to the Orchids."

"Orchids grow everywhere. They are the largest family of flowering plants. We use the Orchids from the region called Vilcabamba – the Sacred Mountain Range. Mountains are natural altars. They are places to connect with the Higher Spirits- with the Masters of the Universe."

"The Vilcabamba Range is the area where I hiked and did my study of Orchids, and started doing their classifications and recognition based on their habits and the way they lived and the pollinating seasons in which they bloomed. The Inca Trail is a stone-paved path through the forest that connects the high cloud forest and the rain forest. From **MACHU PICCHU** *you can see all of the energy lines connected to the rest of the universe. All this creates a perfect setting for the workings of the spirit."*

"The whole Earth is awakening to a new period. A Light period. It is the time of the awakening of the golden light within the hearts of humanity. It means the time of understanding and the time of knowledge. Certainly vibrational medicine like flower essences will open those sources. It will light the fire and bring the golden flame within the heart. The Orchid essences will take healthy people a step beyond."

It is interesting that the one person that I am friends with in Peru turns out to be not only a master guide that speaks impeccably on any subject in five languages- I also find out his hobby is Orchids. MMMMMMmmmm. I love the magic and divinity.

I AM SO GRATEFUL!

MAKING THE ANDEAN ORCHID FLOWER ESSENCES

I FELT VERY STRONGLY ABOUT TRIANGULATION. EVEN THOUGH I WASN'T SURE WHY OR SURE WHAT IT MEANT.

It was my birthday, Feb. 8, 1994, when I made the decision to go make the Essences, and by mid-March all of the details had come together magically, and I was in Peru. It all happened very quickly.

When I first decided to go, I barely had enough money for a plane ticket, and 6 weeks later when we left, I had plenty of money for the trip, which came from surprising sources, and from many directions.

I kept getting a message about triangulation. It felt like there were supposed to be three of us to hold the energy for the essences to be made. I had a new housemate, Renee Sundarum, who had a very nice connection with Roger and I, and she was interested in going to Peru. She didn't think she could get off work for a week, and when she asked, they gave her two weeks off. She was quite pleasantly shocked.

This theory of triangulation was coming clearer. With triangulation, there can't be duality. **TRIANGULATION IS THE KEY TO TRANSCENDING DUALITY.**

One of my big questions was, what was I going to put the Mother Essences in, once I made them? I kept hearing triangles, and had been looking for triangular bottles. They seemed impossible to find, and I had pretty much given up and was going to get Mason jars. A couple of days before we were to leave for Peru, I was trying to get to the store to buy the Mason jars. I kept missing the freeway exit, so I decided that must be a sign to go home and do it another time. On the way home, I made a quick stop at Trader Joe's (a favorite store) for some snacks for the trip. While I was in the check-out line, I noticed some interesting bottles. They were triangular and they had vodka in them. I remember thinking very clearly to myself, "Too bad they have vodka in them." I don't drink vodka. Mostly what I drink at this stage of my life is water (distilled, and preferably with a sacred activation), and occasionally some (preferably) organic wine. I got a little closer and noticed the bottles had stars and a moon embedded in the glass. Oh, now that is really nice, I thought. I decided to buy one bottle in spite of the vodka, because it was such a nice bottle. I was driving home when suddenly I realized what had just happened. I had found triangular bottles!! Perfect ones at that. The vodka in them meant they would be really clean. They had screw tops, which are much better than the cork-topped bottles I thought I had been looking for, and way better than Mason jars! This might not seem so remarkable to you, but to me it was major and magical. The story continued. The vodka company quit making these bottles about a year later. I'm convinced they were made especially for the Orchid Mothers. I bought several cases, and when I ran out, and they weren't making them any more, a friend "coincidentally" found a case in a distributor's garage and bought them for me. I had just enough. Gifts were showering down on me!

Another gift was that I realized that the Orchids wanted to be preserved with vodka- not the traditional brandy used in most flower essences. The graphics that came with this "Jubileam" Vodka were great. It said. "Beyond the ordinary, it's Evolutionary Vodka. Vodka from a higher realm." I'm not kidding. I kept one of the triangular hangtags to remind myself that I didn't make that up. This vodka also had the gift of being quite light, with a tasty flavor. I worried about what I would do when they quit making it. I heard a voice repeating a line from the tag...."Distilled Spirit, flavored with citrus and spice." We now buy "Vodka of the Gods" (yes- that is what it says on the bottle) and add our own citrus and spice. OK, enough about vodka, let's go back to Peru.

There I was, with Renee, armed with my clear glass bowls and triangular bottles, heading off to Peru to meet my good friend, guide superior, botanist and lover of Orchids, Roger Valencia, who just happened to be available for us. This was VERY exciting.

Another interesting thing, for the record, is that I had my last moon (menstrual period) a month before that 49th birthday. I began this essence project in my powerful crone stage, and I feel this is my most important work so far.

We arrived in Cusco, and I didn't really expect to see Roger. I figured he would have someone pick us up and take us to a hotel to rest and acclimate to the altitude. That was not the case. Roger was there with a big smile on his face, saying, "Come on, let's go! The van is packed, the driver is here, the porters are ready, and the cook is waiting for us at Wiñay Wayna." He said he was just at **Machu Picchu**, and we must go NOW because the Orchids were coming into their peak at that moment. I have full appreciation for that "moment of bloom," now that I am a veteran essence maker. So off we went. A little later we stopped at a gorgeous spot where Roger had a beautiful vegetarian picnic prepared for us. Nice start!

We continued the scenic drive on through the Sacred Valley to Ollantaytambo. We stayed at a place called Wendy's Albergue. That was the first time I ever stayed there. (I liked it so much that now I try to stay there whenever I go to **Machu Picchu**!) The Albergue (which means lodge) is right next to the train station. It is so cool for the Hostal to be right on the railroad tracks. You can just go out the hostal gate and right onto the train.

The next day, we hopped aboard the train to **Machu Picchu**. Our porters, who would carry all our stuff, were there to meet us in the town of Aguas Calientes, right below **Machu Picchu**. I had my plan. I figured that we would be making a couple of essences on the Inca Trail during our hike in to Wiñay Wayna. Well, hiking in, it was raining. I began to question my crystal-clear, and many-times-confirmed guidance. Were we really supposed to make these essences? When making an essence, the traditional way is to place the blossoms in the water in the SUN for stabilization. When we got to Wiñay Wayna, the porters greeted us with tea and popcorn (I love it) and they had the tents set up. We meditated and did Tai Chi together, and bonded and rested. The next day the sun was out- it felt like we were in heaven, and we were in a fabulous frame of mind to make the essences. And so we made them. The entire process for 6 days was a sacred ceremony done with the highest frequencies of Love, and Divine choreography, always.

Making these Orchid essences was one of the highest, most memorable experiences of my life. The Orchids are growing at an altitude of about 10,000 feet in the sacred environs of **Machu Picchu** - on energetic ley lines - or seques, as they are called in Peru. All of the Orchids we use are wild, well-adapted, happy in their environment, in full bloom, and plentiful. Of course, the most important ingredient is their willingness to co-create an essence. These are absolute requirements. Roger and I always spend some time with each plant. The volunteers are quite obvious, and usually are saying "CHOOSE ME!" before we even have a chance to ask. The co-creative process is super-gratifying, and joyfully consuming. Sometimes I feel like the flowers are playing me, and I love being their instrument.

Roger was right about the flowers being at their peak. Indeed they were, and we saw over thirty varieties in bloom. I don't think

I have ever seen so many in bloom at one time on any subsequent trip. We made seven essences on that first journey. They are the foundation of the entire Star Essence System. They are: Habenaria ♥ **Balance and Stability**, Epidendrum Ibaguense ♥ **Eternal Youth**, Lycaste Longepetalia ♥ **Ancient Wisdom**, Sobralia Dichotoma ♥ **Anchoring Light**, Trichoceros Parviflorum ♥ **Nature Communion**, Masdevallia Veitchianna ♥ **Divine Goddess**, and Pleurothallis ♥ **High Frequency**.

We used wonderful water from a sacred ceremonial fountain. As we made the essences, we felt reverence, bliss, wonder and awe.

After being in such a rarefied frequency for 6 days, there was a palpable change when we got back to the city of Cusco. I was briefly uncomfortable as I made the adjustment. It made me super-aware of the high vibration we had been co-creating in.

One other huge synchronicity that was happening was that while we were making the essences, there was a very energetically and astrologically auspicious planetary alignment that we had been looking forward to for months. It was called the "Sirius Peristron" (April 23, 1994). Sirius has been known since ancient times as the Dog Star because of its position in the constellation of Canis Major. The portal for this Goddess energy had opened fully only once before in the history of Humankind. It was over 90,000 years ago and with it was born Lemuria. The vortex of the Goddess was going to be open wide on that day and flooding us with a new encodement of light. It was another "cosmic trigger." With that opening dawned a positive future. It opened a new world of dreams, magic and miracles. A world more vast and wonderful than we could previously imagine. On that day, we took the essences to the Temple of the Moon at Sacsayhuaman, right outside Cusco, to be infused with that magical light. It was, again, Divine Choreography in action. What Fun!

Hiking, Planting Trees for Pacha, Sending Love to Rocks

After that, Renee and I went with Roger's brother and another guide to hike in the Urubamba Mountains, into a village called Cuncani. Roger and his friends started a non-profit organization called "Pacha" there, to plant trees around this remote village. We drove as far as the road went, then took horses into Cuncani. We had a great time planting trees and then did a very challenging hike out, over a very tall mountain pass. I used the technique of sending love to the rocks and breathing energy back from them. This helped me considerably, and I made the hike comfortably. Horses carried our gear, and I noticed that there was an extra horse on the way out. Roger told us later that it was the "Red Cross" (ambulance) horse, in case one of us got too tired and couldn't make the entire hike. We both made it. It felt like this communion with Nature was more preparation for what was coming next.

The Big Question:

How do you know what the essences are for?

A question arises for many people. How do you know what the essences are for? Prior to making the first essence, I asked myself this question, too. I didn't know if I was going to have to go to an outside source, if I would have to find a really good channel, or what I would do. I just knew I had to keep taking the steps that came, which is still how I operate. I knew "Magic Happens," and the bumper sticker on my car even said so!

After our hike Renee headed back home to Santa Barbara, and I opted to stay for another few weeks, to see if I could tune in and determine what the essences were for.

I sat with the essences. I took them. I meditated with them. I looked at the flower drawings that Renee had made. I looked at the botanical names and information that Roger had given me. Nothing was coming. I had taken one book with me on the trip. It was *Heart of the Christos*, by Barbara Hand Clow. I opened it up randomly to page 201. It was 3:11a.m. It said, "Flower essences are very important."

That was all I read of the book. Turning to that kept me encouraged. I ended up getting a little bit sick after that, so I stayed in my room and fasted and just drank the corn tea that the sweet hotel folks brought me to settle my stomach. For about 3 days, I just slept and meditated. One morning at 4 a.m., I woke up, wide awake, and suddenly I "knew" what the essences were for! They each had a name. It was all so obvious. It felt like every essence "knew" its name. Fortunately, I wrote down their names and brief descriptions, because when I woke up later, it wasn't nearly so obvious and I couldn't remember what I had written. That is how it happened that time.

The rest of the flowers have different stories. How I find out what they are for happens in all kinds of different ways. In dreams, in visions, 10-second spots on the radio, a book, a conversation, neon signs in my head, information that I am guided to, looking at the Doctrine of Signatures, and, of course, always asking the flowers.

Love Affair

By the time I got back home to Santa Barbara, I was having a love affair with the Orchids that would passionately consume me. I had no idea that I would be starting a business. In fact I never did start it. It started me.

I had been living at the Coyote Road ANGEL HOUSE on borrowed time. The payments were greater than the income, even though there were 13 people living there. (It's a big house on an acre on a hillside.) We had folks living in tents and in every nook and cranny, and it worked. We were still doing *Angel Meetings* every Sunday. I had been taking Light Body classes, learning to work and travel with my *merkaba*, or light vehicle, which is about connecting our electrical grid system. This work helps one to become aligned, activated and capable of running high vibrations and frequencies in order for the higher self and Christed self to anchor and function in physical form. In short, it connects the circuits. Shilea and Zandriel were my teachers, and Shilea made Archangel Essences. I was excited to take her a set of the new Orchid Essences I had just made in Peru. Shilea called me prior to the class, and asked me to bring my new essences to the class.

I said, "Oh yes, of course, I am bringing you a set of the essences." She said, "No, I mean bring them to sell." I had really not thought about selling them. Especially at the class. I hesitated and said "…But you have your Archangel Essences to sell." She said that didn't matter. I had to bring the Orchid Essences. She said, "We have been waiting for them."

ORCHID, THE FLOWER OF ASCENSION…

The amazing thing for me was that I took them to the class, and I sold $400.00 worth! That was a pretty big sign for me! It also gave me money to buy more bottles. That was how the *Star Flower Essence* business began.

THE *Star Flower Essence* BUSINESS

Soon after, a woman named Jeannie Housebrook, who lived in L.A. and was in the Light Body class, called me and said, "Why don't you take the Essences to Fred's Psychic Faire? He lets vendors come for $25.00 a day."

That was my first show. I had at least 8 people helping me at this small, local event. In that safe, small space, I learned how to do a show. We got a super-positive response. That first show got things moving to do more shows, and getting the essences "out there."

I was taking lots of essences (and I still do) and transforming myself all of the time. I continued to get more information about the essences. One in particular, was Eternal Youth. I kept hearing to get it **on the skin**. Be sure and use it topically, as well as orally, I heard. It's **really good for the skin**, I kept hearing. I put it into misters and spray bottles. It did feel really good on the skin. Prior to this time, I used to make these peppermint and lavender facial sprays for Christmas presents. I had never seen sprays made with essences AND oils. I kept trying different combinations of oils, and nothing was really working.

ANGEL SPRAY IS BORN

Then one night, it was that 4 a.m. thing again, and I heard, rather loudly… "Lavender, Frankincense and Geranium"…I got out of bed and tried it, and loved, loved, loved it! Later it was christened Angel Rejuvenation Spray, and it is a wonderful and winning combination of essences and oils.

Everything was new. I had to figure out where to get bottles. My usual source had doubled their price. That turned out to be the gift. (Oh, how usual.) It made me look for other sources. The first one I called said they didn't have the (traditional) amber bottles, but they had blue bottles. Yippee! I hadn't seen blue bottles prior to that. I bought them right away.

Embracing Computers

I wrote my first brochure out by hand, photocopied it, and hand painted the Orchid I had drawn. I had to laugh when someone asked me what font it was! I also handwrote the labels. This, however, was a tedious process. I started praying for a computer. Now, mind you, this was in 1994, and even though a lot of folks knew SOMETHING about personal computers, I knew nothing. I was pretty sure I could use one if I tried. I remember that several years before, I had traded a computer - before I even figured out how to use it - for a trip to Peru, and it was a good trade.

One day, just a month or two before our foreclosure notice on the Angel House, a guy named Joleth came to the door. He said he was an 11:11 angel, and he was guided to come to the Angel House. He wanted to rent a room. I told him we didn't have any vacancies. However, someone had just given me notice, and would be leaving in a month. Joleth and I continued to chat, and somehow my desire for a computer came up in conversation.

Joleth said, "Well, I have one in my car, and if you will let me park in your driveway and sleep in my car for a month, I will let you use my computer, and even show you how to use it."

At first, we put the computer in my bedroom, and I didn't like that at all. I was just getting used to the idea of having a computer itself, and the computer energy was just too much to have so close to me. It was a love/hate thing. We found a little area in the laundry room and made it "The Computer Space."

Now let me tell you, this arrangement with Joleth was way better than me getting a computer on my own. I would have had no idea what to do with it. Joleth became the maker of the Star Essence labels and brochures, and he showed me how to use the computer. What I got was more than money could buy. At first he did everything and I watched. Then I did some of it. Then I would do it and Joleth would be in the living room reading and meditating, and he would be there every time I yelled for help. It was absolutely the best I could have asked for, and I didn't even know what to ask for. I am always impressed how Spirit has the best ideas! I will add that I have definitely embraced computers now. I and the business have five of them, and I love continuously learning new things about them. I practically sleep with Louie Laptop.

We used to have bottling parties, and folks would come and help bottle and label. Oceanna and Shamballa would come and sing and play music for us, and Jeda would give us shoulder massages and it was a party.

Eventually, change was upon us. The flower essence business was growing.

Yanonali Street House

(Yanonali was a Chumash Indian Chief)

Sometime around September of 1994, I got the foreclosure notice on the Angel House. I was financially bankrupt. I was making house payments with credit cards and credit card payments with credit cards. All the lawyers could tell me was that I was in good company. It was the first time in my adult lifetime in Santa Barbara that I had seen the economy- real estate in particular- go down.

It was all divine. It was time for a change. The Archangel Michael miracle loan had served me well, and it was easy to donate the lovely house back to the bank. The essences had priority and they wanted to be sent out and there really wasn't anywhere in the big house to operate. (There were 13 of us living there…) So I let go of the big redwood house that I had built with its gorgeous views of the mountains and harbor and islands, and moved my entire life into the converted carport at my Yanonali Street house. I got to keep this Yanonali Street house in the bankruptcy settlement, because there wasn't any equity in it. It was all rented out and the only place I could afford was the carport, so there I was. Me, my cat, my new Essences, and all of my stuff that used to be in a 3,000-square-foot house on the hill.

I had a garage sale for 3 weekends before I moved. I definitely lightened up. I had a trailer in back of the house, behind the carport, and I thought that I would use that as my bedroom. As it worked out, I was working so much, that I never did make it to the trailer at night. I would just flip out a foam futon on the floor, wherever I could find space. I had a hole made in the door so the cat could get in and out, and it turned out that the raccoons liked the opening, as well as the cat food. I would wake up sometimes in the middle of the night and there I was, eye to eye with "Rocky Raccoon" (as I affectionately named him). He came regularly to have a midnight snack from my cat Lilac's bowl, which was about 2 feet from my head. I was very happy to be in the small space with the Essences. They had taken over my life, and I was

SO GRATEFUL!

THE BEGINNING OF STAR INTERGALACTIC TOURS

Roger had suggested that I take groups to Peru. I thought to myself, NO WAY. I don't speak very good Spanish, and I am not nearly as assertive and organized as my friend Carol, who took groups. I certainly didn't know much about Peru. Carol had studied it a lot, and spoke excellent Spanish. Roger said not to worry, just get the folks to Lima and he would do the rest.

There was another auspicious date coming up: 12:12. I was still hesitant. Then I received a phone call and a letter asking if I would take a group to Peru for 12:12 in 1994. Yikes. I said yes, and the rest is history… I have been taking groups once or twice a year since then.

CHASKALAND

One time when I was in Peru, Roger and I began talking about buying a piece of land there. We talked about what and how we would do it. Then we found ourselves looking around at different spots. This looking went on during a couple of trips to Peru. Then one time, I arrived in Peru, and Roger was excited. He said he had figured out where we should buy land!

There is a small town in the Sacred Valley called San Salvador. It is about an hour from Cusco. You can even hike or take horses over a mountain from Cusco to get there. Tourists don't go there, but thousands of Peruvians make a pilgrimage there every year in September, to travel to the Sacred Valley.

There is a church there called "The Sanctuary of Señor De Huanca." More importantly, in 1973 there was a Kumbhamela there. This was an event where holy people from Tibet came and bathed in the Urubamba River, and brought the Goddess Ray to anchor it in that valley. Roger remembers cutting school that day and going from Cusco over to San Salvador, and seeing and talking to some of the holy men. He remembers it having changed his life. The town, San Salvador, is at the base of a mountain called

PACHATUSAN, which means **"ANCHOR OF THE WORLD."**

After our group was gone, I stayed in Peru, so Roger and I could go have a look in San Salvador. The night before we were to go there, we did a special ceremony with our friend Gonzalo. Gonzalo is an extraordinary artist who painted the Ascended Masters, Sacred Sites, space ships - paintings with cosmic themes. He had done many murals around the Sacred Valley. His physical body has now left this dimension, and he has crossed over to other worlds. It felt like that ceremony prepared us to easily and gracefully go to San Salvador and find a perfect spot the next day. We took a little mini-bus (the local transport) to San Salvador. The driver only spoke Quechua, which was fine, since Roger speaks perfect Quechua. (Quechua is the indigenous language in that part of Peru.)

They had a nice conversation, and the man took us to a piece of property that had been vacant for a long time. There was no house, just a falling-down building and planted corn. We fell in love with it immediately. It was located right on the river. It was one hectare (about 3 acres) and flat- looking directly at the Pachatusan Mountain. I was so excited! I was telling Roger to find the owner, to see if it was for sale, make an offer, do something! (I had no idea how I would get the money; I just knew that I would.)

Roger told me to relax, that we would do things the Peruvian way. We wouldn't do the American thing and barge in and make an offer.

So I waited patiently. (Well, not very patiently, but I waited.) I asked about it every chance I had. We went back and visited the land on subsequent trips to Peru. I waited nearly two years. Then, in the middle of one of my trips there, Roger approached me and was once again excited. His brother-in-law had just called him and said that he heard we were looking for land in San Salvador, and there was a piece coming up for sale. The piece of land he was describing sounded very much like the piece we had been looking at. We quickly made arrangements to go over there with Xavier, and indeed, it was our spot. Then the owners offered to sell it to us (that is what Roger meant by the "Peruvian Way"- they offer it to you). Over the next several months, Roger negotiated for the land, and I managed to borrow some money on my house, because it had a little equity in it by then.

Interestingly enough, the lady who was selling the land was selling it because she wanted money for her son, who was doing a project. In the middle of our escrow, her son suddenly died, from unknown causes. Roger went to talk to her. He told her we would not hold her to the escrow if she didn't want to sell it.

She said, " No, a deal is a deal."

So, we got to buy the land!

At this writing, the only things on the land are a Peace Pole given to us by Danielle Sato of the Peace Pole Project- **PEACE PREVAILS ON EARTH**, a labyrinth, and a little palapa (gazebo) that gives us a nice picnic spot if it is raining. We had a wonderful ceremony there when we planted the Peace Pole and we planted a Pink Mangano Calcite sphere inside the Pole that was given to me by Kathy Kinniard, who was at that time the owner of the Flower Essence Pharmacy. I always visit the land with my travel groups. The lovely Quechua family that lives next door keeps an eye on it, and I am the Godmother to two of their daughters.

Roger, Star & the Peace pole at Chaskaland.

I have made four essences there, which you will hear about in detail later. They are (Chijchipa) I am Generosity, (YuYu/Mustard) I Am Gratitude, (Wild Potato) Wild Feminine, and Chaska. We call the land "Chaska Land." Chaska means "Star" in Quechua.

The Business Grows (The Essences work for Everyone!)

I had borrowed some money to keep going, and borrowing became my way of life. I was the Loan Queen, and also known as the Queen of the ledge, for my willingness to go to the edge-especially economically. To get one of the first loans, I needed to fax my business plan, and I didn't have a fax machine. It wasn't going to make my business look too good, if I didn't even have a fax machine. I had just gotten my phone hooked up, and the line only went to the outside of the house. I managed to buy a fax machine and put it in a plastic bag (it was raining), and hooked it directly to the box on the side of the house. I was faxing! I got the loan and it carried me through, briefly.

The first time I bottled essences, I made 2-dram concentrates. This was pretty standard with essence makers at the time. I soon realized that folks were taking the essences right away, directly from the bottle, without diluting them (they wanted instant gratification and I can certainly understand that)- even though it is way more cost-effective to make dilutions from the concentrates. That is what helped me choose to make dosage bottles, essences ready-to-go, as well as the traditional stock (concentrate) bottles.

In the beginning you could only buy an essence directly from me. I wanted it to go directly from my hand to yours. I wasn't sure how stable the energy was. That shifted the more I found out how well that they work. I remember Roger saying on his first visit to the States after we made the essences -as he was observing reactions to the essences- "I knew they worked for you and I knew they worked for me; I didn't know they worked for EVERYONE!"

That first year I did everything. I bottled, labeled, shipped, learned how to work a computer, created a database, wrote brochures, wrote letters for mailings, went to shows and spoke to whomever would listen.

I put marbled paper on the little boxes- because I knew the essences liked nice houses. I love adding art to a project. Art adds its own nice vibe. (My calligraphy background has helped tremendously because of the design and layout that I learned- and it gave me a great appreciation for fonts. I love the computer for its fonts. I never took the time to practice practice practice to make really beautiful letters- and now you can make beautiful letters right on the computer. (That fact alone has endeared me to the computer.)

The essences told me that they preferred to be standing up, rather than lying down, and thus the corrugated boxes that we use were designed. They also have hand-marbled paper (most of which I marbled myself - and thank you Jean Marie Seaton for teaching me how). A lot of love goes into each piece.

The time came when I needed a computer myself. Up until then, Joleth had shown up with his whole computer (NOT a laptop) and made labels for me, whenever we had a bottling party. I asked all around for money, and finally it was my sister-in-law Norma Howell, who didn't have any money, yet let me put the computer on her credit card. I am eternally grateful. I have often found the people with the least doing the most. That computer served me very well!

One day a housemate and friend, Jeda (combination used-car salesman, telemarketer, massage therapist, crystal healer, energy worker), asked me if he could take the essences to Mt. Shasta to the Mother Mary Conclave happening there. I was hesitant and finally agreed to let them go. It was like leaving the baby with a sitter for the first time. I was happy and a little nervous at the same time. It worked out beautifully and we still have friends and customers from that event.

With miracles abounding- even though money at that time wasn't- I was introduced to Morrie Glaser, who created a web site for me in 1995 for almost free- with a few trades (exactly what my budget called for). Having this website so early on was a gigantic gift.

My Daughter Cara was my first employee and that was a lot of fun. She would come with baby Krista. Kelsea was in school. Of course, back then, many of the days we would choose between roller-skating and working, and often, roller-skating won.

★★★

Teaching became the next phase——

And so for the next section … **LET THE FUNSHOP BEGIN !**

PART TWO

Let the funshop begin

FUNSHOP

Pretend that you have just walked into the Star Essence class. As in other classrooms all across America, you hear the Star Spangled Banner being played. (Think Stars- Think Spangles) - Only the words have been changed... Please hum along to the **EARTH ANTHEM** with these words written by Stephen Longfellow Fiske:

Oh, Say, can we see
By the one Light in all
Our Earth to embrace
At the call of all nations,
Where our children can play
In a world that is free,*
Where we stand hand in hand
In the Grace of Creation,
Where the rivers run clean
Through the forests of green,
where the cities stand tall
In the clear skies of Freedom.

Oh say do our hearts sing out
For Harmony and Love forever
On the planet of our birth
Blessed with P e a c e o n E a r t h.

* The words "without war" were changed to "that is free" - to keep the language positive- I like to operate in the positive and skip those "thou shalt nots" and leave it with "thou shalt."

AN INVOCATION

I surround our space with Peace and Love and Light and Joy and Bliss and Ecstasy. I invite in all of the guides and the Angels and Archangels and Solar Angels and the Ascended Masters of Light that work with us from the highest realms to be with us. Saint Germain in particular, and Dr. Bach and the Overlighting Deva* of this book, and the Overlighting Deva of the *Star Essences*

*Deva = shining one - Elemental - Nature Spirit

and Pan - please join us and overlight the readers of this book… Please impart and infuse your energies and be with us. I ask that every person who reads this book be blessed with a special attunement to the Star Essences, and I ask that every thing that comes through the words and radiation of this book be for the highest good of all life everywhere throughout the universe. And for all of the guidance and the gifts and the blessings that we have and continue to receive,
Please join with me in saying- three times-

I AM SO GRATEFUL!
I AM SO GRATEFUL!
I AM SO GRATEFUL!

And now- Just for Fun,
I AM SO JOYOUS
I AM SO JOYOUS
I AM SO JOYOUS, JOYOUS JOYOUS!

Joyousness is REALLY what we're all about.

If you have any essences, I would suggest that you take an essence. In the class, the bar is open. In fact, at our office, the bar is always open. You can come in any time and help yourself to a flower essence cocktail. (I like to have the essences throughout my house so they remind me to take them, plus they act like little crystals- beaming their very sweet frequencies out and about.) During the funshops we have the interruption rule, which means feel free to interrupt. In upgrading to conscious languaging, we have changed the wording from interruption to conscious addition. Instead of the talking stick where you pass a stick around a circle and each person speaks when it is their turn to hold the stick, my preference is for only one person to talk at a time, and for everyone to listen. Then as you are moved by the energy, when you have something valuable to add, you do it while the energy is there to do it (rather than waiting for that stick to get to you and you have forgotten your brilliant remark, or- you haven't heard anything else because you are concentrating so hard to remember it). That way we have conscious conversations. In fact, while you are reading- if you have something to add, or a question, or a comment, please jot it down and e-mail us. We are in an organic, co-creative process that continues to grow, and everyone that wants to can contribute to our knowledge.

Essences: Who and What They Are:

Essences are powerful and tender, earthly and stellar. Vibrational essences are created for change, for growth, for greater spirituality, for opening the heart. They are high harmonic frequencies.

I'll begin with a little bit of history -

Flower essences have been used throughout time. Indigenous cultures have known about their powers for centuries. Aborigines of Australia, Native America Indians, The Essenes, The Quechua in Peru, and I am sure many others were skilled in the use of flower essences. It is said that Jesus taught his apostles to use oils and essences.

Paracelsus was a 16th century Swiss physician who studied what he called "Essentia," the essential qualities that underlie all phenomena. He had his patients drink the dew from the flowers that he collected. He is also said to be the first one to articulate the theory of the

"Doctrine of Signatures," which states that the external appearance of a plant will give clues to its healing properties. What the plant looks like can reveal its gifts.

(I have read that **Saint Germain**, one of the Ascended Masters who overlights the *Star Essences*, is known to have come in many embodiments. One of them was Paracelsus.) Essences are healing tinctures from Nature. It is said that flower essences were used extensively in the ancient civilizations of Atlantis and Lemuria. They were used for healing as well as for higher states of consciousness. This resonates with me.

♥★ DR BACH ♥★

Dr. Edward Bach, an English pathologist and bacteriologist, resurrected this ancient knowledge, and introduced his innovative system to the medical profession and the general public in a book called Heal Thyself, published in England in 1931. (I highly recommend this big-in-depth, little-in-size book.) Dr. Bach was inspired by the homeopathic principles brought forth by the 18th century German physician, Samuel Hahnemann, who introduced the concept that like cures like and does so in minute quantities. Dr. Bach had a conviction that Nature held the key to more gentle and effective healing. He also became aware of an individual's role in creating their own health. He was inspired to prepare 38 flower essences, which are known today as the Bach flower essences. I have felt connected to Dr. Bach since the moment I first heard of him. I love Dr. Bach and Dr. Bach loves me. I feel his guidance often. Once he told me he was a lot more jolly than the picture on the front of his book portrayed him to be. He has asked me, as well as other essence makers, to take his work to new octaves. He was a pioneer. He was a renegade. I can relate. In 1936, the year he died, Dr. Bach wrote to the British General Medical Council to tell them that it was up to them whether or not to remove his name from the Medical Register (the Medical Register listed the names of those who were approved to practice medicine at that time). He wrote the council that he was leaving the decision in their hands as he considered it " the duty and the privilege of any physician to teach the sick and others how to heal themselves." He closed the letter by stating, "Having proved that the herbs of the field are so simple to use and so wonderfully effective in their healing powers, I deserted orthodox medicine." I, too, turned my back on orthodox medicine. Intuitively I knew there had to be something else, although when I left Nuclear Medicine I didn't yet know what it was. In Nuclear Medicine I did become used to the "unseen" being very powerful. Things you couldn't see or touch or hear or taste or smell: Isotopes. I know that this experience helped prepare me for my discovery of vibrational essences. Now I work literally at the other end of the energy spectrum- with vibrational essences. What a great relief to me that the Divine has a plan that works so masterfully.

ESSENCES ARE INEXPENSIVE, ALWAYS SAFE FOR EVERYONE, AND EASY TO USE. The worst that can happen is nothing, AND THE BEST THAT CAN HAPPEN IS MIRACLES- which happen time and again. Vibrational Essences are among the most powerful and gentle tools for transformation for the 21st Century. They create energetic bridges. They are a cornerstone, and one of the earliest manifestations of what has come to be known as Vibrational Medicine. They are A MOST ELEGANT FORM OF THERAPY AND CONSCIOUS EVOLUTION. The medicine of the future is now, in Nature's pharmacy.

HOW DO ESSENCES WORK?

We have always known the power of the Nature Kingdom to heal and to promote well-being. It is only recently that the deepest secrets of this power are being investigated and used extensively, and integrated into other healing modalities by modern health practitioners. Plants are living beings, part of something much greater than themselves. Flowers are the highest expression of the plant's development, the soul of the plant, containing its sentient life-force and the seeds of its next generation. When we take a flower and put it in water and we use the magnificent energy of sunlight to charge the water, the flower transfers that life energy into the water, which is then used as an essence. Flower essences are the energetic imprints of this life-force of the flower. This creation of a flower remedy is a co-creative act between nature, the environment and humanity to nourish the human soul.

EVERYTHING THAT EXISTS HAS A FREQUENCY. This includes essential oils, diseases, and even emotions. Fear, joy, passion, courage, health, devotion, empathy: each have a particular wave pattern. Stronger and weaker variations of the same emotions show up as the same pattern in a different octave. The essences come in at higher frequencies, in the presence of which the lower frequencies cannot exist. In the Star system of essences, you look for the frequency you desire. If you are feeling depressed - you can take, for instance, **Pure Joy**. It will generally move you out of that feeling. If you take **Pure Joy** when you are already happy-

I have seen it make people all giggly… The essences work from the octave where you are and move you gently- and often (though not always) subtly. When you are choosing *Star Essences*, think about the outcome you desire. Modern physics as well as ancient mystical traditions agree that we live in a world of vibration. Flower essences are based on quantum physics, which defines matter as fields of energy, which oscillate between wave and particle. These fields of energy are impacted by resonance. According to Patricia Kaminsky in her book *Flowers that Heal*: "Flower Essences work according to the principle of resonance. The specific structure and shape of life-force conveyed by each flower essence resonates with and amplifies particular qualities within the human soul." Vibrational essences are based on the same principles as color and sound therapy. Nuclear Medicine (my past profession) is also vibrational medicine. It is a science very interested in counting things. Vibrational pulses, in particular. I love the sign that hung in Albert Einstein's office at Princeton, which said:

"Not everything that counts can be counted, and not everything that can be counted counts."

For a long time we couldn't "count" those vibrational frequencies like we could count isotopes, because of their high frequencies and the density of the instruments. Now we can count more things than ever before. The unseen world is now becoming visible, or at least, measurable. Now bio-energetic tools (machines) are being created that make it possible to measure bodily vibrations. These tools will change the face of diagnosis and healing in western civilization. (Elia Wise talks about this in her book *Letters to Earth*.) Until recently we have had to rely on "anecdotal evidence" - results (actually that works just fine for me). And- it will be nice to see a meter move, to prove what many of us already know, that, yes- everything in the universe has a frequency, countable with human-made instruments, or not.

Let's look at another definition of essences. Gurudas, in his book called *Flower Essences and Vibrational Healing*, defines flower essences as "TINCTURES OF LIQUID CONSCIOUSNESS" within which are stored an evolutionary force, indeed the life force itself, shaped into a particular pattern." He goes on to say that when ingested, flower essences become an evolutionary force in the consciousness of the individual by educating one in psycho-spiritual dynamics, helping us to rediscover the sources and principles of our own true behavioral patterns as spirits and beings of light, by activating ancient doorways to higher levels of consciousness. They open our channels so we are more receptive to our higher self."

They are the art and science of bringing balance. Flower essences are FLORAL OFFERINGS OF THE ANGELS AND ELEMENTALS. They feed our light bodies like a tonic, as they raise our frequencies.

Marcel Vogel, a research scientist who worked for IBM and who made groundbreaking (re-) discoveries about crystals, summed up his research on flower essences by saying: "In flower essences we are dealing with geometric forms which are the precursors for the formation of matter. These codes are absorbed by the etheric body and translated into stimulating vibrational frequencies." Recently, when I was taking the Higher Chakra Trilogy of Orchid essences (you will read about them later), I could see those geometries.

So we have liquid infusions of energies held in water. We have some explanations of how they work. We now have hundreds of thousands of cases of vibrational essences doing their magic all over the world. The essences work and they do so gently, beautifully, elegantly. Our etheric body has receptors for these sweet frequencies that we feed it.

Essences and Oils

Essential oils, which hold the fragrance of a flower, and have therapeutic qualities, also have measurable vibrations. Essential oils have the chemistry of the plant. They are wonderful tools. Essential Oil Therapy (formerly called aromatherapy) is becoming more popular in the United States as we become more educated about them. (It has been popular for a long time in Europe and is used by medical doctors there.)

Flower Essences are totally vibrational. They do not have chemistry and do not have an aroma. The essential oil- which does have an aroma, is like the blood of the plant, and the flower essence is like the soul of the plant. They work very nicely and harmoniously with each other. That is one of the many great beauties of the essences, their compatibility. Use them both.

Compatibility with other Healing Modalities

Star Essences **are compatible with any other modality you are using**, and they will enhance and accelerate your healing process. You can use essences with any kind of medicine, be it occidental (allopathic) or alternative, complementary, Chinese, Ayurvedic, traditional or non-traditional. They can be taken with any other kind of medication with absolute safety. Essences are good adjuncts to any type of therapy and will hasten recovery. You can add them to other liquid preparations (i.e. herbal tinctures, skin creams) to broaden the spectrum of their effectiveness. They are successfully integrated with other modalities of health enhancement. On a rare occasion, especially with very sensitive people, there will be an exacerbation of a situation, because of a need to see the patterns consciously before they are let go. One of the big things that drew me to flower essences after Nuclear Medicine, was the rare and beautiful blessing that there are no side effects or contra-indications with essences. Flower essences fulfill the first premise of the Hippocratic oath: Physician, Do no Harm. And they help miracles abound.

"The greatest gift that you can give to others is to be happy and hopeful yourself; then you draw them up out of their despondency...The action of these remedies is to raise our vibrations and open up our channels for the reception of the Spiritual Self to flood our natures with the particular virtue we need, and wash out from us the fault that is causing the harm. They are able, like beautiful music or any glorious uplifting thing, which gives us inspiration, to raise our very natures, and bring us nearer to our souls and by that very act to bring us peace and relieve our sufferings. They cure, not by attacking the disease, but by flooding our bodies with the beautiful vibrations of our Higher Nature, in the presence of which, disease melts away as snow in the sunshine." —Dr. Bach

Vibrational Essences are super-easy to use.

> *"Let not the simplicity of this method deter you from its use, for you will find the further your researches advance, the greater you will realize the simplicity of all Creation."*
> Edward Bach, MD

> *"True medical advance will always be simple, natural, beautiful, loving and poetic."*
> John Diamond, MD

Do not equate simplicity with primitive or infantile or insignificant. **SIMPLICITY HAS TO DO WITH HARMONY, UNITY AND PERFECTION.**

To ponder: Einstein said,

> *"Any intelligent fool can make things bigger, more complex, and more violent. It takes a touch of genius and a lot of courage to move in the opposite direction."*

The more we evolve, the more we realize the sweetness of simplicity. I will love seeing a new bumper sticker to replace the old one that says, "He who dies with the most toys wins." The new one says: The richest person doesn't have the most- **THE RICHEST PERSON IS THE ONE WHO NEEDS THE LEAST.**

WHO WILL HELP YOU WHEN YOU NEED HELP?

How wealth is measured in Peru

In Peru, your value does not lie in what you own; it is based on your extended family. Roger once went to translate for a German guy who wanted to marry a Peruvian girl and take her to Germany. He had to ask her father. He was all ready with his portfolio and could show his material wealth. The father was not at all interested. What he wanted to know was who the brothers and sisters and aunts and uncles were. Who would take care of her if she needed help? There are some things money can't buy… All of the money saved and property owned - all of the security based on our first two helixes that provide us with identity - is completely irrelevant to the evolution of the planet.

O.K., I slipped off the subject. That can happen in a Funshop…

WATER

Essences are energy patterns held in water. Water, an excellent conductor of electricity, has been called "Nature's floppy disk." It will store information. Water is ubiquitous, in that it is everywhere, including in our bodies and our brains. We are 65-85% water. We become re-encoded by the essences when we take them. It is being shown by scientists, what frequencies can do to a drop of water, changing its geometry. Certain geometries will allow us to hold more compassion in our hearts. This is not a sentimentality- it is mathematics shown scientifically in the language of geometry. Loving intention is a powerful healing force, and there is laboratory evidence to substantiate this. See *Messages from Water* by Masaru Emoto- where Japanese scientists have taken water samples and frozen them and photographed them. There are photographs of water before and after prayer, and other influences. We do a sacred activation on all of the water that we use to make the Star Essences. Water is a universal energy storage system. It is my favorite thing to drink. It will begin to taste better than anything else to you, especially if you do activations on it. The activation that we use is from Patricia Cota Robles, and is available on our website or from our office. We can send you a starter bottle of one ounce of sacred activated water (collected from Sacred Sites around the world) to start your own holy water with.

In Dr. Richard Gerber's 1997 series, "Exploring Vibrational Medicine," he states that **"Flower Essences are healing tinctures of energy from nature...Essences are light patterns of truth expressed in physical form."**

Essences are instruments for peace and for joyful fulfillment. They stimulate inspiration and change.

Please remember- **You can be perfectly well and still use vibrational essences.** They assist us in going to our next step. They work on our subtle bodies, or electrical bodies- where illness and wellness and evolution begin. And by the way- the World Health Organization's definition of health is "health is complete physical, mental and emotional well-being." Perfect health is our natural condition, and it includes all of our bodies. There is a thread that runs through our explanations of essences. The essences themselves are the ones that are doing the teaching. **THE MORE WE TAKE THEM, THE MORE WE KNOW WHAT TO TAKE, AND THE MORE WE "UNDERSTAND" THEM, OR - GIVE UP THE NEED TO UNDERSTAND THEM**...Essences came into existence before we knew how they worked, and the depth of their gifts continues to be revealed. This is enormously exciting. One of my favorite things about the essences is that they address blissful ecstatic states as well as balancing more challenging states of being. Psychotherapists use them in their practices with very powerful results. It is also fun to use them for play. We continue to discover their uses. Essences can broaden the frequency response of our minds. They increase our ability to receive. They move us to different octaves so we can view things with a new perspective.

> *To those who believe, no explanation is necessary. To those who doubt, no explanation is possible.*
>
> –Author unknown

It is nice to put away our doubts and over-active mentality. We don't have to have a belief in essences to have them work.

And then we have the Bible- Ecclesiastes 38:4: The Lord hath created medicines out of the earth and he that is wise will not abhor them. (I'll bet we could find a translation that words that in a more positive way...)

ESSENCES ARE LOVE ELIXIRS OF THE DIVINE MOTHER

AND JUST WHY MIGHT SOMEONE WANT TO TAKE A VIBRATIONAL ESSENCE? TO FACILITATE CHANGE.

I choose health, which is wholeness. Healing has its root in the Greek word holos- where we get the words whole, holy and holistic. Healing means to restore wholeness. Health is an expression of wholeness. The more whole we are, the holier we are. There can be physical healing at a cellular level by affecting our subtle, etheric bodies. We have come to know ourselves as multi-sensory. We know that our thoughts and emotions participate in the creation of our wellness. We KNOW that there is a connection between the body, the mind and the spirit. There are so many zillions of great reasons to take essences. Here are some that I can think of. They remind us to live the present moment to the fullest. They help us to see more on all levels, including becoming more clairvoyant. Essences provide a benevolent form for restoring peace and harmony. They help us remap- and find our divine blueprint. They are catalysts to establish contact between the soul and the personality. They activate and enhance our vital force. Essences strengthen us. They are food that feeds the soul. Yes, they are soul food. They help us move through things without attachment to the outcome.

> ***"The best and the most beautiful things in the***
> ***world cannot be seen, or even touched.***
> ***They must be felt by the heart."***
>
> *Helen Keller*

Essences are the etheric imprint of life-force. They are divine energy impulses. Essences have the ability to raise our vibration to be more at one and in harmony with the universal vibrations that surround us. They balance, stabilize and repair our electrical system. That's big. They are doorways to the infinite (that's bigger). They accelerate our vibratory rate, our frequency. Vibrational essences are gentle and persuasive. They also assist in a harmonious transition for planet Earth. They lubricate the pathways that are now opening- due to the new energies entering through astrological conjunctions, entering through every photon. They move us to a different octave so we can view things with a new perspective. They support our currently accelerating evolution. They assist the openings and expansions, and our waking up to our greatest potentials. They expand our ability to benefit from every other form of healing or therapy we may be using, from traditional medicine to the most esoteric practice.

Flower Essence Cocktails

Essences are safe for children and babies, animals, and even pregnant women. They work on plants as well…Children, pets, births, deaths, parties, tests and interviews. Sounds like a line in a song. They assist in every life situation from birth to death. They are especially useful as learning tools, to learn new ways of knowing oneself, others, and even information. They can be lifesavers in times of stress, shock and trauma. Take essences as friends for life. Experience the world as a beautiful garden of God. Essences affect our energy body. They can melt barriers. They can help us to perceive beauty in all things, all paths, all beings. The essences serve as catalysts to awaken our natural life force and the spiritual consciousness within us, by using the energies of plant nature to stimulate our own creative power- in a way that harmonizes with the planet. We are in a very important, expansive time regarding the evolution of our planet and our consciousness - vibrational essences are more valuable than ever before. They assist us in expressing our gifts gracefully and joyously. It is the job of Nature to achieve balance, and vibrational essences truly help us in this regard.

The Flower Essence Cocktail is the cocktail of the 21st Century… Essences are safe to take on the job. They can only enhance your performance. **Have you taken your *Star Essences* today?**

Making Essences Energy Soup

"If you love something enough,
it will tell you its secrets."

George Washington Carver,
The Man Who Talked To Flowers

Everything in the universe has energy and holds consciousness. Even your car and your clothes and your furniture, as well as the world of Nature; and you can converse with anything. Talk to everything- talk to your body, talk to your food before you eat it, talk to your car, your house… And especially- talk to the flowers.

WHEN WE MAKE ESSENCES, WE ARE ATTUNING TO THE ALCHEMICAL PROCESS OF NATURE.

The plant is the original alchemist - it takes sun and water and soil and creates aroma and beauty and high frequencies.

FIRST I GET A MESSAGE TO MAKE A PARTICULAR ESSENCE.

For me, it always seems to happen that the flowers and gems are shouting, "**choose me.**" I say shouting, because it feels so strongly like they are making sure they get my attention. They want to be chosen. Sometimes I get it right away, and in some cases plants have had a second bloom to get my attention. So, really, the essence chooses me. There is a symbiotic relationship with the flowers (or other element of vibrational energy, i.e. the gems) in making an essence. We are their arms and legs. There are other considerations. For example, the moon cycle, the planetary alignments, and where the plant itself is located. Is it happy in its environment? Is it wild or domestic? If it is domestic, who tended it? The next thing I do is **ask permission**, through love, to make the essence. (The frequency of Love actually bends light. It is the most powerful force in the universe.)

HOW I MAKE FLOWER ESSENCES:

There has to be an abundance of the flowers we plan to use. If there are only a few we leave them there to visit, say hello to and enjoy. The time we made the Xylobium: **Freedom/Libertad**, we saw it the day before- and Roger was quite excited, because he had not written about it. It was a new friend. Since it was getting late and we were almost to camp, we kept going, and didn't look around to see how many there were... I remember that the next day I saw Roger jumping up and down and saying, "Oh, yes, it wants to be an essence. There are plenty. There is a whole family here." (And in Peru their families are extended!) Before I went to Peru on that

Machu Picchu

trip, I wasn't sure if I was supposed to make any more essences (I thought 7 was a nice number). I said the flower would have to be glowing or something. This flower was glowing!

They have to be happy and well adapted to their environment. (They will tell you when they aren't happy. For instance, Roger noted one time that it wouldn't be good to use some particular orchids, because they had been transplanted and were missing their family.)

Another very important thing is that the flower is in its peak. I call it that moment of bloom. I have full appreciation for that. Some flowers are in their peak of perfection for a long time- like Epidendrum Ibaguense Orchid- **Eternal Youth**. Some are at their peak for only a day - like the Sobralia Setigera - The **Gold+Silver/White Chakra**. I have a lot of trust in the Divine to create perfection in the timing. We were in **Machu Picchu** and saw the Sobralia Setigera - this gorgeous large white Orchid with a stunning golden center. I admired it, and didn't think of making it, as it was right inside the site of Machu Picchu. (We make the Orchid essences in the sacred environs off the Inca Trail outside the site.) After we got back to the Cusco area, the flower kept staying in my consciousness - choosing me to make its essence. I was with a group - and magically, everything fell into place for Roger and I to be able to send the group off to do something fun while we hopped back aboard the train to go back to **Machu Picchu**. We had no idea if we would find the flowers outside the site, and - if we did - if we would find any in perfect bloom, since each bloom for the Sobralia Setigera (**Gold+Silver/White Chakra**) is only in its perfect state for one day. As we got out of the train, Roger asked me why I wasn't jumping up and down. I asked, "why?" He said, "Turn around and look up." There was a stand of them right there. We walked a ways away from the train station and found some in a nice spot. We made the essence, and finished just in time to catch the late afternoon train back to Cusco. When it is time to make the essence, I meditate with the plant or gem for a bit before and sometimes have a conversation, and sometimes I just get feelings. Before I cut the blossoms, I ask for permission and I invoke my guides and the Masters that work with me. I also invoke the overlighting Deva of the Star Essences to be with me- to enter into a co-creative union with me. This is often said silently and sometimes out loud. I am extremely interested in the quality of the product. Part of the equation in the Alchemy of making an essence, one of the most important elements, is the state of mind and heart of the essence maker. I know that the clarity and intention of the maker is of utmost significance- even moreso than the chef who prepares food- whose attitude is also important to our well-being. I consistently do the things that feel like they are nourishing me in the highest manner, caring for myself on all levels of my being. On the day I am going to make an essence, I don't eat or I eat very lightly before making it. The Elements are on hand for essence-making: the sun - fire - to potentize and stabilize, the perfect flower and the perfect place (earth), the bowl of water, and the air, and that is combined with a massive amount of love, and the proper attitude. Alchemists were taught that when the four elements are in balance, a fifth substance, called quintessence, can be created… The quintessence, this fifth element, heals the soul.

The essence of something is its purest, most concentrated form.

IT IS TIME TO CUT THE FLOWER. The ones that are to be cut seem to glow. I use a clear glass bowl and the best water available. Here in Santa Barbara it is distilled water from the water store with very nice distillers (people and equipment). We use a sacred activation on all of our water (available on our web site with the permission of Patricia Cota Robles, as well as directly from her - we give her contact information in the bibliography). In Peru we often have water from a magnificent waterfall, sacred fountains, or springs.

I use scissors that are only used for flower essence making. I keep them in a bag with a crystal laser wand. I rinse them with vodka right before I use them and always ask for them to be purified. They have plastic handles- so they transmit as little as possible of my energy. I don't touch the plant, and often Roger goes climbing out on ledges to make this all possible- to get just the right blooms, and not touch them. Sometimes we have to move branches, but we don't touch the flowers that we are cutting. We cut them directly into the water. Someone once said, you mean you carry all that stuff with you? Ah yes, ever prepared. Have bowl (and vodka and clean bottle and scissors and good water), will travel.

When I cut a flower I like to cut it right under its head. I don't include the stem, and I don't cut the petals off. I leave the flower intact, without its stem. And I will repeat- I cut them and let them fall right into the water without touching them.

I have been unsuspectingly guided to make the Star Essences during auspicious planetary alignments. Usually this is very unconscious on my part. I schedule it and then find out later what is happening. It makes my job so fun- to have the abounding synchronicities that surround my mission of preparing and distributing these essences. I know this adds to the energy soup that we are co-creating with Nature.

The flower will tell me how many flowers. Sometimes it will be to cover the entire surface area of the water in the bowl. I did that with the White Ceanothus (**Be Nurtured**) - which was growing all over the hillside, and has very tiny flowers. It took a couple of hours just to cut them. It was my birthday and it was a wonderful meditation. When I had cut all the flowers, they told me the essence was complete and I could go ahead and bottle it or leave it in the sun if I wanted to have a rest. The energy of the flower is transferred right away- should the plant choose to give its energy. The sun stabilizes it- and that is why they will keep for so long (like forever). Usually I leave the bowl in the sun for 1 to 3 hours. I just suddenly know when it is complete. When I made the White Ceanothus (**Be Nurtured**), the first flowers had already been in the water for 2 hours by the time I had cut all of the other flowers. I don't like to leave them in the water past their time. I like to take them out before they get too soggy. The water is full of tiny bubbles and life force from the flower or the gemstone when it is done. (This is real "sparkling water.")

This isn't something where someone can go out, grab some

flowers and toss them in a bowl and have a flower essence. You might have some kind of sun tea- but not an essence. The alchemy is the co-creative process with Nature- and Nature doesn't have to give its energy. I quote from Machaelle Small Wright about Nature Spirits. "They are extremely powerful entities. They are responsible for the existence of all form around us, and at the blink of a flea's eye, they can remove that form. They are many things, but they are never, *never* cute. Nor are they ever controlled by us. They seek a co-creative partnership with humans, and they are in the position to accept nothing less."

So the flower tells me how many flowers. It may be only one, as with the Lotus, or it may be zillions of tiny ones, as with the **White Ceanothus**, or a trilogy, or it may be that each person there cuts one, or I may just hear to cover the surface of the water… The number of flowers cut may have to do with numerology or whatever the message the flower gives. Guess how many flowers ended up in the bowl for **13th Gate**… I use a clean clear glass bowl. I clean the bowl out with vodka (or in Peru we use Pisco) and clean water, before we start- to clear the energy in the bowl. Then I fill it with our good water, and cut the flowers directly into it.

I love making essences.

Sitting with an essence is a fabulous experience. When we were at the sacred site of Wiñay Wayna making the first Orchid essence, we sat and did watercolor painting in this rapturous energy. Roger had never painted before with watercolors, and he did a lovely painting. At some point during the essence-making event, I photograph the flower. It is a very special time. It is a place of no words.

Time in the Sun

I place the bowl near where the flowers came from for about 1-3 hours. One hour is good for some of the gemstones who only want to be in the direct sun for that long. It's usually around 2 hours for flowers- and it can vary. I just feel it. When they are ready they are ready. To take out the blossoms, I use a flower or leaf or a branch of the same plant. I put the flowers out on a rock - or on the earth. Sometimes I eat some, if I am called to. I always express my gratitude to them. The gratitude comes out so easily, because my life is great- and I am truly

SO GRATEFUL!

If it is necessary, I pass the essence through an unbleached paper filter to keep any stray plant material out.

I then put the essence into a **CLEAN BOTTLE**. I use empty alcohol bottles. This assures a clean bottle. If I am in Santa Barbara I leave the bottle 1/2 full of vodka and pour the Mother into that and then we have the preserved Mother (50% alcohol). When I am in Peru I wait until I get home to preserve it, as I want to go through customs with only a bottle of "water." From this preserved Mother essence we will make stock, concentrates and dosage bottles. After experimenting with several techniques for preservation, I have found alcohol to be the best preservative. The alcohol has reminded me that it is a distilled spirit. We use vodka to preserve our bottled essences.

As I said, the vodka we use (I love this) is called Vodka of the Gods. Our concentrates are preserved with 50% vodka because you might have it around for a long time, and we want to make sure that it remains clean. They will keep indefinitely. The dosage bottles are 25% as we do expect you to use them up. As long as the dropper stays clean and you don't introduce anything into the bottle, the dosage bottle will keep indefinitely as well as the concentrates.

Two Flower Essences in a Day

The most flower essences I have ever made in a day is two. One time in the jungle, I was working with John Eddows from Lima, Peru and Arbildo Murayri Mozombite, a vegitalista, curandero and perfumero - a shaman in the Peruvian jungle of Pulcalpa. When we arrived, Arbildo graciously took us around his natural pharmacy growing around his home. I was pretty sure I knew who (which flowers) wanted to be essences. The **Bushilla**, the Chiri Sanango and a third one whose name I don't remember. I do have several beautiful photos of it. The next day we first made the **Bushilla**. It was a gorgeous day - and it was in its finest, most beautiful moment- that moment of bloom. After it was complete, we went to make the next one. And - to my utter surprise, and John's and Julia's and even the Shaman Arbildo's - every blossom on ALL of the bushes was curled up. They were not saying yes. We were so surprised, because the day before there were so many- and we somehow assumed there would be fresh ones.

We went ahead and made the Chiri Sanango- which is a master teacher. It was originally called San Juan, Perfect Temperature- because it was made during the Festival of St. John, during the time when the temperature is perfect in the jungle there. Not too hot, not too cold- just right. One of the many gifts of the Chiri Sanango plant is that it helps regulate temperature. In the jungle this plant is considered a MASTER TEACHER, and so we have changed its name to **Master Teacher**, as its previous name was a bit limiting. It does help with temperatures- and much more. After making that essence, we were all pretty spent - and quite ready for a siesta. We would not have been in top condition to make another essence. The message was that it was so important to make the Chiri Sanango that the other plant curled itself up so we wouldn't make it- and we would have high energy to make the **Master Teacher** essence. (That day was our only window of time.) I have concluded that making two flower essences a day is my maximum. Now for Gemstone essences - that is another story. A couple of times I have made 19 in one day. You will read about that in the Gemmies section.

When I make essences I am in a state of reverence, bliss, wonder and love.

I always (except with poisonous plants) drink some of the Mother essence of the flower essences. I can't say the same for all the gemmies. When we made 19 gemmie Mother essences in one day, after about 7 or 8 I began to feel drunk. And this was before the alcohol was added to preserve it. Drinking a Mother essence is a special and sublime moment. It is also fun to splash it on each other- a flower shower. Sometimes it is nice to make a flower essence for the day- and not even get into the bottling part. Essences have a divine sparkle, a cosmic fizz. I love giving Mother Earth a splash. In Peru folks always give a bit to PachaMama (Mother Earth) when they are drinking anything. (They are mostly outside or in a house with a dirt floor.) Recently in Peru we went to make an essence, and it turned out to be before the flower's time (the Maca flower), and so we had a bottle of vodka with us as we were hiking down the mountain back to the car. We came upon the two caretakers of the land, and Roger shared a bit of the vodka with them. All they had to drink out of was the cap - and even with that tiny amount, each one gave a few drops to PachaMama before they drank it. I love that! And it reminds me to share a bit of the Mother essence with Mother Earth and say a prayer of gratitude. Because

I AM SO GRATEFUL, I AM SO GRATEFUL,
I AM SO GRATEFUL!

Prepare essences with sensitivity, reverence and gratitude, and prepare yourself with prayer, right attitude and dedication... All of the Star Flower and Gemstone essences are co-created with

INTENTION, ATTENTION AND LOVE, ♥ LOVE ♥ LOVE.

A FEW ANSWERS TO A FEW QUESTIONS...

★ HOW DO I DETERMINE THE USES FOR THE ESSENCES?

It happens for me in a variety of ways- like talking to the plant and listening to what it has to say, or looking at the plant signature (doctrine of signatures), i.e., the Orchid for protection having "little teeth" (Odontoglossum- **Faith and Courage**). And a "knowing..." like with the Orchids- waking up at 4 a.m. and just knowing, absolutely. Sometimes the gifts will be expressed in meditation, and sometimes the essence will tell me straight away. They have also told me to do research (Fava). Then confirmation comes- often in amusing ways. I love that magical part.

★ WOULD I MAKE AN ESSENCE FROM AN ENDANGERED SPECIES?

No. As Roger says, think about what the plant is thinking. Imagine you are the flower. What if your pollinator isn't coming- or whatever the reason you are endangered. You are going to know, and as that flower you could be stressed. There is an overlighting Deva of each species, so all of the flowers in that species will know. I only want to make essences from happy plants.

★ What about essences from poison flowers?

I have only made one essence from a poison flower - the Poison Oak- and I haven't put it out for sale. I am not yet sure why I have been called to make it. I was told to put it on the shelf. I would not drink the Mother essence! I do feel the essence is absolutely safe - and I don't feel called to work with poisonous plants.

★ What about putting essences through the X-ray at the airport?

I have had essences in my luggage go through X-Ray many times. These essences have proven to be very stable. Their efficacy remains. I have never let a Mother essence go through X-ray. I ask the authorities to hand search it and I tell them that it is Holy Water.

★ What about reuse of bottles?

I prefer not to reuse a bottle for an essence unless it is for the same essence. Use the bottle to make an essential oil blend- or something else that will enjoy the energy of the essence. It will add a sweet vibration.

★ What about alcoholics using the essences?

First of all I will say that I am told there is less alcohol in a dose of flower essences than there is in a ripe banana - And, you can preserve them with other things. Apple cider vinegar and vegetable glycerin are tried and true. I use vegetable glycerin in the **Happy Kid** Combination - and my granddaughters are so used to the ones with the alcohol that they don't like the super-sweet taste of the glycerin. We use full spectrum light by special request. That works really well as long as you don't introduce anything into the bottle that wants to grow.

★ Should we take essences from around the world- or from our own back yard?

We are global now. Our own back yard IS around the world. Kathy Kinniard, who once owned the Flower Essence Pharmacy, received the message to take essences from every continent, and had superb results. Also, there are some special vibrations available from sacred places that not everyone will be visiting - and so to imbibe the essence is a way to receive those frequencies and encodements.

★ How long do essences last?

The energy remains for seven generations. The rubber in the dropper, however, doesn't.

★ The dosage and concentrate question.

That brings us right away to the economic advantage of buying concentrates versus dosage bottles. Economy, which allows you to put lots of bottles around. (You can make 50 - 60 dosage bottles from a half-ounce concentrate bottle.) The dosage bottles are the most convenient. They are ready to use (for immediate gratification). This is the way to go if you don't choose to take the time to make dosage bottles. You can take concentrates straight from the bottle and they will work fine, it is just not economical. We do put a lot of ♥Love♥ and care into each of our dosage bottles, and you can do the same with yours.

If you use concentrates, you can also make special blends and you can make up lots of bottles, for yourself, friends, relatives, clients, children, animals, plants, to have some in the car, the bathroom, the desk...

If you can't decide which way is best for you, dosage or concentrate, buy the one-ounce dosage bottles and buy concentrates later to refill them.

How to make a dosage bottle from the concentrate (stock) bottle

Take a clean (preferably previously unused - unless with the SAME flower essence) one-ounce bottle with a glass dropper. Add ¾ ounce of water that you feel good about (The water we use is distilled - and we know the distiller, and we feel good about the water. We also do activation on it.) - and ¼ ounce of alcohol to preserve it. (Traditionally, in the past, Brandy was used to preserve flower essences. We were guided to use vodka. Use what you are called to use.) We add four drops of the flower essence concentrate, or seven drops of the gem essence concentrate (some people are guided to use a different number of drops). That's it.

You can use as many essences as you choose - and make a blend (a symphony). The essences play well together. We suggest you use essences that support the same issues, so your neurological system only works on a few issues at a time. Instead of blends you can make up individual bottles and take them as single notes. (I often take several of these single notes at a time.) All of the ways work. Choose the way that feels best for you.

The alcohol in the dosage bottle is so things don't grow in it. If you are going to use the flower essence fairly quickly and if you take care to keep the dropper from touching anything, you don't need to preserve it at all. You can also use glycerin, vinegar, or full spectrum light to preserve the dosage bottle of flower essences. You can also keep them in the refrigerator.

Next Phase of the Funshop – Become Intimate with Nature

We are still pretending you are in class- and it's almost time to stretch and go out into Nature, which is your next assignment. First, notice the words of the love song to the universe by David Pomeranz,

"It's in Every One of Us."

It's in every one of us
to be wise,
find your heart,
open up both your eyes.
We can all know everything
without ever knowing why -
It's in every one of us, by and by...

It is in every one of us to be able to talk to flowers (or whatever else it is we want to talk to). And – Paracelsus said,

"To learn the book of Nature, you must walk its pages with your feet."

The assignment is to go out into Nature and talk to a flower.

"Come forth into the light of things, let nature be your teacher." William Wordsworth

GO SIT WITH A FLOWER. ASK TO BE ATTUNED TO NATURE.

Ask to be attuned to Pan (CEO of the Nature Spirits). If you don't hear anything- start pretending. Now- paint it, draw it, describe it, write down what it says. Get botanical impressions. See what shows up.

The first time that I had this assignment, I was sure nothing would happen for me- so I had an agenda. I was going to sit in a really nice spot and enjoy the day - even if I didn't expect a flower to talk to me. Before I had even a moment to find my perfect spot, a flower began to talk to me. This is what came forth:

Choose Me (by Star Riparetti-and the Tower Butter Weed)

Twinkle Twinkle
Little Flower Fellow
I can't love you
Just because you're Yellow

Choose Me, Choose Me

You're too simple, you're too plain
If I choose you, I'll have no fame.

Please. Choose Me, Choose Me

Are you a Dandelion my friend?
Can I blow your little parachutes into the wind?

No, no, no. But please, choose me. choose me anyway.

How about the precious Manzanita Bell.
To choose THAT would be pretty Swell.
No, no, no. Oh please, Choose Me.

I stopped to take a photograph
And was trying to hold still-
The flower just kept swaying-
A bee was getting his fill.

Silly silly- can't you see?
The bee- it is a sign
CHOOSE ME!

A butterfly stops by to say hello-
How many signs do you need-
Before you'll know?

ChooseMe
Choose Me

I love the sun
I like the shade
I have no fears.
I'm not afraid
Choose Me and you'll KNOW
It's a good choice you've made

The ants came marching in
And said
Choose that flower and it will be WIN, WIN

I looked around and saw a bird
And still I heard-
Choose Me, Choose Me

I kept hearing voices
I was in a fit
Was this REALLY where I wanted to sit?

So I get still
And take time to listen
I hear the birds
And see my baby glisten

Looking down at that flower elicits smiles
And makes my spirits grow
A hundred million miles

Choose Me, Choose Me

Lots of insects stopped on by
They wanted to be sure to just say Hi

Mr. Lizard came to play
Then turned around and went away.

I was near the water,
It could still be heard...

The wind came up and gave me a word-
And then the Sun came into sight

And I said O.K., O.K.- it's right- it's right. 

I **LOVE** Signs.

Now could be a great moment for you to step outside and have a conversation with a flower yourself. The secret to talking to flowers is love. You know what the new kids are saying - how would you act if you found out that YOU ARE AN EMISSARY OF LOVE - right now! Flowers are a doorway to the infinite. The Orchid essence **Nature Communion** is fun to take when you are playing with Nature.

George Washington Carver said,
"Find tongues in trees, books in brooks, sermons in stone and good in everything."

When you are in the presence of Nature, remember to have Love, humility, expectation, wonder and awe.

What if you had a dream And in this dream you went to heaven And in heaven you were given the most beautiful flower you had ever seen and what if, as you were loving this flower, breathing its scent and drinking in its colors, you began to awaken. And what if - as you awoke and opened your eyes - what if that flower was still in your hand..... what then?

Those words are from Ariel Spilsbury, who adapted them from words by Samuel Taylor Coleridge (1772-1834):

If a man would pass through Paradise in a dream and have a flower presented to him as a pledge that his soul had been there, if he found that flower in his hand when he awoke, Aye, and what then.

We can awaken now- and the flower is still in our hand... We are living the dream now. **HEAVEN IS ON EARTH**.

One more thing that I would like to talk about regarding making essences, is what I do to prepare myself for making them- which is also what I do to remain in great health:

Of course I take a lot of essences- and I also get adjustments every week to keep my spine and body in alignment and open to receive and to hold and transmit the maximum Light (Network chiropractic and Bio-geometric Integration). I exercise (doing things that are fun for me- like dancing and hiking and yoga and walking and working on the land) and drink good water and get sunshine every day. I avoid putting chemicals on my skin (sunscreen). By eating all raw my body produces the right amount of Melanin. I let my eyes have some of those solar rays. (I rarely wear sunglasses.) It is important to get sunlight into your system and the eyes are a vehicle.

I do art in some form often. I feel that that, too, feeds my soul.

I breathe good air and I remember to do some simple breathing exercises every day. I mostly wear clothes from Natural fibers so my body can breathe. This includes for sleeping, as well, should I choose to wear clothes. I do my best to see lots of sunrises and sunsets. Those are important times of day. Those energies nourish you in special ways, and they are times when the veil to other dimensions is thinner and it is easier to communicate with the unseen.

ESSENCES ARE MADE WITH REVERENCE, BLISS, WONDER AND LOVE, AND AN ATTITUDE OF GRATITUDE. Gratitude ignites hidden sources of Light and energy, lifting us to new levels of **peace and joy!!!**

I like to conclude the class with a lively song with a Reggae beat. In class I say this is **Jimmy Buffett channeling Dr. Bach.** (I choose to believe that it's O.K. with both of them that I say that.)

From a song called **BAROMETER SOUP** by Jimmy Buffett:

> Come and follow in my wake, you've not that much
> at stake, for I have plowed the seas and smoothed
> the troubled waters.
> Come along, let's have some FUN!
> The hard work has been done.
> We'll barrel roll into the SUN, just for starters.

I AM SO GRATEFUL! I AM SO GRATEFUL!
I AM SO GRATEFUL!

CHOOSING AND USING ESSENCES
THIS IS THE CHOOSING PART

There are many methods for choosing the essences that will serve you best at a given time, and from my experience and from what I have observed, they all work. We get to use the ways that work best for us. One way is to go to a practitioner, a flower essence counselor, for guidance. The counselor helps you determine which essences to use. That will be your special blend. Or as we enjoy calling it, your **CONSTELLATION** of *Star Essences*.

(Dr. Eduardo Grecco, an outstanding Argentinean psychotherapist who now lives in Mexico, works extensively with flower essences, and has written several books on flower essences, came up with this term "constellation" referring to a combination of essences, a blend – and I have adopted it.)

You can also do this for yourself by becoming your own counselor.

COUNSELING
HOW WOULD IT BE IF IT WERE PERFECT?

When counseling clients, that is my favorite question. Write down the answer (for the moment) - How your life would be if it were perfect. Then see what essences come up that will support your most compelling issues. Other questions to ask yourself are: What are your wildest (or fondest) dreams? What is the outcome you desire? By asking and answering these questions, you are strengthening your intuitive nature, learning to trust your inner guide. Your answers will direct you to your essences.

Albert Einstein said, ***"The only really valuable thing is intuition."***

At some point you take a leap of faith and let your intuition guide you to the essences. The flowers are our teachers and are training us to remember.

***According to Dr. Bach**, "Every one of us is a healer, because every one of us at heart has a love for something, for our fellow-man, for animals, for nature, for beauty in some form... We are all healers, and with love and sympathy in our nature. We are also able to help anyone who really desires health... Give all the hope and encouragement you can."*

Star Essences are outcome-oriented. Look at their names… and take that to broader and deeper levels. Their names and subtitles will give you clues and reflect the essences' purpose as you read through them, which will aid in your selection. If you are working on key issues or challenges, think about what the opposite is. (Depressed? How about **Pure Joy**…) Read the names and descriptions to see which relates to your current state of health or attitude. For example, Life changes could call for **Graceful Shift**, or **Let Go and Trust**, and relationships provide a cornucopia of choices: **God/Goddess Unity**, **One♥Heart**, **Mango Paradise**, **Sacred Union,** etc.

INTERVIEWING TIP: PEOPLE WILL OFTEN TELL YOU THE SECRETS OF THEIR LIVES WHEN THEY FEEL SAFE AND LOVED.

Sometimes we will determine the correct essence through lots of talking and interview techniques and deep consultation. Other times we will just intuitively choose. Again - all of the ways work. It might be something as simple as someone saying words that trigger us - and we resonate with it right away. For example, someone might say to us, "Let it go. Have faith." We might immediately get **Faith and Courage** (an Andean Orchid flower essence). We can't take the wrong essence. (The worst that can happen is nothing.) There are no side effects. (And, the best that can happen is miracles.) We want the essences that are most resonant. **THE MORE WE TAKE THEM THE MORE WE KNOW WHICH ONES TO TAKE.**

BODY KNOWLEDGE: A FORM OF INNER KNOWING

People who develop their intuition often have special ways of knowing which essences to choose. You might hear voices, have visions or dreams or a combination of your own secret codes. Skin knowledge (goose flesh/goose bumps- also called God bumps) is another sign. There are many forms of body knowledge. For Dr. Bach, hair stood up on the back of his neck as he passed his hands over the correct essences.

More Ways to Choose Essences:

You can use astrology for clues. People, especially children, often can choose essences very well for themselves by looking at the photos of the flowers. Sometimes you can run your hand over the essences and know by a vibration or a heat which one to choose. During classes and talks, following an invocation, I often pass a box of essences around and have people intuitively choose one. People inevitably come back and tell me something special about the essence they chose and the perfect message they received. You can use them like a divination tool, an oracle of sorts, especially when you choose with that intention. I love the idea that I am my own guru (and you are yours), and it is quite O.K. to self-medicate with essences, and to create our own constellations or choirs or take single notes or symphonies or... That is the beauty and the simplicity. Sometimes it is nice to have someone else help us choose or even choose for us, and it is quite O.K. to choose for ourselves. I have seen all the ways work with grand success. We can make constellations for our friends and family and pets and plants. And sometimes- when it feels appropriate- we can go to a practitioner ourselves. Psychotherapists are doing very deep and profound work using vibrational essences. In Cuba, essences are being used in psychiatric hospitals with exceptional results. When a practitioner suggests essences for me, it is often a deeper issue that I wasn't noticing when I choose them myself.

Communication Through Kinesiology

Kinesiology is a method of communicating with your body through your electrical system. It is also called muscle testing. You get answers from your body to yes or no questions. The key to the effectiveness of this method is learning to ask the right questions. There are various ways to muscle test. I have listed some books that describe different techniques in the bibliography. A simple way to do it for yourself is to make a circle with the thumb and little finger of your non-dominant hand and try to pry it apart with the thumb and forefinger of your other hand. You ask questions, and if the fingers come apart (weaken - the circuit is broken), the answer is no. If they stay together (the circuit is strong) it means yes. With some practice, you will learn to read your own body. Begin with some questions you know the answer to (My name is Mickey Mouse) to get a feel of yes or no. You can become very proficient with this and other kinesiology techniques and move very quickly.

Using a Pendulum

The Pendulum is another technique a person can become adept at quickly. A pendulum is a dowsing tool used to divine answers. You can ask yes or no questions or you can use a chart. I have included some charts at the back of this book for your pendulum pleasure. For more in-depth study I have listed books on pendulums and kinesiology in the bibliography.

The essences are vibrations- and sometimes, just like isotopes, they have different "peaks," i.e., a number of different energy frequencies. If you test for them - and the written description doesn't fit - use them anyway. You may have discovered a new range of an essence's usefulness that we haven't yet translated to words. Sometimes you can think of the organs that the plant would address as an herbal tonic- i.e., Dandelion and the liver. You could extrapolate from there. Don't be concerned that the Dandelion essence is named About Face...

Meditation

Meditation is another method you can use to help you choose essences. If you go deeper with an essence- and you can, especially during a meditation- you may get a lot more insight into how the essence is working. I do this by taking the essence prior to going into meditation. When I want to go totally into one essence, I fast, and then take the essence and meditate. Listen with a totally open heart. In my experience it can be valuable to write down what you are being taught (in order to read it later- in a less altered state).

You can see that there are numerous techniques and combinations of techniques for determining which essences to take. Interview, counseling, kinesiology, dowsing, meditation and intuition- are all viable methods to use. What I have seen is that all of the techniques work. Experiment and see which ones give you the most excellent results.

Important! Name that Constellation

Once I determine what essences I am using, I like to name the constellation. That in itself creates an affirmation. I remember a homesick child naming hers, "I'm having fun now." Some of our practitioners have said that the naming of the essence is one of the most powerful (and empowering) parts of the session- especially when the client is part of the naming process. Here are some samples from a recent class: New Way, Sweetest Life, Inner Serenity, I am a Goddess of Beauty, Life with Peace and Meaning, Yummy Me, I Trust My Abilities, I am Actualizing my Highest Potential, My Mind is Calm and Ordered, Radiant Spirit, Full Bloom, Grounded Expansions, Gramma's Helping Hand, Sovereignty, I am a Luscious River flowing Lucid and Free.

Affirmations (are Prayers)

We add to the effectiveness of the essences with our affirmations, our positive statements of intention. Our affirmations are simple statements that help the soul to express a positive, specific goal of inner development. They work on a conscious and subconscious level. Simply stating the name of Star Essences constitutes an affirmation! We can increase the power of the essences by taking them more frequently, as our system becomes attuned to the higher vibrations they make available, and by using affirmations. The affirmation becomes a vehicle for the Soul to communicate with Nature. Write them, say them, think them, sing them, chant them, dance them, listen to them, meditate with them - whatever is your favorite way. Write them on your bottle, put them on the fridge…

Intention will turn the key to manifest your affirmation.

CHOOSING AND USING ESSENCES
THIS IS THE USING PART

- **WHEN, HOW OFTEN, HOW MUCH: TIMING, CYCLES, DROPS**
- **HOW LONG DO THEY TAKE TO WORK**
- **HOW LONG TO TAKE AN ESSENCE**
- **WAYS TO USE THE ESSENCES**

HOW MANY ESSENCES - HOW MANY DROPS - WHEN AND HOW OFTEN TO TAKE THEM - TIMING, CYCLES

The **NUMBER OF ESSENCES** to use varies. Sometimes I want a capella - a single note. Sometimes I feel called to take them in threes. Trilogies. Most folks agree that 5-7 are plenty- yet some folks want a whole symphony- and they go for dozens- and it seems to work for them. My feeling is that you want to choose essences that support one main issue- and use essences that will support that outcome- sometimes from many directions. (Thus more essences.) Work on the amount of issues that your nervous system would like to take on at once. (If you do more, it won't hurt you, it just takes time for your system to sort through and see what it wants and what to delete.) I like to have my basic constellation that I take for sure every morning and evening, and then if I take other essences during the day- for some momentary reason- I still remember my constellation that I am taking in a cyclical fashion. Taking essences with **REGULARITY, RHYTHM, CONSISTENCY** harmonizes with the natural pulses of the universe. It helps us to tune in to the natural cycles around us that affect us. Modern conditions have lessened our awareness of the natural cycles- and it is valuable to move back into sync. Choose specific times to take essences- especially right when you get up and when you go to bed. These are thresholds when the boundaries between body and soul are shifting- transition times. There is power in the cycle, in taking essences at the same times, regularly. The rhythm builds energy. Watch what happens when you take them on a regular, consistent, cyclical basis! Take the essences **MORE OFTEN RATHER THAN TAKING MORE DROPS,** for more and faster results. You can take them as often as you like- with a minimum of 4 times a day suggested. You can't overdose. Essences are safe and self-regulating. The message I frequently receive is to take them often. The more I remember to take the essences, the more balanced I feel.

How Many Drops

Dr. Bach used to suggest 2 drops. I often squirt a dropper full under my tongue, and this works great. In taking vibrational essences, the number of drops matters and it doesn't matter. First of all - it is not about the volume. In that regard, taking one drop is the same as taking the whole bottle: it is just one dose. I have been guided to recommend 4-7 drops of the flowers and 7 drops of the gems. And still, it isn't about the volume. It is about the geometry. As we get more refined in taking the essences, this goes on. Like if it is four drops of 2 plus 2 or four drops of 3 plus 1, etc. I'm going to leave it at that because I don't yet fully understand this part- and I know there is more to be revealed. It has to do with harmonic sequencing- where you take a certain number of drops in certain patterns at certain times. You will receive your own guidance on this. I have included one simple sequence with the Higher Chakra Trilogy. Some folks douse and get the exact number of drops and the number of times to take the essence. Again- there is magic to cycles. It is another valuable tool to tune into. I know that the uses of vibrational essences are being taken to the next level- AND - let's keep it simple at the same time. Even though I know these special sequences work - and I have had profound experiences using them in esoteric ways- I also mostly squirt a dropper full in my mouth on the run- and the essences do magic for me all the time. It's magic- because what is magic? Learning to affect our own environment.

How Long Do they Take To Work

It can be instantaneous. And, sometimes it can take several doses before things begin to shift. It can depend on how long you have been in the frequency you are shifting, and it doesn't have to. It is different for everyone.

How Long To Take an Essence

Sometimes I take them once- sometimes for several weeks and months. It can depend on how long I have been dealing with an issue. How rooted is what you are changing? Is it long-standing or short-term? It can take a while to be able to hold the new frequency. Things might improve and I might stop taking the essence- and then find I need to start taking it again- to get the frequency back. Take it until you can hold the frequency yourself. The length of time can depend on the strength of the disharmony. If you have had a pattern for a long, long time, it might take a little longer to shift it, and it may be valuable to continue to take a particular essence for a while in order to maintain a particular frequency.

Ways to Use Essences

The most traditional way to take essences is **ORALLY**, dropping the drops on or under the tongue from the dropper. There is faster absorption under the tongue, as there is a major meridian under the tongue that disperses the essence out to the entire meridian and chakra system. Most essences are preserved with alcohol, which gets them into the blood very quickly. You can also put the drops in water and sip it. My first guideline for using flower essences: Take as directed (by your own divine director). Avoid touching the dropper to your tongue (or anything else). We don't want to grow things- like bacteria- in the bottle.

Essences work very nicely **TOPICALLY**, as well. They are absorbed through the skin by osmosis. One of my favorite chiropractors (and good friend), Dr. Margarita Carman, uses them extensively - topically on the points where she is called to put them, and gets magnificent results. One time she dropped some drops onto my solar plexus area and the experience was phenomenal. When I was actually laying still and tuning in, I could feel all of the shifts that were happening. I often drop the drops and move so quickly to the next thing I'm doing that I forget to check out what is happening. Experiment with using the drops and staying still sometimes. When you sit with them for a moment, it will often enhance the whole effect. Chiropractors have reported that adjustments hold better when the person is using essences.

ACUPOINTS

Acupuncturists are getting good results by using the drops on meridians and pressure points, often on q-tips, instead of needles. Essences have been described as liquid acupuncture. They move energy. Put the essence on a cotton swab and pulse it in a stimulating rhythm, and sometimes go in a circular pattern. The ear holds points for all the parts of the body.

Apply essences **topically** to any part of the body that is calling for comfort and support. Put on the 7th vertebra in massage - it is the one that protrudes the most, and it is an entrance for cosmic energy. Put them any other places you are called to drip the drops. Rub or drop drops on pulse points, the temples, wrists, behind ears, behind knees. Rub in the palms of your hands and fan them through the aura. Put drops on the forehead, back of neck, the bottom of feet.

The essences are great in **MISTERS AND SPRAY BOTTLES**. Some people put all of the essences in misters and just spray them into the auric fields with fantastic results. You can mix them with essential oils in the misters.

You can mix essences in with the oils you are using for **MASSAGE**. (This is very powerful, and great for the massage therapist as well as the recipient, as the hands are absorbing.) Mix them with essential oils any time to add to their vibrational energies. You can put them into **OILS, LOTIONS, POTIONS AND CREAMS.**

Essences are especially good put on the bottom of the feet. Manipulate the big toe and rub essences on it. Note: the big toes are very important. Massage your big toe and move it around, often. (This is a tip from very high martial artists.)

Essences are very good in **BATHS**. Bathing with them (and essential oils- I like both) is awesome. It is good to start out with a clean tub. Put the drops in and swirl your hand in the water in a figure 8 to really get them activated. The water (an excellent conductor of electricity) is imprinted with the properties of the essence and the oil. The water enters the body by osmosis.

Here are some ideas for some uses of essences beyond the traditional therapeutic uses. New ones continue to be revealed. Let us know the ones you have discovered.

Doctor's Office

My other good friend and favorite (network) chiropractor, Tim Tupper, has a Star Bar in his office, where patients can help themselves to an essence before (or after) their session.

Altar

Create an altar to support the issues you are working with- using colors and objects and the essences. You can put your affirmations there as well. This can help you be mindful of your intention.

Crystal Bowls

Use essences on and in crystal bowls: Put them on the rim of a crystal bowl, or in the bowl, and the essence will transmit out along with the tone when you play the bowl. Put water in the bowl and put the essences into the water - when you tone the bowls with water in them you can change their notes. And- it is very interesting to have a look at the water and visibly see the geometric patterns that are created when you tone the bowl. It will actually begin to effervesce. It is quite something.

Talismans and Amulets

Wear the essences, as they carry energy just by holding them. The heart, throat and solar plexus chakras are good places to wear them.

Eye Drops

Roland puts the drops straight in his eye from the dosage bottle - alcohol and all, with good results. I like to put the concentrate into a standard eye solution, and then put it in my eyes. I have had good results with **Anchoring Light** in the eye drops.

Contact Lens Solution

In the soaking liquid for contact lenses. I have documented

cases of life extension of the contacts. (Orchid essences- **Anchoring Light** and **High Frequency**)

Nose Drops, Ear Drops

Add the essence concentrate to the standard drops. (The Orchid essence **Balance and Stability** and **Clear Quartz** are good ones to use.)

Auras

Put drops on your hands and then sweep auras with your hands, or spray the aura using essences in misters.

Counseling Practice

Before a session, healer and healee take essences together. (Who is healing who...)

Feng Shui

Feng Shui and essences is a whole new field, and a new book on this is coming out soon, by my good friend and Star Essence teacher Kjerstina Agne.

Earth and Regional Healing

Drop the drops directly on the Earth or in bodies of water. Share essences with the land and bring Light to locations. Put drops on maps to work with parts of countries.

Nature

Take while you are in nature. Take when you are not in Nature and you feel a desire to connect.

For Pets- and Wild Critters, Too

Put the drops in their water or food. Put drops in their mouths, on their nose so they will lick them, or put the drops on their fur and their paws. Spray them. (My cat does not love this- and- she always calms down after.) Spray your hands or drop drops in your hands and pet them, massage into the soles of their feet. Spray or drop drops on their bed and favorite spaces. Use what works for you and your animal companions.

For Plants

Plants love essences. Use them in sprayers or directly into the soil. They will often tell you what essence they would like.

Ceremony, Ritual

We can use ceremony as- a physical vehicle used to ground energy from a higher level, making it accessible. We can use it as a tool to give clarity and form to energy. We can use essences in many ways during ceremony. We can add them to oils and anoint. (Christos means anointed one.) Drink the essences from chalices. Drinking **One♥Heart** will put everyone in the same frequency.

Mudras

Put the essences on our fingertips and do mudras. Mudra: a cosmic sign language formed by the fingers and the hands, often accompanied by vocal sounds. In ancient cultures these mudras were practiced to invoke God. Many statues of Jesus, Buddha and other holy figures are sculpted with various mudras formed by the fingers and the hands. The sign of the cross is a form of a mudra to invoke Spirit in prayer. They have done specific work with mudras in India. Try it out, experiment.

Meditation

Very nice to take essences consciously and observe ourselves quietly. We can do a vision quest with them. Fasting and taking essences can be quite revealing.

Conscious Breathing

is another tool for excellent health- and what I have recently discovered is that I can take an essence and have that trigger my memory to take a deep, conscious breath. When that happens, our posture will correct itself. Take many conscious deep breaths during the day. A useful and easy breathing technique I recommend is alternate nostril breathing. It helps to balance both sides of your brain while raising your frequency.

WITH GROUPS

(High Frequency, One♥Heart, Celebration, Freedom)

Taking essences together works well with groups. Essences (especially **One♥Heart**) are invaluable when traveling with groups. It is especially nice for groups of people that are working together, to take essences together. I love using them in classes and watching the energy shift.

GLOBAL PLANETARY LINK-UPS

Having lots of people take the same essence and connect on that frequency has proven to be very powerful. We have used them for global planetary link-ups. The first time I did this was on a small scale- on 12:12 of 1994. It was so powerful that when the time came for me to connect with the Santa Barbara folks who were connecting with me through the essence, I went into a rarefied space for three days- with water running out of my eyes- and I was hypersensitive to everything going on. Anything that was not love and light was very jarring. And- it was also a blissed-out state. I crossed a threshold into another dimension for a few days. It was so amazing for me that I wanted to do it again on a bigger scale, which I did by sending essences out with a packet that Aluna Joy Yaxkin sent out to groups all over the world who were meditating and connecting on the March Equinox and praying for planetary awakening. The same essence was being taken by literally thousands of people on the same day, all over the world. I have taken a group to Peru for every March Equinox since then- again sending out essences and connecting with folks all over the world on these marvelous frequencies.

"When you infuse yourself with energy and work with intention, you literally send bolts of great change around the globe."
Earth Speaks by Barbara Marciniak

The main uses of essences in Atlantis and Lemuria were for spiritual growth - development of consciousness - and tissue regeneration.

By taking essences we are transmitting them. We become a pillar of light. Some essences, like **Freedom/Libertad** (Xylobium with 24 karat Gold), especially work that way. When we take them we broadcast our frequencies to others, thus tuning up folks that come into our fields. Place them around your house and your car. They radiate energy. Often you will feel good just holding the bottle.

Other Interesting Uses

Put essences in **LAMP OIL**. Infuse them on **PAPERS** and **BUSINESS CARDS** (you can mist them on). Put them in **PAINTS** when you are painting walls or doing art! I've sprinkled them into **CEMENT** being mixed. Put essences in the **WASHING MACHINE** with the clothes. Teachers use them in wash water for cleaning children's desks. Put them in **FOUNTAINS** and other water features. I often put drops of **Faith and Courage** on our **LUGGAGE** to protect it. Put the drops in your car, on your car, in the radiator... **SPRAY YOUR PILLOW** before going to sleep. Roland soaks particular stones in **Anchoring Light** (Orchid essence) during the day and then sleeps with that stone taped to his body during the night. First he cleans the stone by soaking it in **Rhodochrosite** soak water. Put essences in **BUBBLE JUICE**- blow those frequencies around surreptitiously... open portals.

CELEBRATIONS OF ALL KINDS!

Just for the FUN of flower essences

Perk up a party by creating the lovespace with essences (have everyone take **One ♥ Heart**). Or spike the punch with **Pure Joy!** You can put them in drinks of all sorts- hot or cold. Flower essence cocktails and vibrational punch- yum. One of my favorite parts is that essences address blissful ecstatic states as well as doing healing. It is fun to use them for play.

(Not-So-) Secret Recipes from the Stargarita Bar

Stargarita

Juice of ½ fresh organic lemon
Juice of ½ fresh organic lime
About 6 oz. of "bar mix"
(water mixed with a little maple syrup or grape juice or honey or stevia to sweeten it- your choice, and to your taste)

Herbal tincture or tonic of choice
Fun Flower Essences
(i.e. *Zania, Eternal Youth, Pure Joy*)

Run the lemon or lime around the rim of your glass and dip the glass rim into some medium ground Rose-Colored Salt. Put all of the above into the glass and drink up. When you serve this to others, you become an official Startender.

Mai Tai Chi

Fresh pineapple juice
Fresh baby coconut milk
Herbal tincture or tonic of choice
Fun Essences *(the combination called Celebration is fabulous)*

Blend this up with or without ice. Yum!

Holy Mary

Tomato juice or vegetable juice- fresh is best
Herbal tincture or tonic of choice
Fun Essences
Peruvian rose salt mixed with celery powder to put on the rim of the glass
Fresh celery stalk for garnish and to eat
Tabasco and pepper sauces for folks who like it hot

Crystal Flower Essence Punch

Get together with a few friends right before the party - or you can do this on your own. Take a crystal - Clear Quartz works great - and hold it and breathe into it to clear it.

Then breathe into the crystal your intention for the punch. I like to put fun into it, and perfect health, joyousness and bliss. Sometimes I add that everyone will feel like dancing. Put the Crystal into the punch bowl and add:

Fresh Orange Juice

Fresh Lemon Juice

Fresh Lime Juice
(citrus has a very high vibration, and when you mix citrus, the vibration gets even higher)

Grape Juice to sweeten

Fun Essences

Sacred Activated Healing Water *(See Bibliography)*

**Fun Essences- for example-
Zania, Pure Joy, Dance, Eternal Youth, Otter Delight, Wild Feminine...

HAVE ESSENCES WITH YOU ALL THE TIME. THEY ARE GOOD FOR EVERY OCCASION. ♥★

The complimentary Star Bar at Star Essence is always open.

My Obsessions- My Evangelical Moment

This is the part of the book where I get to tell you about my personal perfect universe.

Reverence for All Life Everywhere Throughout the Universe...

I'm writing this chapter for two reasons. One is because this is a book about health, happiness, and rejuvenation through raising your frequency. In the presence of high frequencies, low frequencies can't exist. Higher frequencies are the ones that I enjoy the most, and are part of my heaven on earth...

> ***"Reverence for life is the ethic of love expanded to embrace the universe."*** – Albert Schweitzer

When I hear that, it resonates with the core of my being. That is what ultimately brought me to be a total **vegetarian.**

A note to me from Spirit: This book could be called ***Nutrition of all of the Bodies.*** *You are learning how to have a healthy body by feeding it on all levels. The raw food, the positive thoughts, words, actions and feelings are all nutrition. It is important that you monitor these at all times- diligently, relentlessly - and the rewards are huge. Essences feed your vibrational body. Your body electric. Raw food is close to the Light. The chlorophyll in greens that you eat helps you to hold more light. Feeding your mind good thoughts, and speaking the words that you choose to manifest is equally important.*

The second reason I'm writing this chapter is because it is my book, and so I get my evangelical moment. I get to say how I feel. I love you no matter what you eat- and it is my personal strong belief that it is inappropriate at this time to kill critters to eat them. I also realize that everyone has their own perfect timing.

I quit eating red meat when I realized I was ordering it at restaurants and eating the salad and baked potato, and taking the meat home for my husband to eat later. When I was a kid, *Fairy* (the lady that helped raise me) used to bring me tuna sandwiches in place of the bologna ones that I didn't like. I remember that when I was pregnant I couldn't stand the smell of any meat- cooked or uncooked- and didn't eat any at that time. It didn't occur to me then to be a vegetarian. I had no idea that it was something people did (yes- even though I was right here in California). It was probably talked about, and I wasn't in a frequency to even hear it. Anyway, I quit eating red meat, then chicken, and I only ate fish in the realm of meat. Then one day I saw a big fish in an aquarium- and thought about how beautiful it was. Then I thought about seeing those beautiful fish when I snorkel. Yikes- would I want to bite one? Never. (And I wouldn't like them to bite me back.) (I wonder if they think I'm beautiful?)

Suddenly I became too conscious of what I was eating to be able to eat it. It seems like we have to have spiritual amnesia to be willing to kill something to eat it. It is not in our nature to kill things. Most of us would not want to kill something and eat it. Many of us escort spiders outside. We don't want to smash them! It is in the nature of a cat to kill a bird. Not us. And would you like to put that raw feathery thing in your mouth? We have to turn off our consciousness to slaughter these things. We have been able to do it… We don't want to think Easter Bunny when we have that rabbit stew, or Bambi on the barbeque.

And I would be considered very impolite to bring up what you are eating while you are eating it. It would not be polite for me to ask you how your unborn baby chicken omelet is. Most folks don't want to think about that while they are eating it. On the other hand, it's fine to talk about the grapes or the tomatoes or… Every time I have looked into the big beautiful brown eyes of a cow and asked him (or her) if she would like for me to kill her and eat her- they always say no. Maybe for the Indians they were willing. Maybe back then it was appropriate.

Fruit loves to be eaten and have its seeds scattered and planted.
Leo Tolstoy:

"A vegetarian diet is the acid test of humanitarianism."

Consciousness means awake- by definition. We get to think about what we are doing. When people are eating and don't want to hear about or think about what they are eating, it is denial, in my opinion. An egg is an unborn baby chicken. OK, then there are unfertilized eggs. Just think about what an egg is. What a weird thing to eat. Chicken menstruation. Personally, when I think about eating eggs now, thinking about what they are- it's like thinking about eating monkey brains or gopher guts. It's not a pretty visualization. Now a flower, or an apple or an apricot- a berry or an avocado – there is my picture of heaven. And I get to live it.

I don't eat animals cuz I love them you see, I don't eat animals and they don't eat me. – Line from a "Melanie" song

Animals are my friends... and I don't eat my friends.
– George Bernard Shaw

"I discovered that for remaining staunch to vegetarianism, a man requires a moral basis. For me that was a great discovery in my search after TRUTH. At an early age, I found that a selfish basis would not serve the purpose of taking a man higher and higher along the paths of evolution. What was required was an altruistic purpose. Therefore, vegetarians should have a MORAL BASIS - that a man was not born a carnivorous animal, but was born to live on the fruits and herbs that the earth grows... If anybody said that I should die if I did not take beef tea or mutton, even on medical advice, I would prefer death. THAT IS THE BASIS OF MY VEGETARIANISM!" – Gandhi

Leonardo Da Vinci: *"I have from an early age, abjured the use of meat and the time will come when men such as I will look upon the murder of animals as they now look upon the murder of men."*

I can see that, too. I enjoy what Dr. Bach had to say in his book *Heal Thyself*:

"Internal cleanliness depends on diet, and we should choose everything that is as clean and wholesome and fresh as possible, chiefly natural fruits, vegetables and nuts. Animal flesh should certainly be avoided; first because it gives rise to much physical

poison in the body; secondly because it stimulates an abnormal and excessive appetite; and thirdly because it necessitates cruelty to the animal world. Plenty of fluid should be taken to cleanse the body, such as water and natural wines and products made direct from Nature's storehouse, avoiding the more artificial beverages of distillation."

Even though I have never heard an animal say, "Kill me and eat me" (and my digestive system agrees), I often hear plants say, "pick me." If you listen carefully you will hear. (And the more you eat them the more you will hear them, just like with the essences - the more you take them the more you know which ones to take.) Plato: *"The Gods created certain kinds of beings to replenish our bodies...They are the trees and the plants and the seeds."*

There was a period in my life when tons of information seemed to be being downloaded to me. Sometimes I would have to pull the car into a parking lot and sit - sometimes for 2 hours - not being able to move. My body would be there- and the rest of me was off in Cosmic school. I never knew when it would happen- and fortunately it was during a time when I didn't have a lot of obligations, so it was O.K. The divine has perfect timing...

It was the night before Christmas, 1993. I was on my bed in a semi-altered state, writing. I ended up writing about four pages of stuff that, while it was coming through, I was sure was for my housemate, who was always giving up sugar and then eating it again. The message was all about sugar, and how it is a manipulated energy and will put that manipulation into your system, keeping you in a pattern of mass consciousness, and in the frequencies of mass consciousness thoughtforms. The voice I was hearing said that in order for me to communicate with the higher realms that I was asking to work with, I would have to quit eating all refined sugar. Wow. This message was for ME. I was the candy queen. It had never occurred to me to not eat sugar! I was perfectly healthy and not overweight. And -it was the night before Christmas. My stocking would be filled with sugar.

The message sounded important, so I quit eating sugar on the spot. I committed to 6 months. After that I felt quite an acceleration- and I was afraid to eat any for fear I would become immediately addicted, so it was several years before I ate refined sugar again. When I started again, it was slow at first- and then on to full-fledged addiction. Now with my raw diet it is easy. All of my sugar comes from delicious fruit. And I am satisfied.

It is about frequency. It is about dreaming the new dream. "And the lion shall lay down with the lamb." I can see the lion laying down with the lamb- I see the day when even animals don't eat animals.

Albert Einstein: *"It is my view that the vegetarian manner of living, by its purely physical effect on the human temperament, would most beneficially influence the lot of mankind."* (Remember that even the vegetarian dinosaurs were the peaceful non-aggressive ones.)

Besides being about essences, this book is about health and rejuvenation and higher states of consciousness. Animals are dense and have to be killed to be eaten. We want to eat foods that are filled with life force and high frequencies.

So then there is the question about killing the plant when you eat it. I have asked flowers that question. I actually asked it if it hurt - as I popped one in my mouth one day - and it giggled at me and told me that it was fine for me to eat it.

We do not kill the plant when we pick it. Patricia Cota Robles explains why, and I resonate with what she says:

"All that we consume is part of the Elemental Kingdom. Any Elemental that has evolved to the point of locomotion is no longer appropriate for human consumption. Elementals that walk, slither, fly or swim, in any form, are abiding within their Elemental body, just as you and I who walk, abide in our Elemental (physical) body. If that body is killed, it interrupts the Elemental's opportunity to experience the physical plane. Just as it does for us if someone kills our body. In killing an Elemental body of any kind, we have interfered with the progress of that being, and we have incurred a certain karmic liability. When we consume Elemental substance that has not evolved to the point of locomotion, it is a very

different situation. Stationary Elementals, which include all vegetables, fruits, nuts, seeds, grains, grasses and water, are the outpictured thoughtforms of the Elemental Beings and do not house the Elemental itself. These thoughtforms are specifically created to nourish the physical bodies of mobile Human Beings and mobile Elementals."

We don't need to kill anything to sustain ourselves. For me, I don't want any animal sacrifices in my honor. I know that killing them to eat them is unnecessary. I am perfectly healthy and strong eating fresh fruits and nuts and veggies, all raw. And in terms of sustainability and impact on the planet- it is a major contribution. (Oh, boy- we get to skip all that packaging…My trash has diminished considerably!) Not eating meat is a good way to vote. Eating raw is an even bigger way. I find a blissful simplicity in eating all raw.

It has been interesting on my journeys to Peru. Being vegetarian has made it much easier to communicate with the world of Nature. Intuitively I would eat very little during my flower essence-making journeys. Not by my plan or design, more by a divine plan. A couple of times when I was making essences in Peru I only ate carrots for days. That was all my body wanted at the time.

I met a couple of people who ate only raw food. I thought that was interesting. Then I heard about the Essenes and how they didn't cook their food. I bought Gabriel Cousens' book and a book called *The Christ Diet*. It was all aiming at raw. I met Mark Nasek, a raw food chef, and he agreed to come and do food preparation in exchange for taking my 8-day Teacher Training. So for several years, during the teacher training, I would eat all raw for 8 days.

I was hearing things like: pure, living (raw) organic foods are a necessary and critical part of the Ascension process. Fruits, vegetables, nuts, seeds, sprouted grains and pure water should be our main staples. The less cooked, dead, devitalized food we eat the healthier and lighter we will be. I knew it - and it resonated in my heart - and still, I loved French fries, tortilla chips and other such stuff. A vegetarian diet is not necessarily a healthy diet. You can eat a lot of junk and be a veggie. That would be me (in the past!)

One day I had a look and realized that over the years I had

slowly gained about 25 extra pounds. I have never been fat- and suddenly, it felt like I was. I became a vegetarian for ethical reasons- and I became raw for health and vanity as well as ecology, and, even more important, knowing that the biggest benefit was raising my frequency and helping me to hold more light.

On my birthday in 2001, I went to a talk by Loren Lockman (that birthday thing, again). He said our perfect diet was 70% fruit, 20% leafy greens and 10% nuts and seeds. Everything he said made sense and resonated.

He is also a big advocate of water fasts. I went to Maryland a couple of months after his talk, to his fasting center. I had been eating nearly all raw and was ready to fast and see God. I planned on fasting for 10 days. My body was so excited to have an opportunity to detox, that it went full tilt. I was detoxifying from every orifice. By four days, I gave up and stopped the fast. I was hating it- and yet knowing that it was a great thing to do.

It was powerful and perfect and I will do it again when I choose to take the time. Ending the fast was a good thing for the timing of the moment. I had a lovely 10-day recovery with my good friend Ros in Ocean City, Maryland before I came home to get back to my business.

My clarity after the fast was remarkable, and my sensitivity was super-increased. Sensitivity can be a blessing and a curse... The cleaner I get, the more hyper-sensitive I become to smells and energy and everything else around me. It is the good news and the bad news.

So all that year (2001) I ate mostly raw. I jokingly say 80% raw and 20% chips. I was mostly raw with feast days. **HAPPY DAY FOR GIVING THANKS- HAPPY THANKS FOR GIVING DAY** - Roger came to the States during Thanksgiving that year. That was a feast of 3 weeks. He wanted me to explain the Fiesta of the Turkey to him. The day after Thanksgiving he looked at me and said, I understand this Fiesta of the Turkey now. It's all about the food. Eating raw has its interesting challenges in a culture so based around food.

Raw Raw Raw

Treat Our Body Like a Temple (or at least as well as our car)

As I write this, I am over a year into eating all raw food and loving it. I feel stellar. I feel the rhythm of the universe.

Raw food folks disagree on what the perfect raw food diet is. That's perfect! Because the truth of the matter is, we are the Guru. In the book Seventeen Ways to Eat a Mango, it's the seventeenth way: it's my way (or your way).

The closer food comes to the natural state in which it occurs, or the closer it is to its raw, uncooked form, the higher its quality. The enzymes are found intact. The amino acids are in their finest form. The minerals, vitamins, trace elements, carbohydrates and "life force" are present.

In the lecture Loren Lockman gave, he hooked me on raw - because he gave me permission to eat all the fruit I want and have it be good for me. He says 70% fruit, 20% leafy greens and 10% nuts and seeds is a good ratio. When I was a kid, I was skinny and strong and loved fruit. I knew where all the trees in the neighborhood were and I rescued a lot of the fruit from rotting on the ground (often a long time before it hit the ground).

Fruit presents an open invitation to eat it.

Sunfood is funfood.

Good mood food.

Fruits are the kisses of Mother Earth.

Pythagoras was fruitarian.

I choose to eat raw food. Contrary to some people's opinions, eating raw food is not an eating disorder. Making healthy food choices is not fanatic, it is a good idea! I am at a point in my life where I want all of my food choices to be healthy- and youthing.

This is what Patricia Cota Robles in her book *The Awakening*, has to say: *"Fuel for the Physical body: Raw foods contain not only the usual vitamins and minerals, but the living life force of the food, as well. This life force replenishes the Light energy that rejuvenates the body. It functions as a regenerator to energize the cells and organs of the body, thus maintaining youth, health and beauty. When you consume dead food in any form it registers as a vibration of death in the body. When you consume live food it registers as life in the body. It's very simple: dead food promotes death; live food promotes life."*

From *Letters to Earth* by Elia Wise: *Most inorganically produced foodstuffs are not of our same nature. While inorganically produced or highly processed foods sustain us, they starve essential subtle dimensions of our well-being. As we expand into higher levels of love, consciousness, and integrity, it is valuable to feed our self at those levels. If you are committed to a high level of awareness, it is wise to nourish those frequencies with food that is alive with those same frequencies.*

Albert Schweitzer: *"I am conscious that flesh eating is not in accordance with the finer feelings and I abstain from it."*

In higher states of consciousness, what the body wants when it is there is light-filled food. Of course, there are other important factors that contribute to our good health, well-being, and raising our frequency. It is important to consume pure water. Water is a conductor of light. Sunlight- we need the full spectrum of the sun's light. Sunlight increases our energy level and enables the electrons of our body to absorb more divine light. Clean air. Holy Breath. Deep breathing fills our cells with oxygen and life force as it detoxifies and cleanses our cells. Exercise increases the circulation of the nutrients, pure water and oxygen in our cells and organs. It strengthens every bodily function and enhances our feeling of well-being and vitality. The body is the vehicle for the soul, and it needs care and nourishment and nurturing. Rest/sleep, pleasant surroundings, positive mental attitude, as well as nutritious dietary intake are important. The body wants movement and sound and color and light and love. In addition to the things listed above, we monitor our thoughts, words, actions and most of all, feelings...We discipline ourselves to release ONLY harmonious, peaceful, loving, happy, joy-filled energy through our feelings, every moment of the day.

This happiness thing is VERY important. A key to the universe is humor: **LAUGH!** That is one of the things that differentiates humans from animals. And as Swami Beyondananda says- Remember, laughter is physically healing because it causes the blood vessels in the body to dilate- which beats having them die early....and Swami also says, Be a fundamentalist - be sure the Fun comes before the mental! Laughter is the fastest and most effective way to raise our vibration. It is important that we are laughing through the heart at things that are the result of joy. Laughter opens chakras and actually produces healing chemistry in the body. **PLAYFULNESS, ELATION, WONDER, ECSTASY, CREATIVITY, NATURE, BEAUTIFUL ART AND MUSIC, BLISS, FUN AND LOVE ALL WORK WONDERS.**

Eating raw, I feel more sensitive- and I feel more love in my heart. I feel SUPER happy when I eat food close to Light, and more connected to the source I am choosing to connect with, Nature. I also understand that we are all different and all have our own particular timing. All this being said, there are many people that I know, love, trust and respect that eat meat. I only know what works for me in that arena.

"Whoever sets himself up as a judge of Truth and Knowledge is shipwrecked by the laughter of the Gods." – Albert Einstein

So maybe in heaven they will tell me it is all no big deal. Or it is. Something I AM sure is a good idea:

**CHEW YOUR FOOD. PREPARE IT WITH LOVE,
AND BLESS IT AND INFUSE IT WITH LIGHT.♥♥♥**

Competition Is Replaced by Cooperation And Co-Creation

This is another opportunity for me to talk about my idea of a perfect world. In my vision of Heaven on Earth, there is cooperation, and co-creation, rather than competition. We have a world based on compassion and love.

There was a time in my life when I played a lot of tennis and racquetball. I was very competitive. Then, gradually, I started losing my urge to win, if someone else had to lose. Nancy was a friend I played with a lot. When she became pregnant, we still continued to play. We used to try to psyche each other out - saying "look out - I have my special winning sox on" or whatever goofy thing we could think of to get ourselves into the competitive spirit. There came a time during her pregnancy when I couldn't beat her. What was the point of beating a pregnant woman? I wasn't trying to lose- I just wasn't winning. It wasn't due to a lack of ability. We were equally matched. I just couldn't get that passion to win, to beat Nancy. (You've got to want to.)

Then I went to one Yoga class- and I never went back to the racquetball club that had been my social life for about 4 or 5 years. I fell in love with the practice of Yoga. It made so much sense. Your only competition is yourself - and as we progress on the Yoga path, we are urged not to compete even with ourselves. I turned my carport into a yoga studio and through a vision, called it Laughing Star Studio. (That happened long before I consciously knew my angelic name.)

I only like win/win. I don't want to play something where someone else has to lose in order for me to win. A poignant story that I love is the story of the kids with Downs' Syndrome who were taking part in the Special Olympics. One of the kids fell at the starting line. When his friends, who were also his "competitors," turned around and saw him, they ALL went back to help him. When asked why, one of the kids spoke up for the group and said: "What's the point of running the race if your buddy isn't with you?" I get tears in my eyes each time I think about it. You know that feeling when your nose starts to tickle and water comes to your eyes…

In Nuclear Medicine we played the game of who can serve the

patient best - who can be the nicest - how can we make it more interesting and comfortable for the patient. Everyone is a winner in that game, including the patient.

Another thing I love is one of the practices of the Incas, that if you beat someone at something, it is your obligation to show them how you did it. Ponder the implications of that! This simple practice shows us how to share energy, tolerate differences, learn to harmonize and use diverse energy fields and still have drive and passion and energy to do our personal best.

Win Win Win Win

I love the way Shel Silverstein's poem **Hug O' War** is another way of expressing the essence of the cooperative spirit.

I will not play at tug o' war
I'd rather play at hug o' war
Where everyone hugs
Instead of tugs,
Where everyone giggles
And rolls on the rug,
And everyone kisses,
And everyone grins,
And everyone cuddles,
And everyone WINS.

I skip watching sports on TV. I'd rather play something myself. I still enjoy the energy of going to an event, sometimes even when it is competitive- because of the energy of the crowd.

I still want us all to do our personal best!

I am ready for community at some level that is revealing itself to me. Roger talks about life in the rugged Andes, where they have proven that one person on their own will perish- and yet, working together in community, they can create more than enough for each family, some of their excess is stored for future use, and some is used for taxes. Many of us here, especially in the United States, have learned to do things really well by ourselves. Learning to become self-sufficient is very valuable. Now, as a community, I know we will fly and excel.

WIN WIN WIN WIN

NATURE SUPPORTS THE **WIN-WIN** PHILOSOPHY.

Lessons From Geese (author unknown)

Fact 1: As each goose flaps its wings it creates an "uplift" for the birds that follow. By flying in a "V" formation, the whole flock adds 71% greater flying range than if each bird flew alone. Lesson: People who share a common direction and sense of community can get where they are going more quickly and easily because they are traveling on the thrust of one another.

Fact 2: When a goose falls out of formation, it suddenly feels the drag and resistance of flying alone. It quickly moves back into formation to take advantage of the lifting power of the bird immediately in front of it. Lesson: If we have as much sense as a goose, we stay in formation with those headed where we want to go. We are willing to accept their help and give our help to others.

Fact 3: When the lead goose tires, it rotates back into the formation and another goose flies to the point position. Lesson: It pays to take turns doing the hard tasks and sharing leadership. As with geese, people are interdependent on each other's skills, capabilities and unique arrangements of gifts, talents or resources.

Fact 4: The geese flying in formation honk to encourage those up front to keep up their speed. Lesson: We need to make sure our honking is encouraging. In groups where there is encouragement, the production is much greater. The power of encouragement (to stand by one's heart or core values and encourage the heart and core of others) is the quality of honking we seek.

Fact 5: When a goose gets sick, wounded or shot down, two geese drop out of formation and follow it down to help and protect it. They stay with it until it dies or is able to fly again. Then, they launch out with another formation or catch up with the flock. Lesson: If we have as much sense as geese, we will stand by each other in difficult times as well as when we are strong.

These lessons are all about the group experience. Acting in cooperation. Being together strengthens our resolve, clarifies and reinforces our direction and improves our chances for success. It is valuable to hang out with folks who are on the same wavelength. Together, we travel faster and more gracefully.

The shared experience of initiation into a higher frequency constitutes a quantum leap for each individual.

There is something happening on the planet that is making the group experience even more powerful. Working in groups is awakening the Christ within our hearts. Our luminous solar presence becomes activated. We become clearer, and our creativity and artistic expression expands. We radiate a huge chalice of love and light.

Using essences with all kinds of groups will accelerate the group Light activity even more.

Glorylicious Color

What is my thing with Black? I have one line in the office handbook under dress code: Please wear a minimum of black. Why? Black is the absence of color. It doesn't cheer me up. (This, of course, has nothing to do with black people. They are people of color! I love black people - and they OFTEN cheer me up! - and black critters, too.)

If someone says - "There is nothing wrong with the color black," I will agree. There is nothing wrong with it. I don't enjoy it- so I avoid it. Someone said the other day- it is the void. I looked up the word void in the dictionary. Void is defined as useless, ineffectual, empty space, render invalid, excrete, in vain, pointless. That's how I feel about black. On the other hand, colors are therapeutic. They can balance and harmonize us with their frequencies.

I truly know that we are moving beyond duality. We don't have to have dark to have light. It can be all light and funner than we can imagine.

Love has no opposite. The opposite of fear is freedom.
There does not have to be dark to appreciate the light.
Skip polarity, duality and opposites.
Evil is not the opposite of good.
Evil is a word to describe the absence of love, which is how God manifests- through Love.
It is a lack of something- not the presence of something else.
Darkness is not the opposite of light or the other side of light- it is the absence of light.
Black is seeking light.
Quiet is not the opposite of music. Colors bring joy- and healing vibrations.
Black absorbs energy- black roofs, cars, solar stuff. It is non-therapeutic.
With white you stay in your own auric field and can transmit more light.

In my world, it is gloryliciously all magnificent light.

Do you know why we don't wear black in hospitals- and, in fact, wear white? Because the black will absorb the energy of everyone around us. That is probably why white has been the standard for doctors and nurses. It helps to reflect the healer's light as well as to protect them. Black helps you become invisible (which is very useful when you are a stagehand in a play or something of that nature). Otherwise, I prefer to reflect and radiate and absorb colors into my aura and energy field that will strengthen and feed them, which colors do. I love color. White is all colors. (Take a color wheel and spin it and it will turn white.) I put my distilled activated water into colored glass bottles in the window and continuously treat myself to colored water. I love the gemmies because they are color therapy. I am excited to experience the colors of the higher dimensions. We get tastes of them in our iridescents and opalescents and luminous colors, which have sweet high energies. Glitter. Sparkle. Spangle. Little girls know them and love them.

It all fits in with raising our frequency.

Light is Illumination

Light is absence of weight

Enlightenment

Color is a language that Spirit can understand. Spirit uses color to experience life. In some universes color is used to create. Color is the game outside time and space. Color is used to communicate from being to being. Spirits have carried that love for color. Color changes consciousness - there is a reality shift.

SOMETIMES I CAN SEE THE COLORS OF THE ESSENCES.

CRYSTALLINE ★ RAINBOW ★ LUMINOUS
OPALESCENT COLORS.
YUM!

If You Say So

The Universal Truth of Deliberate Creation

Good Oral Hygiene Good Mental Hygiene Good Emotional Hygiene

Oral Hygiene is important and this goes beyond brushing your teeth. I'm talking about **conscious languaging**. Saying what you choose to manifest.

Life IS a self-fulfilling prophecy.

I said, "Uh-Oh, I'm going to be late." "**If you say so**," said Roger. It took me a minute to get it. Oh - if you say so... Roger is such a quick study - he had just been to a talk on Mastery of Language.* Now my mantra in that regard is: I always get everywhere in perfect timing. So whatever the clock says is fine. My timing is perfect. I remember that whatever I say is what is true for me. If you say so...Watch carefully what follows when you say I am. When we say I am- our body believes it. It is an affirmation. Instead of I am sick, the preferred comment could be, "I'm choosing health." "I'm choosing a strong ankle." "I am choosing for my head to feel clear and great," etc.

I became interested in conscious languaging sometime around 1979 when I took an EST seminar (now called The Forum). I remember they taught us to stop using the word try - because we either do something or we don't. There is hardly any such thing as try. The other thing was to change the word *but* to *and*- and see how the sentence feels. Saying "but" negates everything we just said. For instance - I love to eat raw food but my family eats cooked food. Instead, I can say I love to eat raw food AND my family eats cooked food. Those little hints made huge differences in my life and I became very interested in how things were worded.

I then heard some tapes from Jonathon Parker talking about surrounding things with white light to protect them, and I began using that in my car. It is a great tool. (I consciously surround my car with white light especially when I am traveling.) And - another trick I learned was to speak in the positive. Instead of saying don't fall down, say, have a perfect performance. It is also valuable in the sense that it is a higher choice than hearing "fall down." The last thing that you hear, that you leave up on your "screen," is "perfect performance." Instead of saying don't forget your lunch, remember to say, remember your lunch. The brain works in "do" mode, so we want to focus on what we want.

When my daughter Cara was young, I taught her to only say good things about herself and her abilities. When she was around fourteen I was studying for a test for the Bach Flower Essence course I was taking, and I mentioned to Cara that I was lousy at memorizing. She said, MOM, how can you SAY that. You would never let ME say that. Whoa- watch what you teach those kids - it comes right back at you. So I immediately changed my affirmation: I easily memorize things. I took a dose of some flower essences - and memorized those essences, and got 100% correct. I always thank Cara for reminding me of what I taught her, and being my teacher.

Having our words express our plan, with feeling, is essential to manifestation. It is valuable to be specific with our thoughts and to come from our hearts. Instead of moving away from something, move toward something. Instead of moving away from fear, move toward confidence. Instead of stating what is not, state what is. Speak and think all of the time - only that which we choose to have come into reality. What we speak of, what we focus our energy on, we attract. If we speak of what we lack, we will have more lack. Rather than say, "I don't have enough money," (which attracts lack of money) we can say, "I create plenty of money."

By having our words saying one thing and our feelings saying another, we can be in self-sabotage. If we say something and realize right after that it wasn't what we choose to say, we can say "cancel/clear" to erase it. When we are expressing a characteristic of ourselves that we choose to shift, we can end our sentence with "in the past"- or- "up until now." For instance, "It's hard to eat healthy (then you notice what you just affirmed - and you add - in the past." That way we are not locked into continuing a particular behavior. Thoughts, words, and emotions create our reality. "Decree a thing thus, and it shall be established unto you." –The Bible. We all get to imagine our perfect universes. The more we imagine them, the more they come true.

"Imagination is more important than knowledge. It is the most powerful force available to humanity." Albert Einstein

I vote for conscious conversations. When we give something the fullness of our attention, we give it life. We can live as if the world were already as we wish it would be, and it will be so. Remember that what we fight weakens us and what we support strengthens us.

Another brush with words I had was in Jekyll Island, Georgia, at the Solar Heart Conference, where I met Robert Tennyson Stevens. Robert teaches **Mastery of Language*** - and takes this all to the next level and the next. He teaches us to avoid saying I want, I must, I might, I should. The mantra he teaches is:

I can, I am, I will, I choose, I have, I love, I create, I enjoy. From quantum physics we know that the behavior of a "particle" (energy) is dependent on the expectation of the observer. In other words, reality behaves the way we expect it to. We can take control of our thoughts, words, actions and feelings.

Good Mental Hygiene is also important. This line says it: ***A Golden Mind, a Golden Life*** - Gurumayi Chidvilasananda

Here is an affirmation that I like:

I cultivate a practice of holy speech in which my words are directed to increasing the love and caring in the world. I use my speech to increase harmony, health, social justice, kindness, trust and unity. I am generous in praise and support of others.

The **DECLARATION OF DIVINITY** is an invocation that people all over the world are decreeing, and I invite you to join... It was brought to me by Danielle Sato of the Divinity Project and the Peace Pole Project, which originates in Japan. Peace Prevails on Earth.

The Declaration of Divinity
Ware Soku Kame Nari
I am a Divine Being

The words I speak are the words of God
The thoughts I emit are the thoughts of God
The actions I take are the actions of God
The words, thoughts, and actions of God are abundantly overflowing with Infinite Love, Infinite Wisdom, Infinite Joy, Infinite Happiness, Infinite Gratitude, Infinite Life, Infinite Health, Infinite Light, Infinite Energy, Infinite Power, Infinite Success, and Infinite Supply.
They are nothing more, nothing else.

Therefore, Ware Soku Kame Nari
I am a divine being who thinks, speaks and acts just as God does.
I will brighten and elevate myself so that when others see me they cannot help but think they have seen God. Those who have seen me have seen God.
I emanate light and continue to radiate the most supreme infinite love of God to all humanity.

Every time you say this decree, its influence is multiplied many times over, as people all over the world are saying it. They are also saying **PEACE PREVAILS ON EARTH** every day at noon.

Spiritual warriorship calls for us to remain in appreciation even when the environment is giving us signals that we have the right and reason and justification for being less than happy and peaceful and compassionate. It is our choice to make our life Beautiful, Joyous, Easy, Graceful, Prosperous, and Fulfilling.

We get to take responsibility for how we feel. How we radiate out our emotions affects our entire eco-system: another reason that it is important AND a service, to take essences. (It is said the deserts of the Middle East were not deserts until hugging became forbidden.) We are responsible for our feelings. We can, we have the ability, to change our reaction to any given event. We can take control of our thoughts, words, actions and feelings. Things happen and we get to choose our reaction. The world is as we dream it. The mind decides - the body obeys.

Essences can be useful for good mental, emotional, physical and spiritual hygiene. We take command of our thoughts, words, actions and feelings. We say it because we mean it, want it, intend it. How would God say it? How would an emissary of love say it?

Every thought is a prayer.

Espavo This powerful word was used in the ancient days of Mu (Lemuria) as a greeting for hello and goodbye. Literally translated, it means: "Thank you for taking your power." ESPAVO. It is time for us to re-member this important word... Ponder that one for a moment.

Namaste (Sanskrit) The divinity in me honors the divinity in you.

Pronoia (the opposite of paranoia) "The theory that life is constantly conspiring to shower you with blessings. Pronoia is the unshakable conviction that there is a secret conspiracy to liberate you from suffering, fill you with joy, and make you really smart." -Rob Brezsny

Expect it to be easy!

* Visit Robert's website masterysystems.com - and you can find his complete contact information after the bibliography.

PART THREE

All about the *Star Essences*

ALL ABOUT THE *Star Essences*

Here is my understanding and experience of the *Star Essences*. Each essences has its own story about how it was created and the energy surrounding the event.

I encourage you to go beyond the words I've written, to use any clues that you get, including their essence names, to go deeper and to a more personal perspective, even to other octaves - when you are choosing and using essences.

ANDEAN ORCHIDS OF MACHU PICCHU

"High in the Vilcabamba (Sacred Place) Mountains in and around **MACHU PICCHU, PERU,** are growing many species of Orchids that have within their matrix the ability to affect global consciousness. These flowers are resonating to a frequency which can be directly translated by the vibrational bodies of all who encounter them."

The Orchid is the most evolved species of the plant world. These plants carry in their DNA the information of all the other plants, which is evident by their adaptability. Their growth pattern in the plant world is like that of the growth pattern of dolphins and humans in the animal world. One of the main purposes of the Andean Orchid Flower Essences is to assist us in balancing our energies as we go through shifts into expanded consciousness.

Growing wild and free in Nature's laboratory, at an altitude of 10,000 feet, these orchids are well-adapted and very happy in their environment. They are growing on energetic ley lines, at the sacred center of **MACHU PICCHU**. They have a strong energetic field. I feel there is a correlation between the efficacy of the flower and the location at which it is made, as well as the time it is made, who makes it, and the state of its maker.

The Andean Orchid Flower Essences open and expand our hearts, allowing us to love more. This is one of the reasons the flower essences work so well. Love is a magnet which draws all things to it. "It is the force which holds the stars on their course."

★ ANCIENT WISDOM *(Lycaste longepetalia)*

DISCOVER SOUL PURPOSE ♦ TRUTH ♦ DREAMS

Enhances awareness and openness to the wisdom of the ancients that is returning now to Earth. This is an important dream essence. It aids in opening the chakra at the back of the neck to allow information to come in, so that we can remember ancient truths and also remember who we are. It assists in discovering soul purpose, and awakening to our divine potential. This essence has been found to be useful for areas of awareness in the base of the head. Use it on the back of the neck, the cave of wind, the moon tunnel, also known as the "mouth of God." (Use topically on this area, and take it orally.)

- ♥ Connection of vibrational and physical bodies
- ♥ Opens holographic awareness
- ♥ Focusing
- ♥ Connects with the ancients to receive knowledge
- ♥ Lemurian and Atlantian work
- ♥ Assists in gaining perspective
- ♥ Connects us to our tribes, soul groupings, and spiritual families
- ♥ Connection with and balancing of Master level energies
- ♥ "Re-Minds" us of our truest identities
- ♥ Dreamwork
- ♥ Stillness
- ♥ Remember ancient truths
- ♥ Reveal soul purpose

EXPERIENCES WITH ANCIENT WISDOM:

"Taking Ancient Wisdom, I experienced a heightened sense of awareness that was awesome. I felt like a Sage." – Christopher

Orchid drawings by Oceanna

"I took the Ancient Wisdom drops and immediately went into nature and spontaneously wrote (channeled?) an inspiring poem." – Sharon

"I started taking Ancient Wisdom and then my whole life changed. I quit my job, have gone back to school, and started a new career." – Jeff

"When I take Ancient Wisdom I can remember my dreams." – Anne

★ **Anchoring Light** *(Sobralia dichotoma)*
Grounding ♦ Planetary Light Work

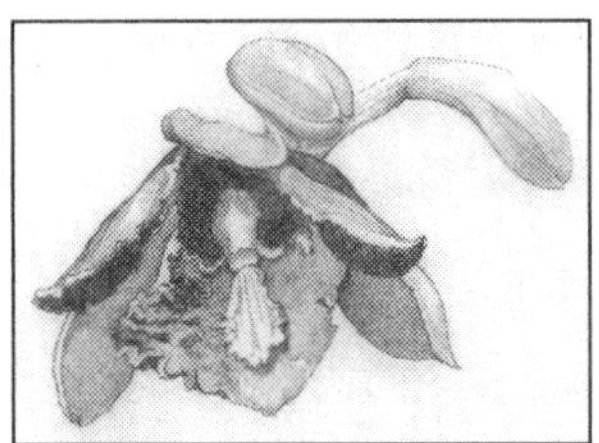

This essence is useful when we are consciously serving as a divine instrument for anchoring light, connecting ley lines and healing the planetary grids. We are transducers of energy, and this essence helps us remain stable, grounded and loving, adhering to the concept of peace, while doing this very powerful work. Also good to use during Yoga, Tai Chi, Planetary Acupuncture, and all forms of sacred movement. This essence lubricates the pathways so that energy can flow, enabling us to be more effective conductors of the new frequencies entering the planet. It is also good to use when feeling over-energized, as it brings grounding energy. It helps with spontaneous kundalini, and allows the energy to flow freely through us, while assisting us in grounding that energy. Apply drops on head to bring energy in, or put drops on feet to ground and anchor energy.

- ♥ Grounding
- ♥ Opening crown chakra
- ♥ Releasing density
- ♥ Holding space
- ♥ Opening portals and stargates
- ♥ Assisting passage into light bodies
- ♥ Master level energies

This is the **Machu Picchu** Orchid. It is the guardian standing at the entry of **Machu Picchu**. When we were making the essences, at one point I looked at Roger and he was talking to an Orchid. I asked him what he was doing and he said he was asking it to open, so he could photograph it. When the photo came back, I could see the Light Being in it. This photo experience happened after calling it **Anchoring Light**. I loved having confirmation that this essence was christened with the proper name.

Experiences with Anchoring Light:

When I was teaching classes, and so much energy was coming in that I felt like I would implode, I used to run down to the beach and put my feet in the ocean. The salt water helped to dissipate the energy. One of the ways I have found this essence to be useful is to put it on my feet, especially when I am teaching classes- and it works as well, and saves a trip to the ocean. – Star

★ Balance and Stability *(Habenaria)*

Emergency Remedy ♦ Harmony

This is an aptly named broad spectrum essence. It helps us to feel balanced in our environment. Take it for any kind of stress or ***emergency situation***. Use it whenever feeling out-of-balance. Very fast results! Brings things back into present time and focus immediately. Keep a bottle in your car, your bag, or anywhere. Use as often as necessary. Aligns all of our bodies and gives stability throughout the dimensions. Assists the body in adapting to the new high frequencies pouring onto the planet. Many say this is the most profound essence they have ever experienced. It promotes serenity. Good for children and animals. Chiropractors also report that this essence helps people hold their adjustments. Use topically as well as orally. Use it to help gracefully surf the waves of light that are rolling in. It might be considered the "rescue remedy for the 21st century." Use it for nervousness, stress, visits to the dentist or doctor, or apprehension about interviews and exams. Another use for **Balance and Stability** is when working with planetary healing and disharmonic energy patterns. Share this essence with the environment.

- Emergencies
- Strength - physical, mental, emotional, spiritual
- Energy balancing, whether hyperactive or hypoactive
- An earth tonic
- Inter-dimensional travel
- Soothes the energy field during deep emotional release
- Supports clinicians and healers during professional practice
- Provides clarity on all levels
- Broad spectrum essence
- Peacefulness
- Tests, interviews, speeches, performances

Experiences with Balance and Stability:

"The Habenaria (Balance and Stability) is the most profound essence I have ever experienced. I have (and am) experiencing a release and balancing of my chakras, especially for me the 1st, 4th and 5th. I am sharing this remedy with everyone, and I have yet to meet anyone who does not experience a balancing or healing on some level." – Sharon

"I have had so many profound experiences with your essences that I cannot possibly list them all here. One that is worth mentioning, is when I began to take the Balance and Stability for insomnia that has plagued me for several (10) years. I took 4 drops an hour before bedtime, then 4 more drops as I was getting ready to go to bed. I don't remember getting into bed." – Mary

"Your Orchid essences are the highest vibrational quality that I have yet to encounter. As you witnessed, the Balance and Stability assisted me greatly; to sustain and maintain my energetic fields in a situation of great potential for emotional upset, and to begin the integration process with grace." – Mary Jo

"Just returned from vacation and am enjoying the flower essences, especially Habenaria (Balance and Stability). Great for jet lag and hotel room jeebies." – Teri Sue

"The longer I took Habenaria (Balance and Stability) the more it helped me clean out the pollution, and it definitely supported me in controlling my asthma." – Michael

"The Balance and Stability, within 18 hours, began opening up my sacrum." – Kevin

"I recently rented a car. I noticed immediately that the energy in the car was horrible. I felt like I was going to get in a wreck, the energy was so chaotic. I carry Balance and Stability in my purse. I put drops in the front and back seats, on the dash and the steering. The negative energy cleared right away! And all became peaceful again." – Michelle

"Habenaria (Balance and Stability) has become my best friend." – Yolanda

"In my opinion, Balance and Stability had a lot more in mind than just balancing and stabilizing things for humans. In my estimation, and from my viewpoint, Habenaria (Balance and Stability) balances and stabilizes across all physical and etheric realms. It heals, by bringing into harmony, ills that have been performed on the Earth and to the Earth. As one participates in sharing this essence with the environment, the effect is rather profound as we observe the moving of stuck and sickened energy. "As I moved close to the Teepee-shaped glyph it was clearly Balance and Stability who called out to me for recognition and usage. We are valuable as humans. I was used as a vehicle at that moment to deliver a sacred tonic: Habenaria. As this miraculous orchid essence was applied to the glyph itself, a most healing and equalizing effect happened throughout a few square miles of this site. Ghosts were freed. A reality that was created with pain and deep suffering was transformed into a freshly balanced energetic pattern. A blank pallet. New. A fresh star provided. Peace filtered all around this site in Nevada. The glyphs sang. Moments, simply a few brief moments, and all was again well. I walked slowly away and felt deeply honored to have this opportunity. "As I quiet even further, I am brought into the presence of the vibration of Habenaria. "Restorative" is the first word I hear and I feel my body at a cellular level, pulsating in a more synchronistic pattern. Pattern, yes a pattern; that is what is happening here. My typically random thoughts and feelings are given form and pattern as a result of this beautiful flower. As this pattern increased in its strength throughout my body, I am permitted access to both

thought and feeling without the judgment of one or the other as superior or inferior. Simply I am. I am here. I am whole. I am resonant. Star, I just love you, and pray that your efforts with the flowers reach the full spectrum of their potential. If I can assist this process in any way I would most certainly be honored." – Daniel Pry

(who went on to write a book on our **Andean Orchid Essences of Machu Picchu**)

★ **Divine Child** *(Ponthieva montana)*

Sensitive Children and Adults

This essence is especially effective for the very sensitive, very special beings who are being born now, to assist them in staying in balance with their gifts. Also, this essence will help the sensitive child and adult to reconnect with and reestablish gifts that in the past were suppressed or repressed. It is now safe to be sensitive and to stay in the realm of delight and express our divine brilliance. I suggest 4 drops every day or as indicated. This essence is good to take with Blue Ceanothus (**Soul Family**) before and during pregnancy, to connect with the soul of the new child. It is especially good for the newborn. Put a drop on pulse points and the third eye.

- ♥ Support for sensitive beings
- ♥ Joy
- ♥ Pleasure
- ♥ Connection with Divine Child & Self
- ♥ Protective
- ♥ Polarity work
- ♥ Celebration
- ♥ Enhances music appreciation and creation
- ♥ Pregnancy
- ♥ Assists spirit in developing fetus

Experiences with Divine Child:

"I remember to play, relax, and joke around." - Daniel

Co-Creating the Divine Child Essence:

It is a beautiful, delicate, baby white flower, and it was shown to me by Skip, a 12-year-old boy. I was not wanting to be told what to do by this boy, so I asked in meditation if I should make it and what the essence would be good for. A big "A.D.D." flashed before me. Later that morning, I found out that Skip had been diagnosed with A.D.D. Oh how usual.

★ **Divine Goddess** *(Masdevallia veitchianna)*

Intuition ♦ Deep Issues

This essence is an aid in birthing, anchoring, attuning to, and balancing the **Divine Goddess** energies. It assists in developing intuition. It is quite good for building self-esteem. It is useful for both men and women. This is an extremely powerful essence when working on deep issues. On a physical level, this essence has been shown to be useful in shifting PMS and hot flashes. The heat may still be there; what shifts is your attitude about it. There is not thrashing about- the heat is very smooth, very graceful. It holds the energy of the Mother/Goddess, acknowledging the feminine as the source of creativity. It has a quality of compassion that is reflected in those who take it.

- ♥ Attuning to Goddess energy
- ♥ Awakening intuition
- ♥ Living in the base of our personal power
- ♥ Third-dimensional healing
- ♥ Moontime and Menopause
- ♥ When feeling less than divine
- ♥ Can diminish long emotional processing time
- ♥ Balances pace of healing and expansion

Experiences with Divine Goddess:

"We (all our family and our friends and cats) have been enjoying the essences. I actually can get thru my usually painful periods with no ibuprophen, just Divine Goddess!" – Ellen

★ **Eternal Youth** *(Epidendrum ibaguense)*

Rejuvenation ♦ Regenesis

This is called the Wiñay Wayna Orchid, which means "forever young" in the indigenous Peruvian language, Quechua. It promotes rejuvenation, by retraining our cells to remember the optimum frequency of life, and by raising our frequency into a place beyond disease and aging into super health and youthfulness. It is also good for regaining our childlike fun qualities. A few drops every day are recommended. Put some in your drinking water. This essence can be put right on the skin. Eternal Youth can avert the effects of premature aging of the skin. My message from the very beginning about the Epidendrum Ibaguense (**Eternal Youth**) was to use it every day and to get it on the skin. It is especially good in the bath. It is an important ingredient in our Angel Rejuvenation Spray. It also addresses homesickness. Put it in all your creams, lotions, potions, go through your stuff and add essences. Try it in shampoo and conditioner. It helps to bring sparkling eyes, exuberance, vitality, and radiance.

- ♥ Energy
- ♥ Brightness
- ♥ Clarity
- ♥ Expansive Joy
- ♥ Self-realization
- ♥ Playfulness
- ♥ Rejuvenation
- ♥ Youthful Passion

- Fertility
- Skin
- Refreshes spirit body

Experiences with Eternal Youth:

"Eternal Youth is an energetic essence, a booster of body and mind. It has powerful reactions- people look younger, it cleans the skin energetically. People have reported more interest in sexuality." – John Eddowes

I have many reports of people feeling that it helped reverse premature aging.

★ **Faith and Courage** *(Odontoglossum)*

Protection

We were divinely guided to this orchid, botanically described as having little teeth. This essence creates a frequency around us so that nothing disruptive can enter our field. This "protection essence" is like having a powerful, yet gentle watchdog at the outer edges of our etheric body. Take this essence frequently when you feel vulnerable, in order to build up a force field of invincible protection, or when you feel you want more faith and courage. It helps us to wake up to our inner courage. Excellent to use in hospitals and courthouses. Great with all kinds of healing modes, as well as for inter-dimensional protection. **Faith and Courage** is soft and gentle, like a sweet, protective friend. It offers protection for the transfer through the void space to the next worlds. It also helps to protect from all the x-ray and fluorescent and "wiggy" energy from airports, train and bus stations, and even crazy freeway energy. It assists us in becoming more optimistic. It is useful to us as we willingly and lovingly open to the higher frequencies. This flower essence protects boundaries, and knowing we have this protection gives us faith and courage.

- Protective
- Supportive

- Energy to take action
- Speaking truth
- Living truth
- Interdimensional protection
- Helps create an inner safe space

Experiences with Faith and Courage:

"When I look at a photo of the flower, I can imagine those fairy flowers all in a circle around me radiating love, so I am invincible." – Lesley

"Since I have first taken Faith and Courage, I have been able to face many problems that have always been in my life. I have had the courage to walk through the pain and come out the other side. This has made a difference in my entire life and all my relationships. I have used Faith and Courage on my dog who is 14 ½ years old and giving me subtle signals that she will be leaving. I am giving her the essence to help her face her own passing." – Sidney

Here is one of my many personal stories about **Faith and Courage**...

I kept hearing "keep the faith," and took lots of this essence. Go to the edge. Stay balanced and stay committed. I was five house payments behind. It appeared that I had no money to pay my one employee, my worst fear. I needed bottles, I was committed to teach a class in Maui and needed plane tickets, and I needed money to pay for our Star Essence booth at a show we were attending the following weekend. It was Friday. I said to my employee, "Yes, Shamara, I will pay you on Monday." I had to choose between panic and depression, or going to a birthday party and having fun. I chose the birthday party. (And taking the essence every 5 minutes to stay mellow in the midst of ...) Shortly after I got to the party, I got a phone call. $1,600 was deposited into my account from overseas. Another person that owed me money got a loan and paid me off! My friend Diamond got three tickets (Me, Roger and Diamond) to Maui with his frequent flyer miles. The next day, my neighbor bought an equity share in my house and did it in 20 minutes, standing in the front yard on a Sunday, saving me from foreclosure. All easy. And this happens all the time. I am SO grateful - for Faith and Courage.

Right before I left for Peru to take my first group, I was asked by five different people for a flower essence for protection. Spirit really wanted me to get the message, and I was ignoring it at first. We needed something beyond the ordinary protection essences; something more outer-dimensional. It is interesting that when we take this essence, people around us act differently toward us. I'm sure it is because we are feeling differently about ourselves. It's like having a protective friend with us. Normally-abrasive people have turned soft and sweet (yes, even someone opposing me in court!). Take this essence frequently to build up a protective field, especially when you are feeling vulnerable. And- take it for faith and courage.

★ **FREEDOM/LIBERTAD** *(Xylobium with 24 karat Gold)*

MANIFESTATION ♦ ASCENSION

This essence addresses freedom on all levels, especially the freedom to express ourselves, and freedom to manifest truth at all levels. It assists in realigning us to our original divine blueprint. It assists our evolution into our multi-dimensional identities. It enhances other modalities. The frequency of Gold added to the Xylobium works synergistically and assists in opening dimensional doorways. We have been guided to take this essence several times every day, as a service to others, to the planet and to ourselves, to maintain a frequency beyond mass consciousness - regardless of what other essences we are taking. We are researching this essence in regard to alcoholism and fetal alcohol syndrome. A friend who took it said that it diminished his craving for alcohol, but actually he would rather drink, so he didn't want to take the essence. You have to want to shift.

FREEDOM/LIBERTAD is here to assist and balance our outer-dimensional bodies as we cross the threshold and take the first steps of ascension. I recommend taking this essence 1-2 times a day with meditation. This essence radiates the vibration of the number 12. It helps us to evolve into our multi-dimensional identities. As we build our frequency we radiate out that frequency, which will automatically assist anyone entering our field. In this way, we are serving others and the planet as well as ourselves. The frequency of the gold assists in opening dimensional doorways. It is a premier conductor that conveys codes, and it is the container of light on the metallic plane. It raises our vibration to a frequency where we are free to be who we really are.

FREEDOM/LIBERTAD reminds us that everything is within us. After experimenting with this essence, we have found it to be quite freeing. People have reported feeling free enough to dance, and many other varied, happy reactions. (This essence is fun to pass around in a group. People loosen right up. It's like having a cocktail.) I invite you to feel for yourself what it does. When you are with a few people and the energy is low, try giving everyone a few drops of this essence and then notice the shift.

If you want to evolve really quickly, take this essence VERY regularly- in a cyclical fashion- 4 drops 4 times a day. Be consistent with the times each day. You will be amazed. Sometimes it might feel like you are evolving too fast, and then you will magically slow down. The 5th dimension really comes in when taking this essence. Total truth - no duality, only unity and oneness, all light, time and space collapse...

Taking **FREEDOM/LIBERTAD** is like taking a truth serum. Are you ready for the truth? We, as humans are rebuilding our matrix - our DNA structure - and this essence supports that activity. When we take this essence, it rhythmically builds momentum. As we find our frequency being raised, our behavior will likely become consistently more "wholesome." Taking this essence, we can only tell the truth, and we know more and more when others are telling it. In telepathy, which is getting stronger and stronger for all of us, we can only be telling the truth.

♥ Expansion
♥ Liberation

- Opening universal flow
- Supports action
- Unconditional love
- Ascension
- Access to inter-dimensional realities
- Energetic Truth Serum

Co-Creating Freedom/Libertad Essence:

Right after we made this essence, I told Roger that I was getting the message that it was supposed to have Gold in it. His immediate response was, "It has to be 24 karat gold." Shortly after that, in another discussion, I overheard Roger describing to someone this totally pure, spongy-shaped, 24 karat gold that you could get in Puerto Maldonado, which is on the Amazon River. In still another conversation, Roger was debating whether to pick up a group in La Paz or in Puerto Maldonado. I said, "If you go to Puerto Maldonado you can pick up the gold for the essence." "Decision made," he said immediately. "I'm going to Puerto Maldonado." When he called me on Christmas Day, I asked him if he had gotten the gold for the essence. He said, "Funny thing, our bus broke down, right in front of the place where they sell the gold. I went in, bought the gold, came back, and the bus started, and that was it." He had planned to get the gold on the way back out. As it worked out there was a storm on the way out and they had to leave at 4 in the morning, and wouldn't have been able to get the gold… The name of this essence originally was **Ascension - First Step**. This essence is especially beneficial to those of us who offer ourselves as instruments for service to the light, and consciously choose Ascension in this lifetime, and continue to ask for the steps to be presented. It is great for balancing the "stepping up" that is going on. We are ascending in steps. The cone shape of this flower is a Lemurian key. I was told in a dream that the shape and message of this flower is very symbolic. You can see the photo on the web. The flowers on the bottom are open and as time goes on, more open up. We open to the next level. The name then shifted to **Freedom/Libertad**. It is especially overlit by **St. Germain** - on the 7th Ray of Freedom.

Experiences with Freedom/Libertad:

"Taking Freedom every hour, I saw myself really move into the flow with everything happening magically." – Ryan Evans

"I became more clear about myself with this essence. Who I really am. It was a catalyst that moved me quickly to the next step." – John

★ **High Frequency** *(Pleurothallis)*

Meditation ♦ Heart and Lungs

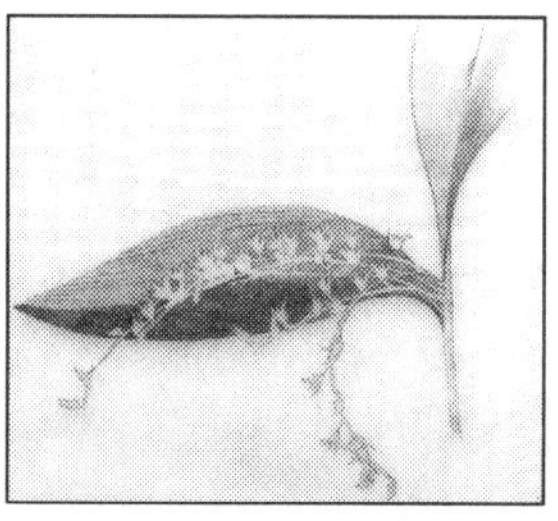

An extremely high frequency essence! Aids in opening channels to the highest dimensions, and to the Ascension energies. Take a few drops and meditate. Many have had profound experiences after taking this essence. Flower essences facilitate your highest conscious and unconscious desires. This essence is also useful with issues around heart, lungs and grief (you can actually move from grief into bliss). An example for me of the different octaves, was when we realized that **High Frequency** will take us to very high places when it is appropriate, and if we are starting at a level of sadness and/or grief-it can lift us out of that. We noticed that it dealt with issues around the heart and lungs. "Pleura" is the root word for lungs and is also in the name of the orchid (Pleurothallis).

- ♥ Increased awareness
- ♥ New perspectives
- ♥ Elevation of vibratory patterns
- ♥ Working with Master level energies
- ♥ Living in Highest Expression
- ♥ Supports individual choice
- ♥ Expression of highest consciousness
- ♥ Takes us to a rarefied space
- ♥ Meditation

Experiences with High Frequency:

I was with my friend Susan Ward and she pulled out High Frequency and took a few drops. She dropped into an immediate and unexpected meditation. For the next 45 minutes she sat and described to me in vivid detail, how the essence went to each one of her chakras and lit it up. She was totally altered, and yet she could come out of that state (unlike with drugs) any time she wanted. She quite enjoyed the experience.

★ **Nature Communion** *(Trichoceros parviflorum)*

Connection to Nature ♦ Reverence for All Life

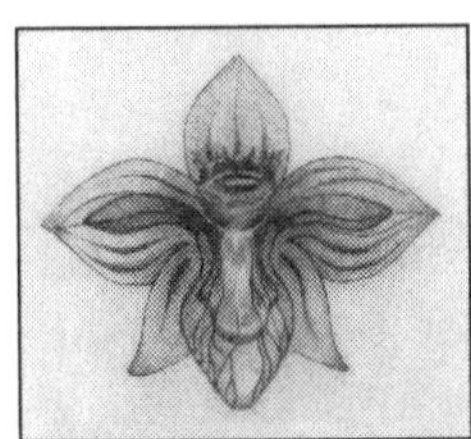

This essence enhances your level of consciousness and your connection to the Nature Kingdom. The unseen world becomes palpable. **Nature Communion** supports your connection to your physical body, and is also good for fertility. It is fun to use when working in the garden and when hiking, because it assists, as its name indicates, in communing with Nature. Use it when working with the plant world in any form. Often this essence shows up to be mixed with other essences to accelerate their energy. It synergistically enhances herbal preparations. It is also useful when you have been inside too long, i.e., too much computer...It is like a hike in a bottle.

- ♥ Connection to Earth energies
- ♥ Connection to Devas and Nature Spirits and Pan
- ♥ Connection to plant and animal kingdoms
- ♥ Connection to gems, minerals, and stones
- ♥ Awareness of physical body and physical sensations
- ♥ A hike in a bottle
- ♥ Awakening of Natural Kingdom in Dreamworld

Roger and I first called this one “Little Bee” because of how it looks. From the front, it looks very much like a little bee, and sometimes from the side, it looks like a miniature hummingbird.

Birds and bees… I called it "Plant World." This flower was for communicating with the plants, that's for sure. One day when I was talking about Plant World as my favorite essence, I also mentioned that other people were hardly noticing it. Roger said, "Well, you know that isn't its name."

I said, "whoaaaa! ... well then, what is it?"

He said, "Nature Communion, or something like that." Zip! I got it immediately. I said, "YES, that IS it! It isn't just plants, it's all of Nature." Thus, it was re-baptized as **Nature Communion**.

★ One ♥ Heart *(Epidendrum cuscoense)*

Acceptance ♦ Love ♦ Unity

This essence addresses the merging and balancing of male and female by unifying both sides of ourselves. It is about oneness, unity, unconditional love. This essence will assist the "pioneer" relationships between people that are happening; relationships that defy definition and social confines, and that are beyond language. It does this by moving us into a frequency to accept the paradigm shift in our perception of relationships, and into the frequency of unconditional love. We can revel in the ecstasy of being Love itself, of finding reunion. This is an excellent essence to share with groups. It immediately unifies people into the high frequency love space. It opens the heart chakra, and many have had a profound experience of feeling it physically in the heart; feeling the heart expand. It can also be called in for healing broken hearts. Love returns. This essence connects us on the heart frequency and vibrates the frequencies of unification and acceptance. It was made on a Mother's Day which was also the *Wesak full moon. We sometimes call it "Love Drops." *Note: The Wesak Full Moon is Buddha's Birthday, and is a Sacred Day during which tremendous divine dispensations occur, spiritual gifts are given and major blessings are experienced. It always occurs on the first full moon in the sun sign Taurus. (See footnote for more information on Wesak.)*

This essence is sweet and gentle, yet good for powerful issues. Use it after you have worked on deep heart issues to smooth things out in the emotional body. **One ♥ Heart** is great for balancing male/female energies within oneself, for increasing telepathy and non-verbal communication. It offers the ability to (as the Dalai Lama says) bless everyone. **One ♥ Heart** feels full as in a Mother's love. Unconditional love. There is a blending, merging and attracting. It assists in magnetizing love to us, and moving our love to a higher form. As we take this essence, we notice the love frequency all around us. When taking **One ♥ Heart**, it is so easy to love everyone. It inspires relationship at a new level, in a new form.

Love unconditionally is the message of the new paradigm. It is time for total acceptance and time to love one another.

- ♥ Group work
- ♥ Gatherings
- ♥ Unconditional love
- ♥ Self-acceptance
- ♥ Unification
- ♥ Connection with source
- ♥ Opening fourth chakra
- ♥ Issues of the heart
- ♥ Heart connections

Co-Creating One ♥ Heart Essence:

I received a strong message to go back to Peru with another group in May of 1995, for the Wesak full moon. The words "One Heart" kept coming up everywhere, and even when I closed my eyes, sometimes I would see it spelled out. When we came upon this particular beautiful, deep maroon-colored Orchid on the trail (which has since become **One ♥ Heart**, Epidendrum Cuscoense) it called out to be made into an essence. In my early morning meditation the next day, I got messages to cut the flowers after 4 p.m. That was unusual. I usually make essences right around noon. I didn't give it much thought, although I did choose to not rush into making it.

Later on, we were all having a siesta when suddenly, I got up and out of my tent. Roger was just coming out of his tent. (I love the magic of even simple synchronicities like this.) We looked at each other, and got the essence-making gear and headed for the Orchids. It was about a 20-minute hike. We got there and sat with the flower a bit, and then realized that we hadn't brought the camera.

We like to photograph the Orchids before we make the essence. Since we weren't in a hurry, we stashed the essence-making equipment and hiked back and got the camera. When we got back, some more of our group were awake and wanted to come with us. We hiked back and by that time, it was EXACTLY 4 o'clock when we cut the first flower. The time that I had heard in my meditation. Nature has her way with me…

The other message I heard, was to have the flowers in the water as day became night and night became day. So it was. I left them in the water dusk until dawn, to absorb that wonderful full moon energy. It was the night of the Wesak full moon, and Mother's Day as well (May 14, 1995). We sat with the essence all night inside the sacred site of Wiñay Wayna (one of my very most favorite places on the planet), in the heart of the rainforest/cloudforest in the Andes Mountains. As the sun rose in the morning, it shone directly into the bowl, illuminating it. The early morning sun feeds our hearts. Magically, the early morning sun was the only sun we saw that day. The rest of the day was foggy and rainy.

The waters we used to make the essence were 1.) water taken from a ceremonial fountain on the "Island of the Sun" in Lake Titicaca, 2.) water from a ceremonial fountain at Wiñay Wayna, and 3.) some water that my friend Susan Winter Ward had collected from Mary's Well in Nazareth (that she just "happened" to bring along). And it was, as I mentioned, Mother's Day. Oh how usual.

Experience with One♥Heart:

This is an essence that I have with me at all times, when I take groups to Peru or anywhere. In the beginning, I used essences a little to help create a common experience. Finally I noticed that the days that didn't go as nicely as I would like, were the days that we didn't use and share the essences. **One ♥ Heart** especially helps to increase everyone's tolerance, so that everyone loves everyone, even in the goofiest of situations. At times when we were all taking **One ♥ Heart**, we couldn't even get the group to split up into 2 boats. Everyone loved everyone so much that they always wanted to be together. These are "love drops" with freedom built in. You get to be loved just how you are, and return the love in the same way.

At home, I have tried it with my granddaughters when they were arguing in the car, and afterwards, suddenly they were helping each other. I also use this essence in many combinations, because it is so good for unification and blending.

★ **Sacred Union** *(Maxillaria)*
Oneness

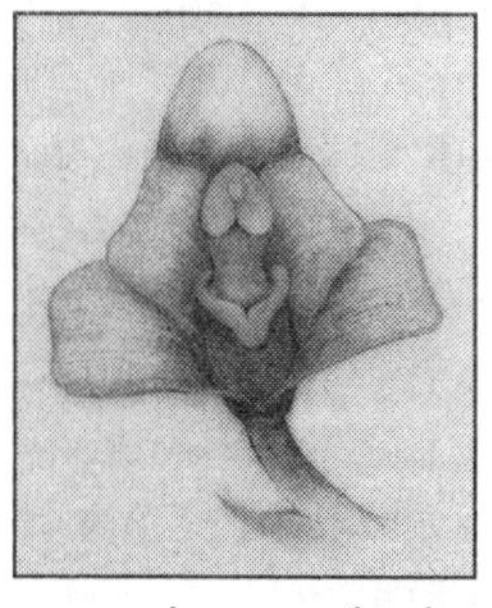

Addresses integrated sacred sexuality. It is a vibrational catalyst to move us to a new level of heavenly union, with ourselves, or with a partner. Rejoice in ecstatic fulfillment conjoined to make one soul, one body in love, which gives bliss to the divine presence. This love in itself is an instrument for peace in the world. Be zealous to bask in this joy. It is very nice to take in conjunction with **One ♥ Heart**, and also good with **Divine Child**. Use alone for tantra. This essence portrays the tantric visions of celestial bodies. It was made during the March Equinox of 1996, as the energy on the planet was balanced in every direction. Take it with your beloved. It is for taking sexuality to a heavenly level.

- ♥ Re-Union of self with SELF
- ♥ Tantra
- ♥ Honoring the heaven in this moment
- ♥ Merging on any level
- ♥ Connection with other life forces
- ♥ Greater depths in relationships of all sorts
- ♥ Sacred Sexuality

It is fun to note that right after we made **Sacred Union**, we made **Divine Child**.
These Orchid essences are like notes in a symphony that play well together.

★ Wesak Full Moon Information

Through the Wesak Ceremony, a wave of spiritual energy comes to the planet. This is the same current of energy from Source that comes each Wesak Full Moon and increases in frequency each year, with each spiritual cycle. This wave is known as "The Wave of Enlightenment" and each of us can choose to be connected to it energetically through a Wesak Ceremony. It is recommended that you enter the ceremony just prior to Full Moon, after you have already cleansed your energy body and raised its vibration. Ask for this wave of Enlightenment to fill and flood through you.

Here is a prayer that I have used for Wesak:

I call to Beloved God/Goddess and My God Presence to assist me at this time of Wesak, to prepare my energy body for this sacred ceremony by clearing my fields and chakras with a concentration of violet-platinum and white golden light. I ask to be purified with the cosmic white fire of The Christ I Am… "I Am That I Am" …I call to Lord Buddha and All Bodhisattvas, the Inner Plane Ascended Masters of Shambalah, The Archangels and Angels of Light, The Inner Earth Temple Workers, Mother Earth and all Earth Kingdoms, Divine Mother, The Sisterhood of The Rays and Rose, The Ashtar Command, The Elohim and The Masters of The Great White Lodge, to assist me in connecting to the Wesak Ceremony. I ask to be taken to the Wesak Valley by linking my merkaba, my light vehicle, with other groups who are traveling on the Inner Spiritual Planes to Wesak at this time. I ask that I receive all I need to fulfill my divine mission and my puzzle piece of the Divine Plan at this time, and that I be guided by I Am Presence to offer my gifts to the fulfillment of The Divine Plan on Earth. So Be It. So it IS.

Orchid drawings by Oceanna

The Higher Chakra Trilogy

This Trilogy of Essences, Gold+Silver/White, Zeal Point, and Awakened Thymus, is useful in preparing for the activation of the higher chakras

Zeal Point

Gold + Silver / White

Awakened Thymus

These essences can be used on their own or in any combination. Using all three of them, and doing numeric harmonic sequencing, can be very powerful. This is explained after the definitions.

The **Zeal Point Chakra** essence was the first essence to be made in this Trilogy. It was a most interesting thing. I was feeling pretty complete with the 12 Orchid essences, when this magenta flower came in my face. Literally. I was walking around a corner, a couple of hours from **Machu Picchu**, and there it was hanging down. I had to see it- even if my mind was 10,000 miles away. We had just done a meditation the day before that had included the magenta chakra. Someone came up after and said that the part about the Zeal Point chakra (magenta chakra) really resonated. Then the next day- zip, zap, zing- there was a magenta orchid greeting me. Oh how usual- that everything fell into place the following day to go and make the essence (on 11:11-1996). I felt like I had legions of Angels assisting me on this particular hike. We made this essence in perfect harmony and grace in a perfect location after it rained (which is always a great sign to me that I am supposed to make the essence, as rain cleans and purifies everything). I made a mental note to find Brenda Montgomery, who had written the magenta chakra meditation.

This is the even more interesting part. When I got home, I put out a newsletter about this essence, and I invited folks for a

Christmas party. The day of the party, guess who walked up. Brenda Montgomery was already on my mailing list. She saw what I had written. She came a little early and I was still getting ready for the party- and I was in shock, sort of, from seeing her. She said she came especially to give me something that she had written. She thought it was important for me to have. She didn't even stay for the party- and I got so busy that I didn't read what she had written until Christmas Eve - around midnight. Just reading it catapulted me into a new octave- and I was ecstatic to have made the essence for the Magenta- the Zeal Point- Chakra.

Channeled by Brenda Montgomery (on 11:11, 1996! The same day that we made the essence!)

Peace and everlasting joy, my sisters and brothers. You are in the final stages of life, as it is known on the planet today. Yes, this is the final gift- you are being given a jubilant gift, a gift of evolvement and of enlightenment.

Yes, brothers and sisters, the time is now for the final chakra point to be announced. This point of light within the body is now a necessity and a powerful energy realization.

In this time on Earth, before and during the ascension, it is necessary for each one to begin the process of rising to the height of spiritual consciousness. This new chakra is the answer. No more is it necessary to work for years to cause the movement of the kundalini as did the sages of old (if you do not choose to). No longer is it necessary to learn the many mudras of the merkaba and spend time in meditation trying to enlarge the energy field, and create the lightbody through this practice- if you do not choose to.

Now with the simple opening and movement of the Zeal Point Chakra, your destiny is set. As you begin to use the Zeal Point

Chakra the rush of energy will, on its own, create a powerful lightbody that readies you for ascension. The same movement also completes the chakra system- uniting it forever in a powerful flow with the universe. There is a light so bright- a power so infinite- and you know that the energies are forever changed by the action of the Zeal Point Chakra.

How does this work? Where is the point of light? The Zeal Point Chakra is at the lower-most curve of the skull, where the curve makes a downward flow to the top of the neck... this area has been called the "old brain," or the medulla oblongata. Looking to the side view, it is just about a straight line through the mouth to the Zeal Point Chakra- also a gift of placement. The gift?

A fully conscious mind to express the spiritual powers through the voice.

The Zeal Point Chakra draws the color red and the energy and power from the first chakra, and it also draws the color violet of the crown chakra with its highly spiritual energies and the bliss and the pure knowing of the heart/mind. These potent colors and energies meet at the Zeal Point Chakra in a burst of MAGENTA color and energy that immediately transforms into supreme white light flowing upwards through the soul chakra (the transpersonal chakra above the head). In this action it carries your vibration to its heights and causes the flow of energy to unite with the celestial energies of all knowledge- attainment of enlightenment. Full bliss is the next step. Several tries may be necessary to accelerate into full bliss. This is easy if one can let go of all human fear.

As the energies rise and the supreme white light is released, your lightbody is empowered and charged- lighting the way for the final ascension. These are the new times- the way is smooth and the lessons made easy. You are on your way now, no more false starts. The final days are present.

Do not try to come back from this action too quickly, for the moments of bliss are needed to expand your understanding of this place of beauty in mind and body and spirit. This is a moment in time of great peace, joy and true balance with all that is. This is your gift, your birthright. You have done the work of each of the chakras, you have found your peace and you now look forward to making your way to the ascension with full understanding in heart, mind, body and spirit.

Dearest sisters and brothers, use this gift with care. Do short periods of energy expansion at a time. It is crucial that you are fully aware that as these energies move to the expansion of the lightbody- the lightbody will expand and take you into bliss. In this state you will be in the state of full knowledge-YOU ARE ready to handle the results of this.

As you come back from your experience of truth, you may not remember the knowledge that was given you in the deliverance into bliss. As you give up the need to control the experience, more will come. The future is in your hands- enlightenment is pure joy. You are being readied for the full ascension.

At the time of the full ascension you will immediately go through the zeal point chakra, and without hesitation be into the full lightbody flow- easily- and into the next stage- all fear gone forever- ALL LOVE ACCELERATED- all bliss at hand.

We offer you the Zeal Point Chakra now at the **11:11** *1996 as a completion of your flow into oneness with your creator- The Light. You will be fully in readiness. No matter how long the process of change takes or how quickly, you are now readied- a pure light. Now it's time to help others- those who are slower to come to this information. No matter how long the process of change takes, or how quickly, you are being readied in pure love. Take this information and use it to help others in your circles of energy, of LIGHT.*

I love you endlessly- fully. Our bliss and joy is yours now. My father's wish is that you understand and move forward in the light.
-Jesus Christ the Son channeled by Brenda Montgomery

★ Magenta-Zeal Point Chakra

(Epidendrum Federicci Guillemi)
Expression Through the Voice

Assists in opening and balancing the Magenta Zeal Point chakra, which is located in the back of the head at the base of the skull. This area is referred to as the "Mouth of God." This essence balances the body, mind and emotions. It assists in moving Kundalini energy through the body. It opens us to the next level of initiation in divine harmony. It also helps release energy that collects and becomes stuck in the neck. It is useful in conjunction with many other essences, and especially in blends made for children. **Zeal Point Chakra** helps us to speak our truth. There is a gift of **Zeal Point Chakra**, which is having a fully conscious mind to express the spiritual powers through the voice. It is beneficial to have bodywork done while opening this chakra. The Color magenta is aligned with the number 44, which in numerology, indicates it is an entry point into a new evolution. Magenta is a combination of red and violet, a marriage of sun and moon, and the unification of polarities. It is a launching pad and entry point to a new evolutionary spiral.

The **Gold+Silver/White Chakra** essence was made next. Looking at the photograph of this Orchid, like some of the other Orchids, creates activation in itself! This exquisite essence was made from the outrageously beautiful white Orchid with a gold center, the Sobralia Setigera. We first saw this Orchid while we were in **Machu Picchu**, and did not make an essence of it. After leaving **Machu Picchu**, that outrageous Orchid became compelling to me. It kept leaping into my consciousness. Miraculously (or as we say now, "how usual"), everything fell perfectly into place for Roger and I to go back to **Machu Picchu** to make the essence. Roger got the train tickets and we were off. When we arrived Roger looked at me and said, " I thought you would be jumping up and down by now." I had to take a look around to notice that the hillside was filled with those gorgeous white orchids greeting us. It was such an awesome thing that we found plenty of Orchids in full bloom. (After the coffee flower incident I had become humble- especially in reference to the moment of bloom.) And for this particular Orchid, this is rare, because they have ONE DAY when they are in their perfect, prime, peak state; essentially a fleeting moment of bloom. The Orchids greeted us as we got off the train, saying "YES!" We hiked a bit and found some pristine specimens saying "CHOOSE ME!" We made the essence and got back just in time for the train back to Cusco. I am so grateful for the divine choreography.

★ **Gold + Silver / White Chakra** *(Sobralia setigera)*

Balanced Light Body ♦ Peace ♦ Serenity ♦ Harmony

This exquisite Orchid essence encompasses 2 chakras: the gold chakra is like a halo, about an arm's length above the head. The wisdom of the gold chakra is love and acceptance. It holds the Christ energy. From the gold halo, this chakra cascades out to the silver/white chakra encompassing the luminescent light body. This **Gold + Silver / White Chakra** essence contains the new energies for us to access the space where truth and peace flow out of our ecstatic hearts: we feel enraptured in bliss, peace, serenity and harmony. When we go into this space, we ride the currents of the universe through our consciousness and feel wisdom and love and acceptance of all that is. In this space, we also have recognition of pure self. This essence assists our subtle bodies in sustaining balance, tranquility, peacefulness, and divine contentment. Taking the **Gold + Silver / White** essence with intention to bring this high-vibrational light into our body, will assist the activation of these chakras. This essence helps us stay balanced while this activation is happening. There are ways to assist and prepare ourselves for the activation of this chakra… What we eat makes a difference. It is useful to eat live foods rich in chlorophyll. Chlorophyll assimilates light; and thus it helps us assimilate light more gracefully. Doing breathing exercises is also helpful.

★ AWAKENED THYMUS *(Erythrodes simplex)*

HIGH HEART ♦ GRACIOUSNESS

This special essence helps to filter and convert 5th dimensional energy to make it more easily acceptable to the human body. It is useful for telepathy, and connecting the 3rd and 6th chakras. The thymus, being between the heart and the throat, empowers loving communication. The thymus is also called the high heart. It is useful when healing with voice and sound. (On the physical plane, the thymus relates to the immune system.) It was made in the moment of the March Equinox at Wiñay Wayna. There were eight of us, and we each cut a blossom into the bowl of water taken from a nearby awesome waterfall. To energize it, we had carried the water bowl to the ruins of Wiñay Wayna, to a place that we call The Point of No Fear. This Point is a triangular-shaped stone, jutting out from the window of the ruins, that seems to hang in mid-air, with thousands of feet of drop-off and the rainforest below. It feels like an energy vortex, where fear disappears and time and space stand still.

The thymus gland, a small gland located in the chest, and the heart chakra have different locations and are inter-related. The thymus gland is said to have been much larger. It is our job to wake it up again to its previous function. The thymus receives spiritual life force energies and transforms them for use in the etheric, subtle body and physical vehicle. Thymus tapping is a valuable thing to do to stimulate it. Activating it stimulates the immune system. We can put our conscious attention on building it up. Take the essence to strengthen and nourish it.

These enchanting essences that are called the HIGHER CHAKRA TRILOGY, have many levels of activity that reveal themselves, especially when you take them together.

Be Merry.

Experimenting with the Higher Chakra Trilogy

There are exciting things to be discovered as we use these three Andean Orchid flower essences from **Machu Picchu**. Use them alone and in combination; by yourself, and especially in groups. The following is a suggestion, and I urge you to experiment. The number of drops as well as the order they are used in, all create a specific sacred geometry, and we are the explorers and scientists in this arena.

Take 3 drops of **Zeal Point Chakra** essence under your tongue.

Next put 3 drops of **Zeal Point Chakra** in the palm of your left hand- and then place your palm on the back of your head, at the base. Do 3 rounds of ***PLANETARY ACUPUNCTURE**.

Take 4 drops of the **Awakened Thymus** essence under your tongue. Next put 4 drops of Awakened Thymus into your right hand, and rub the drops on the skin in front of the thymus (center of chest a bit above your heart).

Do four rounds of planetary acupuncture.

Now take 5 drops of **Gold + Silver/White Chakra** essence under your tongue, and put 5 drops of the essence in either hand. Rub your hands together and lightly brush your head/hair with it. Continue to do planetary acupuncture- 5 rounds - and then go into meditation.

If you are doing this in a group, which is VERY powerful, you can do the **Gold + Silver/White** part to each other - You can add these essences to an essential oil and anoint yourself and each other with it. When you do, these essences can activate and open a major conduit through which the heart can have an immediate, profound opening.

This special anointing - whether self-administered or whether you anoint each other - opens up a space for very beautiful, high information to come through, with the geometries of the flowers. The essences trigger things on a very deep level and put us into the frequency of well-being, gratitude and openheartedness. You can also do this while someone is playing crystal bowls, and you can put the drops, in the same ratios, into the bowl, to be amplified and broadcast. You can do this with and without the planetary acupuncture.

The **Zeal Point** moves energy. The **Awakened Thymus** opens the heart with love and compassion. And the **Gold + Silver/White** puts us into the Light Body field.

Through the laws of resonance, these essences will raise our frequency - to a place where we will access rarefied energies - where we become enveloped in a column of light - where beauty and harmony abound. As more of this energy becomes anchored into the Earth through us, it is for everyone to get into these higher aspects. In this refined state of awareness, we tap into the strengths, height and majesty of our Divine Self. We wield our power with love and compassion.
When taking these essences with a group, we can achieve Illumination and Unity Consciousness.

"In flower essences we are dealing with geometric forms which are the precursors for the formation of matter. These codes are absorbed by the etheric body and translated into stimulating vibrational frequencies." – Marcel Vogel

More information is coming regarding using the Higher Chakra Trilogy and other essences as well, in harmonic sequences. Ask for guidance, and experiment with using them in different patterns and ratios.

★Planetary Acupuncture:

Take a deep breath in from Mother Earth, into your heart.♥
Hold it for a moment and fill the breath with love and breathe
out into the stars.

Take another deep love-filled breath in from the stars
to our heart ♥ hold it- then breathe our love into
Mother Earth.

Now take a deep breath in from the Earth and the stars
at the same time into our heart, hold it, fill it with love, and
breathe that love-filled breath out all around.

This meditation is adapted from **Martin Gray**. It was given to him to do at sacred sites around the world at the request of the Earth. We can do it any time. It is a win/win for us and for Mother Earth. You can get more clever and more complex and expand this meditation and move through your chakras, and you can visualize the energies coming in as tetrahedrons, and visualize them intersecting, and then you can spin them…

We can take lots of flower essences to attune our alignment to subtle vibrations and work toward the harmony of all, and there are also things we all can do to assist ourselves in assimilating more gracefully, the increased Light on the Planet. Some of these things are: We can eat live foods rich in chlorophyll, as chlorophyll synthesizes the sun and light into food for our being. We can practice conscious breathing, as breath is the very essence of taking in life. We can practice joy, de-light and bliss, by spinning, dancing and laughing, which also opens Chakras.

The Peruvian Flower Essence Collection

I was happy making Orchid Essences and having them be "my thing," and then the Coca began to talk to me… and that was the beginning of the Peruvian collection of essences.

Mama Coca

Coca Flower and leaves

In Peru there is a ceremonial plant. It is often referred to as Mama Coca, and is considered a symbol of freedom to the Andean people. It is a sacred plant worshipped and used in ceremony and ritual. The Andean people use the leaves to make prayers and payments to the mountains, always taking special care to pick out the most perfect leaves for their offering. Coca is also used in all manner of healing, including licking and pasting a leaf onto a particular area. To the Andeans, Coca is also a working tool that helps with adaptation to the altitude. When you are in the high Andes in Peru, going somewhere you can only get to by horse or on foot, and you really want to take photos and you would like to give the folks you photograph a gift, you would be advised to take them some sacred Coca leaves - a gift much nicer than money. Even though they might have their own, they like to trade, and get leaves from other regions.

Now Coca has received a very poor reputation. We have adulterated and manipulated it and turned it into paste. Cocaine. Coca is not only cocaine. It is made up of 14 alkaloids (one of which is cocaine) and some nutritious elements as well, for example protein and amino acids. Some of the alkaloids that coca has are well known for soothing stomach disorders. The Andean people drink it as a tea. It is chewed and used for altitude adjustment. It also has a couple of chains associated to opiates, and it has others that are currently under research. Coca has even been used in the Andes to make toothpaste, and there are many other uses that are NOT associated with the cocaine alkaloid. The most important use of Coca is for sacred rituals.

For about a year, the spirit of the Coca plant kept coming and asking me to make a flower essence of it. It also wanted me to go to a Coca plantation and do a ritual. I told Roger that I was getting a strong message to make the Coca flower essence, and that we had to do it with a group. Any other person might have said, "Take fifteen gringos to a Coca plantation? You've got to be crazy!" But once it was put into Roger's consciousness, the magic began to happen.

Nasario- a great shaman blowing coca leaves for ritual.

Our mission was not only to make the flower essence, but also to shift the energy for all of the Coca plantations, who were feeling very misused and misunderstood. The Coca was feeling sad that so many people knew it for only one thing, when in reality it has so many gifts. There is a beautiful song by a Bolivian composer, Ernesto Cavor, that says "Coca, beautiful companion of our lives in the Andes, beautiful Mother that brings freedom to us, what have we done to you to make you a jailer of our consciousness…" The song goes on to say how sacred the leaves are. There is a T-shirt you can buy in Cusco that says, "The Coca leaf is not a drug."

Nasario- a great shaman blowing bubbles for fun.

Roger's Story

When Star called me up and asked if we could go visit a Coca plantation, my first response was, "This is not an easy request." Although I was internally expressing that it was not easy,

I allowed Spirit to help me, and my answer was "yes we can, we can visit a Coca plantation." I didn't know how, I didn't know where, because normally Coca plantations in Peru, Bolivia and Columbia are areas (because of the name of Coca and because this beautiful plant has been misused to extract Cocaine out of it) - politically speaking, are very sensitive areas where foreigners are not welcome. With Star's request now in my consciousness, I continued doing my everyday thing - traveling and guiding in **Machu Picchu**. Then several synchronicities started happening. While traveling on the train that goes from Cusco down to Ollantaytambo to **Machu Picchu** to Quillabamba (the same train that we would take later with the group), I met with some friends I hadn't seen for several years who are dedicated mainly to the cultivation of Coffee and Cacao. I asked them if they knew when the blooming period of Coca was. Their general answer was that Coca does not have flowers. I told them it *must* have flowers, that botanically it belongs to a group of flowering plants. The flowers could be very small or hard to see or could last for only a short time, but they do have flowers. Coca is a dicot, and dicots are flowering plants. However, they affirmed that there were no flowers. Coca plants are not allowed to go to seed, so by taking the leaves before the plant is mature, the plant never gets to the flowering stage, or *almost* never gets to the flowering stage. Plants will be cloned, anyway, to extend cultivation of Coca.

The harvest of Coca, like the harvest of tea, happens 3-4 times a year. They wait for the leaves to be a little bit mature, and then they collect them by hand. After that, the leaves are put into a solar dryer or are first left out in the open, then dried in the shade - the first softening of the leaves is done in the sun and then a day or two later when the leaves are softer, they are put into packs in the shade. When the Coca leaves are sold, they're sold in big bundles that weigh 45-46 lbs. each and they are well-pressed, compressed to make a smaller bundle.

We were talking about Uña de Gato and how good it would be to start planting Uña de Gato as a substitute crop for Coca in the valley of Quillabamba. At this time, the government was paying for and running a program of substituting other crops for Coca. My friends mentioned something very interesting; that because of this crop substitution program, the Coca was not favored any more, the price of Coca leaves had dropped down dramatically in the region and Coca plants were not being harvested. It's not legal any more in Peru, so they have to fill in requests and so on through "Inako," which is a national nursery that controls the expansion of Coca plantations in the area. All of this was news to me, yet I started looking for a place.

The same day I met those people, I was also talking to one of our cooks who was traveling with us - an excellent person. He said he had family down near Maranuda and that there they have Coca plantations and Cacao and Coffee, among other things, and that they live very close to the train line. Little did we know that they lived at the train line! I talked to my friend and said we would like to visit with the family. He promised to let me know and to organize a little bit in the area of Maranuda. I went back to the States and told Star, "I think we've got a winner, I've got something going here and I think it is going to be possible." Up until then I was a bit dubious about going to a Coca plantation because of it being quite politically sensitive to have Americans visiting in the region.

Arriving in Cusco

When the group arrived the following March, Roger's first impression was, "Wow, we have a very diverse group." We had several women, we had a young kid about 12 years old, and we had a 6 foot 6 inches tall e.t. gentle giant, Jonathan. We took them around Cusco and explained to them that the visit to the plantation was still a big intention for our trip, still not confirmed but in the works, in the hands of Spirit. We visited **Machu Picchu** and had a great time going to Wiñay Wayna. In the meantime, Roger's office had requested the permits from the government to go and visit the region and though the police officers in Cusco granted the permit, they said that we would go there at our own personal risk. The police would not take any responsibility over the journey. Peru is a free country. You can travel anywhere, is what he said, as long as you take responsibility. Roger asked what kind of responsibility he meant and was told by them that "…it just means we are waiving for you to go and saying we don't want to mess with anything of that." After this encouraging statement, Roger decided to totally ignore it and continue with our program.

We left **Machu Picchu** on the afternoon train and by 6:30 we arrived in the lowlands. You feel the humidity. You feel you are in the sub-tropical forest. There were plantations of Banana, Cacao and Coffee. Roger had made special arrangements with the conductor for the train to make an unscheduled stop for us. The train stopped only for what seemed to be about one minute, just long enough to allow us to jump off. All fifteen of us. We tossed off our luggage and landed in the middle of Doña Inocencia's field.

It was dark when we got there. It was a very, very simple house. The second floor was a large room with three openings for windows, with no glass in them. The room had been recently whitewashed - just for us, and the family had moved out to give us the space. This was the place where we started to make a home for ourselves. Enthusiasm was high. We brought in the mattresses and our sleeping bags, and waited for our cook to prepare dinner. We had brought some children's clothes in anticipation of our visit - and we passed them out, which was really fun. Many of the neighbors came to have a look at us. Because of who Roger is - and I'm sure because of the look of this group - they were not afraid of us. (I figure they must have thought that spies wouldn't be bringing a 12-year-old kid…) These folks had never seen the likes of us (and probably never will again).

In Search of Coca

The next morning we woke early (with lots of dogs and roosters for alarm clocks). We all started coming out to the patio, where there was a single water faucet to wash. We talked with the family (and extended family) and expressed our intention to go into a Coca plantation to recognize Coca as a sacred plant - a very special gift brought to us by the Spirit of the Andes as a symbol of freedom and the linkage of all the different ecosystems in the Andean region. We could see how every Quechua man and woman was nodding and smiling and happy and pleased that we had come to participate in this reverence to Mother Coca. Mother Coca's true nature was going to be recognized. (It was due to human nature that a jailer's quality got assigned to this plant that was intended to support and symbolize Freedom.) The intention was to allow the world, energetically, to know that Coca has many gifts, and to shift some heavy energy. Our Quechua friends were happy about this.

We were off to search for the Coca blooms. A few had been spotted in the past weeks, so we were in the right season. Still, we weren't sure if we would find them. I have truly come to appreciate the moment of bloom. On this adventure we had a one-day window (that now or never thing)…

We went out to the field, walked down and went through a coffee plantation. The owner of the plantation and some of the workers joined us. He was very proud to show us how the coffee plantations were done following the natural curves and lines of the terrain. He showed us the water canals to irrigate them. We hiked. And we hiked. And we hiked. We had our bowl and our good water and we were ready. We hiked some more. We spotted a flower here and there. It was a beautiful day and a beautiful hike. And we kept hiking.

We went through the Cacao plantation, saw some Citrus and Banana and other fruit trees. At the end of the Cacao plantation we got to the first small lot. Until then nobody was certain that there were going to be Coca flowers in the Coca plantation. When we got there we found that they hadn't been harvested - yes! - for the reasons expressed before - and there were a lot of Coca leaves. The plants had reached maturity and, thank you to Spirit and to the devas of the Coca flowers, there were lots of yellow five-petaled flowers on almost every single one of the plants in this beautiful, one-acre, untouched Coca plantation.

We made a circle. We recognized the Spirit. We looked at the flowers. We held hands and I led a prayer and meditation to shift the energy for the Coca plantations. As Roger translated everything to Spanish so the owner and workers could understand, they nodded their heads "yes," and we enjoyed the wondrous moment. Taking water from one of the natural fountains nearby, we proceeded to make our Coca essence. We all took part and the energy was awesome.

It just so happened that it was the birthday of the plantation owner and Roger had managed to send someone on a mission of going into the town and getting some beer, so we went back to the house and celebrated.

We named the essence **Inocencia Coca**, after the mother of the plantation owner. It is associated strongly with freedom and with strength and with the other positive qualities that Coca has. The plant- in its natural form- is innocent. The **Inocencia Coca** essence is used for breaking non-productive holding patterns, and is also good for metabolism, restoring energy, and improving stamina. It helps you to align with your true source of joy. The magic held in the Coca plant is very powerful. It is used to help you gain your own power, as opposed to taking your power away (as does cocaine). I am SO grateful that Coca chose to show up for us to make its essence. It has proven to be extremely valuable for many people.

The Coca was the beginning of making other essences in Peru, besides Orchids. Now we have a collection of 13 Peruvian Essences. **Thirteenth Gate** was the 13th Peruvian essence to be made.

Circle of energy at the Coca Plantation.

♥ ABOUT FACE *(Dandelion - Taraxicum officionale)*
ALL ABOUT THE FACE ♦ FACING ISSUES

Helps us face issues we may have been avoiding. This is a powerful essence to keep us on track. It alleviates procrastination. It addresses "facing things" at all levels, and sometimes doing a complete about-face. This can even mean storage, closets, drawers, relationships, jobs, etc. It also addresses actual face problems like acne. Make a cream or oil for the face and add the essences Eternal Youth and **ABOUT FACE**. It is about turning around the aging process. It will help reduce wrinkles, and strengthen and tone the face. It is also good for liver balance and de-tox, especially if alcohol has been used to numb feelings. It is about growing in the face of adversity. It helps balance and stabilize old feelings. It is about all kinds of face things. Face the music. Face the facts, lift your face to the sun, especially face ourselves and reflect light. Continue to grow. Make a wish every time you take the drops.

MAKING THE DANDELION ESSENCE - ABOUT FACE:

Near Lima, Peru, during a full moon in 1998, I went to the desert with an 87-year-old priest, who is an expert on herbs a nd traditional medicine and knows all of the healing plants, and John Eddows, a brilliant psychotherapist who uses lots of flower essences. Also accompanying us was John's three-old-son.

We went to Lomas de Lachay to see what special flowers would be growing following the "Phenomena el Niño," which had brought a lot of rain to this usually dry area. I was ready for something exotic. To my surprise, the flower that was calling me was the Dandelion. Now, the Dandelion is a favorite of mine. I just figured that I could make it anywhere, and I knew that I was only making one essence that day, because I had only brought one bowl, one bottle, etc.

The three-year-old-boy would not move until I took its photograph. (And Nicolas can be very stubborn.) The Padre looked me in the eye, and told me that the Dandelion was a VERY important plant. The flower told me it was **ABOUT FACE**. It was growing in the face of adversity. It was important to make the essence at that time and at that place.

It was funny, when I got back, I spoke to my sister and she had just had some minor surgery on her face. She said, "You know, it's all about the face." This was just another little confirmation for me… about my choice of names. This is also a good essence to put into face creams.

This is an essence that has become near and dear to me. I am always taking essences, and I pick them intuitively, or by their names or an idea that jumps out. While I was newly acquainted with **About Face**, I had a session with a massage therapist that was more than amazing. I was in Ocean City, Maryland, and this was the only session I ever had with her. I had just met her. I had mentioned that I made flower essences. After the session, she asked me if I worked with Dandelion, because it kept coming up. I told her yes, I had an essence of it. She said, "Take it."

She had no idea what it was for. It was super-perfect for me in that moment, and yet probably not an essence I would have thought of. I began taking it, and everything in my life appeared before me so I could face it, and gracefully. As I looked at (faced) them, the issues shifted into an even more beautiful existence. This is an example of how sometimes it is very valuable to step out of the way and to have someone else pick essences for you.

Experiences with About Face:

"About Face helped me face things I was in denial about. I had to change jobs! And I did that. I found another job that pays twice as much."
– Beverly.

♥ **Bushilla** *(Bushilla)*

So far, we know this essence is good with female issues, especially reproduction at any stage. Men have had success with this essence, working on mother issues. We are told that more is being revealed, especially as to its uses with men. Experiment. Arbildo Murayari Mozombite, who is a vegitalista, curandero and perfumero, and who is the shaman in the Pulcalpa jungle that I made this essence with, said that it is very important and that it is very valuable. I look forward to your feedback.

♥ I Am Generosity *(Chijchipa - Tagetes Multiflora)*
Grand Fortune

This essence is a treasure. It is about prosperity consciousness, opulent manifestation, full-flavored magnanimous flow, affluence, and prosperous abundance. Share a universal cornucopia of expanded grand fortune. We are reminded to give generously.

♥ I Am Gratitude *(Yuyu - Mustard)*
Holy Grace

This precious essence reminds us of our exquisitely rich rewards, of our holy grace. We are pure channels of divine love, filled with gratitude. This essence magnifies the higher octave love energy. Affirm "I am so grateful" three times, as you take these drops. Gratitude is a magnet that attracts more of what we are grateful for into our lives. The mustard plant also grows in Santa Barbara, and it wanted to be made in Peru in the particular rarefied energy of Chaska Land.

♥ Inocencia Coca *(Coca)*
Shifting Patterns ♦ Stamina

The Coca plant is greatly used for ceremony and healing in Peru. This sacramental plant is multi-faceted. It is invigorating. This flower essence is being used to increase stamina. It balances appetite and metabolism, in addition to assisting with shifting addictive patterns. Use for dieting, rejuvenation, raising metabolism. It helps align the will and intent, and breaks non-productive holding patterns. It aligns us with our source of joy and effectiveness. It brings us into alignment with our dharma, our true service, and aligns us with what is passionate and productive. It will raise the intellect to meet the messages of the 3rd eye chakra, thus aiding psychic ability. It is also very good for altitude.

♥ Integration *(Mutuy - Cassia hookeriana)*
Open & Clear Mind

Helps balance your mental and emotional bodies in preparation for emergence into 5th dimensional reality. Works with the pancreas. Sweetness. Self-esteem. Useful for integrating shifts, and during chaotic times. According to Maximo, the 87-year-young medicine man who helped make the essence, it helps soothe your head when you are scared.

♥ Mango Paradise *(Mango)*
Celebration of Life in the Physical Form

This essence is about robust sexuality, sensuality. Juiciness! It also has the energy of the pink dolphins who were jumping in front of us while the essence was being made. It is about jubilance and enthusiasm. It is also primal, uncomplicated and earthy, free of belief systems, and filled with wind and the spirit of the Sun. This essence is a gift and a celebration of life in the physical form. Juicy and magnificently tropically sweet.

Making Yummy Mango Paradise:
While this essence was being made, my friend Julia, who is the archetype of Mango, slathered herself in what she referred to as "spa quality" mud and baked in the sun. It looked so fun that I followed suit- or lack of suit… This essence is very sensuous, as is the fruit of the mango.

♥ Master Teacher *(Chiri sanango)*
Master Teacher ♦ Expansion

This is considered a Master plant in the Jungle, meaning that it teaches us. It can connect us with the overlighting Deva of healing. It is about expansion, and about temperature regulation. Many people report hot flashes or "power surges" have disappeared while using this essence. Cold extremities warm up. In fact, the essence was originally called San Juan/Perfect Temperature. This is because it was made during the festival of San Juan, at the time of year when the temperature in the jungle is perfect, and because as a plant teacher, Chiri Sanango regulates temperature, and is good for the blood and bones. It got re-christened, as we realized its gifts were much broader than temperature regulation. **Master Teacher** takes us when we are ready to go to a next step. It helps clear paths and balance things in our aura, so we can come to a peaceful place.

Personal experiences with Master Teacher:

"Master Teacher in combination with the Rainbow Crystal Chakra essence (Clear Quartz) - my life patterns are being brought to consciousness and they are able to be released." – Sidney

"I just started to use Master Teacher, and it's working! I have been sweating for the last five years, and this appears to be the first thing in my whole life that I've taken that is helping me. I am ecstatic and like jumping for the ceiling with ecstasy. I'm so happy!" – Rosemary

♥ **Purification** *(Muña - High Andean Mint)*

Sanctify ♦ Cleanse

Assists connection with our guides, and in passing through the veils of the other dimensions. Use it for balance, especially during purification. Good for cleansing and clearing (it's in our Crystal Clear Mist). Use this essence to sanctify and purify in multitudes of ways. Get creative! Also good for altitude.

Making Muña:

On one particular trip, I crossed paths with friend and Shaman Jorge Luis Delgado. He asked me if I had made an essence from the Muña - the High Andean Mint. I said no. He said it would be a good idea. He said that they planted it on purpose at the sacred sites, so you are automatically purified as you walk through. In perfect timing, we found the Muña in bloom and offering itself at the Temple of Fire (Purification Temple) at the sacred site of Sacsayhuaman outside Cusco, Peru- on Easter Sunday, and made its essence.

♥ Strength and Chi *(Fava - Vicia fabia)*

Well-Being ♦ Vitality

This noble flower essence facilitates all functions of brain activity, including memory, energy and sense of well-being. It is useful for balancing hormones. Strength, energy and radiant vitality come from being in balance. Good during a parasite cleanse, to sustain balance in your subtle bodies. Good for menopause.

Personal Experiences with Strength and Chi:

In a sequence of research and synergistic events after making this essence, we found that Fava contains a high concentration of the amino acid L-dopamine. Later, we found L-Dopamine is a factor that is being considered in treatment of Attention Deficit Disorder (A.D.D.). Strength and Chi is an ingredient in our Attention Formula.

"Strength and Chi works like magic with hot flashes." - Dina

♥ Sublime chocolate *(Cacao)*

Balance Metabolism ♦ Feed the Channel

"God gave Angels wings, and humans, chocolate." This essence balances metabolism. Excellent to use when you crave chocolate. Helpful for remembering dreams. Good for women during their moontime (menstruation). Stimulates psychic abilities. Improves appetite for healthy food. Provides energy after meals. Etheric endorphins. Assists in clearing ancient DNA. Assists connection to Mayan and Incan cultures, by clearing the channel. Feeds the Light Body. Yummy! It is for awakening, and getting in touch with the ancestors. Chocolate correlates with pleasure. It enjoys a rich history.

Co-Creating the Sublime Chocolate essence:

The importance of the moment of bloom: The reason we took the whole group to the Quillabamba area, was to make the coffee flower essence (or so I thought). Roger had been there checking the flowers two weeks before our arrival, and the fields were covered with them. Now I will say here, that I have never had a whole cup of coffee in my life. Only a mouthful by accident once or twice when I thought it was chocolate… I don't know or understand coffee.

Chocolate, on the other hand, is a different story… I do have a connection there. Anyway, we headed out to find the coffee plantations. We went high into the mountains, because we wanted totally organic plants. Our bus driver, Juan, was from the Quillabamba area, so he brought his wife and daughter along for the adventure. This included driving our bus over a 17,000-foot snowy mountain pass. There was also Leo, our cook, and Patti, our local guide. She was very good at getting the bulldozers to move, so we could get our bus into places I didn't expect a big bus to go. On the way, we stopped at a known-to-be-magical spot: a special mountain called Urusaya or Blue Mountain. We hiked in, and several of us ended up in a completely rejuvenating waterfall.

After bathing and purification in the gorgeous waterfall, we found ourselves making the Cacao flower essence. Once we became attuned to the tiny flowers that grew right out of the trunks of the trees, they stood out like little fireflies saying, "Choose me!" It was beautiful energy that connected us for the making of this essence. Juan and Patti and Leo were all interested in the Cacao flower essence, and Roger was, as usual, super at explaining and translating to everyone what was going on. We were definitely in an area rarely visited by non-Peruvian tourists. Two days before we made this essence, I was visited by the Deva of the Cacao. I hadn't paid much attention, as I was focused on the coffee essence.

We continued our journey to the coffee plantation, and when we got there, hardly any of the plants were blooming. To find the flowers was like an Easter egg hunt. There were a few stray bloomers, and lots of buds for a later bloom. We went ahead and collected enough flowers. It took a long time. It wasn't easy. The signs weren't there. We tried with a few blooms that took us hours to find. It was just too hard. It was also not in keeping with our standards of excellence, which require plenty of blossoms, in full bloom, at their peak. The Coffee flower was NOT in the perfect moment of bloom. That night, I returned the Coffee flower essence we had made to the Earth. We were two weeks late for

Coffee, but in perfect time for Cacao. Sometimes we have to learn how to do something, by learning how NOT to do it. Coffee brought so many lessons!

The Cacao flower is a beautiful star-shaped flower that grows right out of the bark. We saw the Cacao in every stage. We saw the green fruit coming right out of the bark on the trunk and branches (right where the flowers were), then yellow fruit, which, when totally ripe, was orange. Yum. We saw some fruit cracked open, so we sucked on the seeds. They had a little bit of tasty pulp on the outside of the seed that you could suck off. As they dry, these seeds are harvested and are ground up to make chocolate powder.

Personal Experiences with Sublime Chocolate:

"Sublime Chocolate and Let Go and Trust are really impacting my life! I haven't craved chocolate…" – Talasteena

♥ **Wild Feminine** *(Wild Potato - Solanum diploide)*

Uninhibited ♦ Spontaneous ♦ Nourishing

The **Wild Feminine** brings all of our aspects together in joyous relation, whether our gender is male or female. We express our unique diversity as we choose. We remain cohesive, yet gloriously individual. It also has a nurturing feminine quality to it. This essence carries a vibration that just became available during the powerful solar eclipse of March 1998. It helps to anchor important feminine aspects of us in a new way. Enliven & awaken sensations with enthusiasm. Savor the rhapsody.

Making Wild Feminine:

The potato had called me for a long time, nearly a year. I was concerned about finding potatoes growing in the Sacred Valley that hadn't been poisoned with pesticides. I wanted chemical-free and grown with love. I was delighted when the Wild Potato showed up on Chaska Land. We made the essence on the day of a very powerful eclipse. I had been very drawn to the date, Feb. 26. The eclipse and alignment of planets were happening the day we made the essence. When we returned only a few days later, the flower was gone. (That moment of bloom thing again.)

When we arrived at Chaska Land, the neighbors had a little crop growing on our land. We had given them permission to grow, and didn't know what crop they would choose. It was, you guessed it, POTATOES! That day, there were a few flowers. The neighbors were quick to show me the bugs eating the leaves. I have told them that I never want any pesticides put on them. The bugs are a good sign. Most of the one hectare (approximately three acres) just has weeds and some seeds that we have sown to put nitrogen back in the soil. Since the potato flowers were so sparse, I was thinking that it wasn't prime time for this essence. Then Roger was down on his knees and had something to show me. One of the "weeds" growing all over the ground in the height of its bloom was the Wild Potato! Perfect! Ah- again the perfection of being at the right place at the moment of the bloom. This essence, made with the special energies of the planetary alignment, carries a very powerful and divine frequency. Potato says, "My tuber grows deep under the earth. My flower feeds me and I feed my flower. I am nourishing. My roots, growing in the Mother, are fed continuously with her energies in the dark, in the yin. I send and transform that yin energy into my flower with the light."

♥ 13TH GATE *(Cantu Flower - Cantua buxifolia)*
OPEN PORTALS

The 13th Peruvian Essence

Cantu Flower Essence being made.

Good for integrating those energies of the number 13. You have the pleasure of interpreting for yourself what that means. This essence also carries hummingbird medicine. It has been found to be a very pleasant and peaceful essence, smoothing edges, during these interesting accelerated times. It also helps with changing frequencies and solar flares.

The number 13 is a very sacred number, and as part of the grand illusion of the third dimension, we were taught to be afraid of it. The perfect relationship of Jesus the Christ with his twelve disciples is a fine representation of the sacred power of a group of 13. Numerologically, Jesus the Christ equates to the number 13. Jesus = 74 the = 33 Christ = 77 Total 184 = 1+8+4 = 13.

This essence was made around the time of the March Equinox at the sacred Lake Titicaca, from the Cantu flower, which is the national flower of Peru. It helps us move through and integrate gracefully the portals, the octaves and gates that we are moving through.

In March of 1999 while in Peru, I received the message to go back to Lake Titicaca in the year 2000. There was something about the energy of 13 - some work we would do in that regard. Lake Titicaca is the 13th Chakra of Earth and the frequencies of 13 are beginning to return. (I can't say that I exactly understand what this means - I just hear what I hear & enjoy the signs and synchronicities.)

At the beginning of the trip, Roger had been telling us how the stones were laid at 13-degree angles and Cusco was 13 degrees latitude. Oh those 13's again. So, on to Lake Titicaca. I had a strong feeling I would make one flower essence this trip. The Cantu kept coming and when I asked Roger if it would be in bloom - the guy who knows nearly everything said he didn't think so (based logically on the time of year and the weather). Several years before, I had made an essence from Cantu and was told to let it go - it wasn't time yet. It was curious that it kept coming to me.

When I packed for Taquille Island I had to think about the bowl. Should I take it? This is a pack-light-for-one-night, carry-your-own-stuff affair. I packed the bowl. We got off the boat and regrouped in a beautiful meadow. Beautiful does not aptly describe Taquille. You have to go there to feel it. It is peaceful and pure. No cars, no electricity. (Now a little solar stuff is happening). They speak in whispers. Located in the middle of the lake of the Eternal City - Lake Titicaca.

I began the hike to our host's home, where our group would stay. At the top of a hill a young boy greeted me with - YES! - a Cantu necklace. Of course I immediately knew that today was the day, and the Cantu was it! Cantu is the national flower of Peru and Bolivia. It is bright red and a natural hummingbird flower. We arrived at our host's home, where lunch was served. The Cantu was calling. I often fast while I am making essences - so I easily made the choice to skip the tempting meal. I grabbed my equipment and went off to make the essence. Pure ecstasy is the way I can describe it. I found a perfect terrace with Cantu surrounding me. I had the perfect spot to sit with the flowers - who were all saying "YES" and "choose me." I began cutting flowers into the bowl of water. At one point I stopped and thought, "How many flowers?" and I thought, well, maybe 22. I began to count the flowers in the bowl - and then got a good laugh. There were 13. That was perfect. I sat with the flower essence. I went into euphoria. When the essence felt complete, I was thinking it was time to bottle it. Two little kids and a baby, maybe 18 months old, approached. They were quite intrigued by me and watched my process, the two bigger ones (a girl and a boy - maybe 4 and 5 years old) smiling - the baby a bit apprehensive. When I finished, I took what was left in the bowl and splashed some on the kids - then went ahead and splashed the baby. She started giggling and laughing. What a blast! It was another peak moment. I bottled the Cantu. The next morning I returned right after sunrise to the special terrace - to sit with the Cantu again.

I LOVE making (and taking) flower essences!

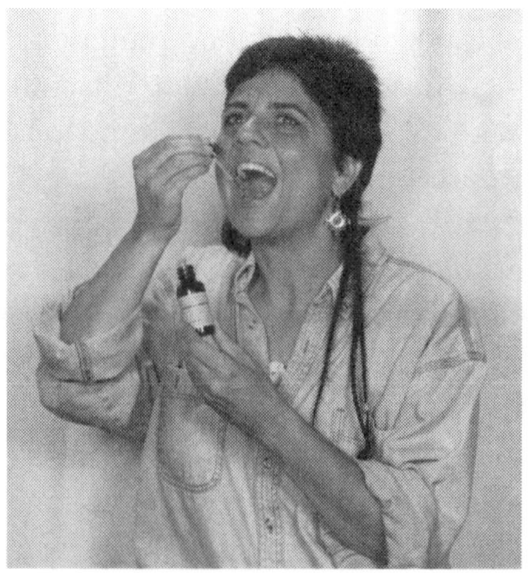

Santa Barbara Flower Essence Collection

Pink Lotus

I have always had a love for flowers. I remember making bracelets and soups and salads and bouquets and arrangements and anything else I could think of to make with flowers. For years, I have taken numerous medicinal and edible wildflower classes/walks. My favorite ones have been with our local Teacher Extraordinaire, Peggy Lane. I am always hoping her vast knowledge of the Santa Barbara flora will rub off on me, and I always appreciate her rampant enthusiasm. When I first heard about flower essences, I had a secret desire to make Santa Barbara essences, but I somehow didn't feel worthy. I also felt sure someone else would do it at any moment. I figured since I was interested, everyone else must be as well. Several years went by and no one made them. I made a few for fun, and to teach others how to make them. I remember that I made the Orange Blossom (Pure Joy) essence with several of my Angel friends, and the Lavender (Full Moonlight), and Male Strength from Mr. Agave, all before I thought about being an "essence producer." Each one of them spoke to me so strongly that I made their essences. I had these essences even before I made the Orchid Essences. I didn't think much about them, especially after the Orchid Essences came to be. Then one day the Santa Barbara flowers let me know that they wanted to be recognized, so I started talking about them more in the classes. Then I realized I was the person who was supposed to make the Santa Barbara Essences. I was born here in Santa Barbara, and I love it here! I have been hiking the hills and mountains forever (my forever). Also, Santa Barbara is one of the important sites to make essences, as it carries **Lemurian* energy.

Lemuria - There were two Lemurias in the history of the Earth. The first Lemuria began just after the Fall about four and a half million years ago and continued until just prior to the beginnings of Atlantis about one million years ago. At that time it simply vanished. It was not a physical world and therefore no archeological remains exist. The second Lemuria coincided with Atlantis and is also known as Mu. It was a landmass in what is today the Pacific Ocean. This second Lemuria was physical and left behind indicators of its culture, such as Easter Island, etc. Both the first and second Lemurias were typified by their alliance with Nature and art, contrasting with Atlantis which was mental and unnatural. Received by Bob Fickes

I now have 24 Santa Barbara flower essences. The following are descriptions of some of their expressions. They are divine gifts from Nature that bring us into blessed perfection. I like to take them all the time and I remain pretty "blissed out," which now feels "normal" to me. I really notice the difference when I DON'T take them... I invite you to expand your capacity to experience ecstasy.

♥ **Be Nurtured** *(White Ceanothus)*

Mother's Milk

Soothes our soul. Nature refers to this flower as Mother's Milk, as it is filled with the Divine Mother's energy. Feel safe and nurtured. This essence is especially good for children and babies. We are surrounded with an abundance of love from a higher realm. There is plenty of it, it is spilling over. Be nurtured.

Made on the auspicious occasion of my birthday- as a nurturing treat to myself. I saw a beautiful rattlesnake that day- right on a very wide part of the trail, and we had a pleasant exchange. I felt safe and felt like the snake was an old friend and guardian. (With reverence and good sense, I also let him have the trail, and I walked around him- letting him have some space...) It was truly a magnificent day, nurtured by Nature.

♥ **Creation/Focus** *(Jacaranda)*
Creative Vision

Assists our ability to hold the energy to dream the new dream. Supports creative vision and staying focused. Stimulates new ideas. Great when working on computers. Helpful for studying. A constant companion to me while writing this book. (In the Combination Brilliant Student)

Creation/Focus was made as the comets were entering Jupiter- in a super force-field of meditation. It was a second bloom in one season for this tree - the Jacaranda very strongly offered itself during this timing for this important essence.

♥ **Dance** *(Bougainvilla)*
Grace ♦ Beauty ♦ Brilliance

This essence gives assistance for flowing through life gracefully. It gets us moving. It is good for all forms of sacred movement, especially dancing. Take it for dancing through life gracefully. Also, use it in relationship, which is a "dance" of harmony and of perfect rhythm. Dance the journey into the self, and then to the source of supreme energy: this is the cosmic dance. Try dancing at dawn with your eyes looking east. Watch for a profound state of ecstasy. Travel to the future that comes before the past. Activate your imagination and awaken. When we are dancing, we can make contact with the trees and the animals and learn many things. Experience innocence, spontaneity, and naturalness. This essence assists in our evolution. Feel good for no particular reason - or any reason!

♥ **Deep Breath** *(Eucalyptus)*
Divine Inspiration

This essence is about breathing. Take life in and let it out. It is all about inhaling and exhaling. Open and expand the chest and the lungs, and remember to breathe. Breathing connects all systems in our bodies. Watch for the automatic deep breath, which is

God Breathing Us. The breath of God that happens when God breathes us is so yummy. Inspire = to breathe air/life into the soul. The best way to get more air is to exercise outside. Do complete inhalations and exhalations to eliminate the carbon dioxide. Mastery of breath is mastery of health. This essence will assist in the journey.

♥ **Early Bloomer** *(Oxalis)*

Family Harmony ♦ Trust

For those who awaken early - to have certainty of self. This essence assists in adapting to accelerated, early growth and maturity. Use our advancement to awaken to our divine potential and become a positive instrument. Great for children and teenagers who are advancing at an accelerated rate. Be alert. Expect, Trust, Know.

Krista Skyler Peace with Oxalis.

♥ **Emancipation** *(Tobacco Flower- Nicotiniana)*

Physical and Emotional Well-Being ♦ Peace

Freedom from anything that has power over us. Liberation. Release cravings gracefully (especially nicotine and marijuana). Focus your intention, take the drops, remember your intent, and breathe out again. Do this each time you take the drops. Tobacco is grounding and good for traveling between worlds. Emancipation of potentiality. The tobacco flower essence cleans the meridians. If you are choosing to quit smoking, this essence assists with grace and ease. Remember the importance of the sacred breath, and the intention that goes with the breath.

My friend Ros was working with the "Youth at Risk," and I volunteered there from time to time. Ros is great about using flower essences with the kids. They kept asking for an essence that would help them quit smoking. About the same time, the tobacco was in bloom and showing up everywhere, no matter how much I tried to ignore it. It told me it would help to emancipate those kids. We find that it does help a lot. And another important thing - you have to want to quit, and change your patterns in order to get results.

♥ For ♥ Giving *(Acacia)*

For Giving and Receiving ♦ Worthiness

For giving and for receiving gracefully. This essence reminds us to give and receive from the heart to assist in moving into the frequency of forgiving-ness. For forgiving ourselves and for giving TO ourselves. Know that you are perfect. We have also found Acacia is useful when working with allergies. They can be released. It can move our vibration into an elevated state of acceptance, giving the ability for giving even more. Remember, ultimately the gift goes to the giver. Release. Give, and you receive. And- it is time to transcend the need to forgive anyone for anything.

After doing major construction/remodel and addition to my house, the yard was down to just dirt. After all of the building equipment left, I had carefully landscaped my very small yard. I planted a couple of trees and the area was beautiful and happy, and EVERYTHING I planted, grew. I planted an apricot tree because I love them. I also really wanted a tree to separate the front house from the back studio. As I was inspecting "Herb Mountain" (my 5 by 8 ft. plot of herbs), I noticed a little "weed" about an inch tall. I love letting little things grow, especially when I don't know what they are. It is a nice surprise to see what it turns into. I watched it and one day I thought, this is not a weed. Only a couple of years later, that little weed had grown in the perfect spot to do exactly what I wanted, so perfectly. It volunteered. It gives a full, generous bloom every year of gorgeous, deep golden yellow puffed flowers, and it perfectly gives privacy to the front and the back house. One day, as I was thanking the Acacia for the fine display and for so kindly doing such a great job, I immediately heard back, "That's what I am good for…For-giving. For giving, Forgiving, For Giving."

♥ Full Moonlight *(Lavender)*
Full Moon Energy

Excellent for addressing full moon weirdness or sleeplessness or out-of-sortedness. This essence helps to balance full moon energy so it can be harnessed and used beneficially.

This was the first flower essence I ever made, and it was unorthodox, because it was made with the energy of the full moon instead of the sun! A Friday the 13th, full moon, Valentine's Eve, I might add. It worked for me immediately. I was having that "out-of-sorts" feeling- like I might implode- and as soon as I began to make the essence- I became peaceful. This essence has helped me again and again to use the powerful full moon energy in a creative way.

♥ God/Goddess Unity *(Banana Flower)*
Masculine Balance

For merging of the male / female. There is now unified oneness in our sexuality. This essence assists gender healing at very deep levels, and balances the first chakra. Banana flower essence is useful for dealing with sexual issues in relationship, enabling us to view them from a higher, balanced frequency.

♥ Graceful Shift *(Fennel)*
Change with Ease

This is an excellent essence when you are going through great changes. Useful for balancing physical energy when going through dimensional shifts. Should an influx of light cause discomfort, this essence will address it. Often good in conjunction with Anchoring Light. Excellent for grounding. Fennel addresses nausea, especially when caused by shifting frequencies. Gives those hungry butterflies in the tummy something to eat. Little by little everything is handled, and becomes settled and perfect.

♥ **Initiation of the HeartLight** *(Pink Lotus)*
Open-Heartedness

Reach a new level of open-heartedness. This essence goes in very, very deep to open the heart. It will help us to recognize any judgment we may still have. A threefold flame resides in our hearts, and the Pink Lotus fans the spark and ignites that flame within us. Sometimes you will feel warmth in your heart after taking the essence. In ancient Egypt, the Lotus is associated with resurrection, rejuvenation, and eternal life. It is said to have mind-altering capabilities. The Pink Lotus is also associated with Lakshmi, the Hindu Goddess of spiritual wealth, spiritual abundance, and spiritual evolution.

The Co-Creation of the Pink Lotus Essence – Initiation of the HeartLight:

The Lotus flower spoke to me in meditation for ten months before I made its essence. In my meditations, it told me it was about "initiation." It was about reaching a new level of open-heartedness.

We were linked with people all around the globe who knew that we were preparing a Lotus Essence. The essence-making ceremony was held during that magical, auspicious August 11, 1999 eclipse and Grand-Cross planetary alignment. The Earth energy was phenomenal. It was that day that we went to Lotusland in Montecito and made the enchanting Pink Lotus Flower Essence. It has called itself **Initiation of the HeartLight**. It is helping to open our hearts wider than ever.

In 1999, I held a Star Essence Teacher Class and our entire class received an invitation to visit Lotusland, a magnificent garden in Montecito. They only allow a certain number of visitors each season, and you have to get on a waiting list, so we were excited to receive this special invitation. We had a wonderful time; I viewed each flower as a prospective volunteer for a new essence. As I listened to my inner voice, I heard a resounding NO, regarding the making of a Lotus flower essence. A couple of months later in meditation, I started getting regular visitations from the Deva of the Lotus, asking me to make its essence. When I inquired about its blooming time, I was told the time was past. Remember, obtaining the flower at the moment of bloom is very important for creating a perfect essence. The Lotus said "of course," because I was to make the essence the next year. I then heard that there would be specific energy anchored into it. It was to be a very special essence.

At some point during the year, I set a date for the teacher training. Out of curiosity, I called my friend and highly respected astrologer Ken Kalb (author of "*The Grand Catharsis*" and "*Lightshift 2000*"). I am not an astrologer, and yet inevitably, I have been and am guided to make essences and go to Peru and be in specific places during auspicious planetary alignments. I asked Ken if there was anything special happening during the time I had chosen. He laughed a lot and didn't even have to check his ephemeris. He told me August 11 was a time he was calling a "flashpoint;" a very important time. I was happy that once again I had unknowingly chosen an important time for the class.

Later the Lotus came to me and said that we were to make its essence during the class and after the eclipse (which was happening around 4 a.m. on the day of August 11th). I love to have confirmation, so I started making stipulations to the Universe, to the Lotus Deva… to make certain this was really what I was supposed to do. I said that first we would have to get permission to go to Lotusland again. Then we would have to get permission to cut a Lotus! And… I wanted it to be EASY.

We got the permission easily, thanks to Super Star Essence Teacher, Lovely Lea Parker. The challenge was that the main Curator, who was giving us permission, was going to be out of town that day, so we had to find one of the Docents who could be there for us. We ended up with a more than perfect situation. How usual! My friend and Visionary Artist, Oceanna, walked into my office. For some reason, it just came out of my mouth that we needed a docent for Lotusland. Well, guess what, Oceanna had just been painting Lotuses there, and working with the Lotus… and she happened to know that our friend Lori Ann David was a Docent. One phone call and it was done. So, with us we had the perfect Docent, who was totally attuned to what we were doing, plus Oceanna, who had been having a love affair with the Lotus!

Our class of 12 had been together (day and night) for 12 days. There were folks from Japan, Switzerland, South Africa, and all over the US, as well as Santa Barbara, and we had a Vandenberg Air Force Base spiritual lady rocket scientist.

The energy between us was resonant. We had been eating primarily live, raw food, and then we did a 24-hour watermelon fast in preparation for making the essence. I find this allows for much greater clarity when communicating with the flowers. We had gone to Namaste Santuario at 3:45 a.m. to join in meditation during the eclipse.

Following the group meditation, at sunrise, I went out by myself for a walk on the beach. The Lotus came to me again with more information. It said it would be PINK and it would be "about initiation." It said we would recognize the specific flower. Up until then I had been thinking it would be white.

During the actual tour and ceremony, I will mention that there were some folks in our group who were apprehensive about cutting the Lotus. They weren't sure that was such a good idea. We looked at all the Lotuses (all the ones in bloom were pink) and we noticed that there was one that stood out amidst the others. There was one that we all knew was THE ONE. As soon as we cut her, everyone became delighted, because they could feel the delight of the chosen Lotus, and how happy she was to serve this very high and honorable purpose. The Lotus energy had been preparing itself for us for months. The Lotus literally danced into the water, and continued to dance and spin in it. It brought tears of joy to our eyes. There were 18 of us participating and witnessing this special event.

Regarding the planetary alignment on August 11, 1999, all the astrologers I know took it to be an auspicious life-changing time. There was a huge outpouring of rarefied energy, and folks all over the planet were in alignment, praying peace.

A message from the Ascended Masters at that time said, "It was pure galactic geometry… All the moving parts of the galaxy and our solar system came into an alignment IN THE PHYSICAL PLANE, bypassing the dimensions by opening the dimensional doorways. The descent of Grace and Light came through unobstructed, penetrating the densest of matter."

We have seen an extraordinary change in collective consciousness as a consequence of the Light that has come in.

"Pink Lotus – wow – it almost made me cry." – David

♥ INNER GURU *(Purple Sage)*

INNER GUIDANCE ♦ HIGHER SELF ♦ INDIVIDUALITY

The Purple Sage essence helps access that part of us that knows the answers; the Sage within. Be our own Guru. Knowingness. Omniscience.

♥ I REMEMBER *(Rosemary officionalis)*

REMEMBERING ♦ CLARITY

This essence deals with remembering on all levels. "I remember who I am, I remember my gifts, I remember what I came here to do, I remember how to manifest." (I even remember where my keys are.) Excellent for clarity in all realms. Certainty of self. Creativity, inner peace that creates prosperity, to heal oneself, and to be one with Spirit. It also strengthens the immune system. Awakens the full memory of our own potential. When we remember what we are really supposed to do in life, it can restore our health. When we remember what all of humanity is supposed to do, we can heal the world…

♥ LET GO AND TRUST *(Oregano)*

RELEASE

This essence helps us let go of attachments. Release, with ease, things that no longer serve us. It is good for use during a cleanse. It is excellent for Birthing. It is also like an "etheric colonic." It gets rid of gunk in our auras. Space is created for something new.

♥ **Light Navigator** *(California Pepper Tree)*
Inter-Dimensional Journeys

This tree is called **"Molle"** in Peru. It is a Peruvian native plant. This essence can take us to places where we are connected on the inner planes. It helps us to know our direction. It lights the path, with the radiant light of our God Presence. It is good to use in specific meditations. It is great alone, and in combination with other essences. There is a very strong Grandmother connection with this powerful essence. Inner vision lights the path, and helps us to get where we are going, and to know our direction. It is a direct portal to Peru. This essence assists in time travel, and inter-dimensional travel. Take it, meditate and move forward in time.

Co-Creating The California Pepper Tree Flower Essence:

This essence was made from a huge grandmother Pepper Tree at the Namaste Santuario in Santa Barbara. It has a very strong connection to Peru. John Eddowes was here from Peru and sang beautiful Icaros (songs of the plants) the entire time the essence was being made. Another friend from Peru, Puma, had done a ceremony under this very tree, the day before we made the essence. It is said that the Guru Krishnamurti attained his enlightenment under a Pepper Tree (in Ojai, about 30 miles from Santa Barbara).

♥ **Magic Healer** *(Plantain)*
Accelerated Healing

This essence is a catalyst for healing the body, especially skin-related issues. It aligns body, mind, and spirit. Great with anything pertaining to the skin. Use alone or to boost other healing modalities. It works like magic to accelerate healing. Use on plants to balance insect population (put drops in water or a mister).

"I am still amazed at the power of the Magic Healer. Awesome. I have been having various challenges with sores in my mouth, including biting the side of my mouth. I just put some drops in my mouth and it immediately stopped being sore and was gone the next day." – Susan

♥ Male Strength *(Agave)*

Power ♦ Virility ♦ Enhances Masculine Aspects

This essence speaks for itself. Additionally, we have had positive reports back about this essence's effectiveness. It is also useful for women who wish to be more in touch with their masculine aspects. Addresses issues of power and virility.

Making His Essence

I'm Agave; you can call me Mr. Agave, please! Notice me. He kept talking. He was most persistent. He said it would be a long time before I'd find another specimen like him, so super-erect. And he stayed that way for a long time. He continued to volunteer his bloom until I made the essence. This guy was awesome. I had no idea how true his statement was. Usually I photograph the flower before I make the essence- and this time I didn't, so I am always looking for a similar Agave to photograph. I haven't seen one like him yet. It was so funny how he was adamant about being male. Agave is what they make Tequila out of. He kind of sounded like he had had a couple of Margaritas… I have been pondering the things that differentiate us from animals- and a sense of humor and laughing may be one thing. Flowers, however, definitely have a sense of humor.

♥ My Passion *(Passion Flower)*

In the Moment ♦ Compassion

This essence teaches us to be in the moment and love that moment. Focus during anything, and it becomes our passion. (i.e. studying, lovemaking, artistic endeavors…) It brings out the highest aspects of our passion. Expands awareness and ability to recognize magic. Receives, circulates and broadcasts energy. Addresses Soul Purpose, Right Livelihood, and Divine Will.

♥ Open Mind / Future Vision *(Mugwort)*
Dreams ♦ Visionary

This essence has many qualities. It is good for clairvoyant dreams and divinatory acuity; to increase our visionary capabilities and insights, and to trust them. On a physical level, we are experimenting with using it on the skin as a protection from Poison Oak, bug and spider bites. It is great to take this essence with a partner to envision and co-create your perfect future and dreams. It heightens openness and spiritual perceptions. It is about openness at all levels, including sexuality. Mugwort is a good essence to use on q-tips with acupressure points and meridians. Stimulates and expands our sensibilities. Addresses and aligns with Moon magic, dreams, safety, getting close to others. Works in many dimensions.

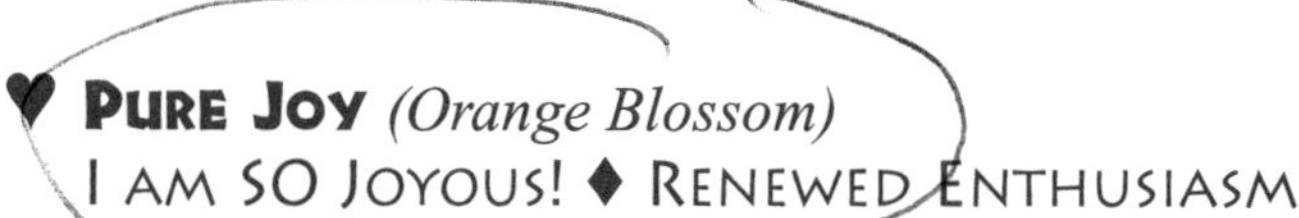

♥ Pure Joy *(Orange Blossom)*
I am SO Joyous! ♦ Renewed Enthusiasm

This essence takes us an octave higher than wherever we are. Abounding excitement and enthusiasm. When used in conjunction with other essences, it will give them a boost. Mix **Balance and Stability** and **Pure Joy** instead of a cocktail. Great in party punches. Be merry.

Talking Trees

One day I went to ask the big rock at my house on Coyote Road some questions. That day the Orange tree that was growing right next to the boulder started talking - even louder than the big rock… so much so, that I forgot what I had gone to ask the rock… The Orange Blossom wanted its essence made and that seemed to preempt any other subject I had in mind. It is called **Pure Joy**. I have taken this essence for years- and I must admit, I am nearly always happy. Happiness: A state of well-being characterized by relative permanence… and by a natural desire for its continuation. The state of pleasurable content of mind.

♥ **Solar Power** *(Sunflower)*

Heart Opening ♦ Personal Power ♦ Sovereignty

The flower of the Incas. Sunflower calls forth our personal power at its highest level and gives us strength through an open heart. It reminds us to stand up straight and tall (good for the spine). Assists with father and fathering issues. It reflects the energy of the Sun. Enjoy the power of the Solar Christ Consciousness.

♥ **Soul Family** *(Blue Ceanothus)*

Precious Connection ♦ Births and Deaths

This etheric blue flower helps to unify soul groups, or tribes. It assists with connecting to the Soul of an unborn baby. This essence is especially good for Hospice work. It is good for the people passing over during the death process, and it is good for the ones assisting them. The flower is etheric blue with five tiny petals. The blue pearl, a little focused beam of light, will guide a person out of the crown chakra when the person is ready to leave their body. In this way, the person may go out directly into their soul group at the moment of transition. In the physically healthy person here on Earth, this essence aligns us with our soul collective and/or guides and teachers.

♥ **Sweet New Beginnings** *(Pink Jasmine)*

Clarity and Ease with New Things

This essence is useful for remaining balanced during these new, ever-changing times and energies we are in. It is very helpful to take each time we feel a shift to another octave. Helps us remain clear and connected to the Divine as we expand and adjust easily to the new frequencies and changes. Helps affirm that there is sweetness everywhere. With this essence, we can go through change from a clear vantage point, because it provides clarity.

♥ **ZANIA** *(Zinnia)*

FUN ♦ PLAYFUL ♦ LIGHTEN UP ♦ BE ZANY

All seriousness aside. This essence helps us relax and open up. We can see things in a brighter, more colorful light. It encourages relaxation and **FUN FUN FUN**.

Star with Ryan in his Zania graduation cap.

The Birth of the Gemmies

Sometime around 1983 I took some classes that were offered through Cerena's Astrological Store. I learned about Tarot and Mandalas and - the one course that got a lot of my attention was studying with Michael Bromley from England, about Crystals. Crystals had begun to call out to me. The class was extraordinary. Something enchanting would always happen. Sometimes he would put a huge crystal in the middle of the room and have us all go into the crystal. The remarkable thing to me was how similar our stories would be of where we went and what we saw. Sometimes we would close our eyes and he would come around and drop a crystal into our hands. I was surprised at how the crystal would begin to tell me things the minute it hit my hand. Whenever anyone would ask Michael about a specific quality of a crystal he would say "ask the crystal." He was a (wonderfully) pushy sort of teacher, and while he was around, amazing things happened and folks had great openings.

Eventually his classes shifted to happening at my house, and they shifted to include healing, and of all things, channeling. He had a belief that everyone could channel - and if you showed up at the class, you channeled. Some folks would channel very high beings - and I would usually channel some Light Deva or a flower. I thought I was making it up to bring a little lightness to the activity, and when I tried to make it up, I couldn't.

I have always enjoyed crystals - and they haven't been my passion. I have never collected them. I have had many of them along the way. Flowers are the path that I have intensely pursued. In the second or third Flower Essence class I ever taught, which was in Las Vegas, someone said she was directed to give me a book. It was Melody's *Love Is In The Earth*. It is a fabulous comprehensive book. I wondered why - since I didn't really do much with crystals.

It was in **1997** that, through serendipitous events, I rented a room to Virendra and Nirmoha. They were here from India where they had been living at Osho's ashram for around 10 years. At the time they were a couple. They had a passion for stones and were here to study with Gemisphere, a place in Portland, Oregon, that deals with therapeutic gemstone necklaces, and to do Light Body work with Amora Quan Yin. They stayed here several months and ate mostly raw food and meditated a lot and strung beads - and Nirmoha did some bottling for us. She is originally from Australia and is adept at several different healing methods. Virendra is originally from Germany and is an extremely adept healer. It was lovely to have them around. Eventually they headed back to India.

I returned from another intense adventure in Peru. I had a lot to integrate when I got home. I was barely functional for about 4 weeks. I wasn't sick, I just couldn't do much of anything. I mostly meditated and slept, and let the frequencies form Peru integrate. On the day that I felt like I had finally come back into my body and could be present with people, Virendra came walking down my driveway. I was happy to see him. I was telling him all about my most recent trip to Peru. As he was listening, he started shaking his head. He was wearing a beautiful Pink Tourmaline necklace. He said, "I just made this necklace - I thought for myself, for this trip, yet somehow I knew that it was not for me. Now after hearing your story, I know this necklace is for you." And he took off the necklace and gave it to me. Pink Tourmaline has many qualities. One in particular is that it is good for protection - from people, places and things. I was so open that I needed some protection.

After that, we started looking at his other necklaces. He had come to the States this time to go to the Wesak Festival happening in Mt. Shasta and to visit again with Gemisphere. Gemisphere had hired him and Nirmoha to collect Gemstones for them, because they have such well-trained eyes and are extremely energy-sensitive. They know the therapeutic quality stones. He had his best necklaces with him. It felt so high to just sit and hold them and look at them. We spent hours playing with them. I learned more about the quality of spherical gemstones. I had read the Gemisphere book about the Guardians of the stones.

The next day Virendra came back, this time with Nirmoha, who met him here in Santa Barbara. They were no longer a couple, and they were still good friends and had decided to travel to the

Wesak Festival in Mt. Shasta together. Nirmoha had brought her collection of exquisite necklaces as well, and again we got high playing with the necklaces. I mentioned to them that they ought to make Gem Essences with those awesome gems. They agreed. It was sort of like yeah, someday…

Well, that night Spirit was speaking loudly to me. I was getting a very strong message that I was supposed to make the Gem Essences. I thought that was pretty crazy, because I didn't own a single high quality gem, and besides that, I didn't even know very much about them. I didn't have any idea how Nirmoha and Virendra would feel about my message. When I saw them the next day I brought up the subject and I had barely gotten the words out of my mouth when they both excitedly jumped for joy and said YES! I was saying that I wanted to make the seven chakra essences. Ruby-Red, Emerald-Green, that was easy. Nirmoha and Virendra thought I should use them all.

They love the stones and love collecting them. They love making the necklaces. They go through thousands of beads to find the perfect ones. They sell 3A quality and 4A quality and the 6A quality they often keep. If there are enough, they sell some, and as I said, they keep the very best for their own collections. They were happy to have these superb stones used for essences- and I have a vehicle to get them out to the world (which is, I assume, why I was chosen to create them). I might interject here that making essences is charming work - and such a small, and critically important, part of the work. The rest is filling bottles and standing in line at the post office and less glamorous stuff like that.

So as usual, everything fell perfectly into place. They had one day that they were available before they left for Wesak. We set a time. I had the message to get new bowls. I had no idea how many to even get. I miraculously found 18 bowls and bought them all. By then I thought that I could deal with 12 - for the 12 chakras - and they would nicely fit into our boxes. I have since determined that Spirit does not care about fitting the essences into my boxes! I was still sort of arguing in my head about this. It had been foggy for several days - and of course the day we were making the essences, the sun came out right on cue. There were 19 necklaces. Thousands of dollars worth. 6A quality full strands of Sapphires and Topaz and Rubies and Emeralds… I had 17 bowls (one bowl had disappeared). I finally agreed to make 17 essences and we took out the Quartz and the Lavender. I (mistakenly) thought the Lavender was close to Amethyst. Then another bowl disappeared, so I had to take another gemstone from the lineup. I decided (at least I thought it was me who decided) to take out moonstone because it was pretty common.

It was a totally awesome day. Virendra and Nirmoha called in the Guardians of the stones. They work with the Guardians, and you could tell that the Guardians were more than happy to come. (Guardians of the stones are comparable to the Devas of the flowers.) The bowls of water seemed to actually change color. They looked like bowls of Easter egg dye. Magic abounded. After making the Mother Essences, the first one I wanted to try was Tanzanite. We always make extra so we can drink some of the Mother Essence. It is so fun. Brain blast into love. Wow! I was immediately high - like intoxicated. (This is before they were preserved with alcohol, by the way.) Then we proceeded to sample all of them for the rest of the afternoon. I was gemstoned! That night I was reading about some of the qualities of the stones and when I got to Moonstone, I realized I needed it. Bummer. We didn't make that one. (The missing bowl showed up after we were finished.) Well, of course I didn't make that one. It is supposed to be made in the full moon. Moonstone. Duh.

The next day Nirmoha and Virendra stopped by on their way to Mt. Shasta. They wanted to bring me some Clear Quartz, because they thought that it would be good to make that essence on the day of the Wesak Full Moon. They would connect with me from there. When I told them about the Moonstone- they got the perfection right away. They left me the Moonstone necklace to use to make the essence on the night of the Wesak full moon.

On the day of the Wesak I made the Clear Quartz essence. As I was preparing to make the essence, it reminded me that Quartz is programmable. I asked it what it wanted to be programmed with. It said, "all the love in the universe." Oh. So that is what went into the Clear Quartz.

That night I took all of the bottles of mother essences down to the beach- where I had been guided to make the Moonstone essence. There were several of us and we did a beautiful ceremony. It (of course) was perfect. The moon rose early- right over the water. The moonlight on the water looked as if it ended up right in the bowl. Yummy! The Moonstone essence was made and the other essences were infused with that energy of the Wesak, while telepathically connecting with the thousands of people that were doing ceremony at Mt. Shasta and around the world. Yes- very powerful.

For the next ten days I sat with the essences. It was one of the most dramatic and rapturous times of my life. As I would work with each one of the twelve chakra essences- a Master would come to me - actually in a precipitated fog-like form. They each infused their energy into an essence. I don't really have words to describe this, so I will leave it at that.

When Virendra and Nirmoha returned from their Lightwork adventure at Mt. Shasta, it became apparent that the Lavender essence was choosing to be made. With a beautiful ceremony, we added the nineteenth gem essence. (The same number of essences Dr. Bach started with…) The first twelve addressed the chakras, and I called the other seven the Beyond the Beyonds. All of our Gemstone Essences are unique because they are made with spherical or rounded gemstones (except Diamond, which was faceted). They are pure. They do not have the matrix of anything else with them (often uncut stones have other things attached to them). The roundness makes these essences very gentle. They work nicely with the aura of the body. And I had these extraordinary experiences with the Masters. I felt complete.

This is the announcement we sent out:

Star Flower Essences joyously announces the brand new Star Gemstone Essences. There is an abundance of Magic and Marvelousness surrounding these gemstone essences (affectionately nicknamed "Gemmies"). They are made co-creatively with the mineral kingdom; the Guardians of the stones; the current caretakers of the stones, Virendra and Nirmoha, who love and adore them, and me (Star- who also loves and adores them). These gemstone essences are made with the finest quality therapeutic spherical and rounded gemstones *available on the planet. The sphere represents wholeness and infinite potential. The rounded crystals teach us of worlds within worlds, and catalyze our consciousness to grow and expand. (Some more!) The sphere is the safest way to use gemstones (with pointed gemstones it is important to know which way the energy is flowing and to use them appropriately). These special essences, made from beautiful brilliant spheres, carry the color radiance which provides color therapy, as well as the specific vibration of each stone. They nourish, purify, strengthen, balance and stabilize our subtle and physical bodies. They will open, activate, and balance the chakras. Chakra means "wheel" in Sanskrit. Chakras are vortices, revolving or rotating wheels of energy located in our body, through which we draw energy from our environment. Many Angels, Archangels and Ascended Masters infused their energy into these marvelous essences, which were also infused with the energy of the Wesak* Full Moon.*

The Guardians say to bring these essences into your life with gratitude and you will see even greater benefits. As with all of our essences, these Gemmies are true treasures lovingly bottled into a base of Sacred Activated Healing Water.

Putting out nineteen new essences meant nineteen new labels and new brochures and price lists - well, all of our paper work got to change again. I was used to that by now. I felt complete with the gems. I was just getting comfortable with these nineteen when several months later Virendra came back to town. He had some more beautiful necklaces that I hadn't seen before. There was a very auspicious planetary alignment coming up. Virendra was happy to make more essences.

Spirit was telling me **GEMSTONE PHARMACY.** I was feeling like it was just too much. Too many essences. Getting complicated. Spirit said we are complex beings and some of the essences are very specific. It is very difficult to find this quality of stone - and also have it held by a person who loves the stones so much. Virendra was willing, the stones were willing, I said yes. I still thought that we wouldn't make every one. We checked to see who wanted to come out of the line-up. None of them. They all wanted to be used. O.K., O.K.

During this time Virendra and Sia fell in love. (Sia was part owner of Paradise Found- a metaphysical/New Age store in Santa Barbara. She also volunteered at Star Flower Essences - because she loves the essences.) Virendra went back to India, and didn't stay very long, as he wanted to return to his beloved, for her birthday. When he came back what did he bring? You guessed it: nineteen more exquisite gemstone necklaces. Wow! Oh what Fun! Here we go again. It's the Summer of 2000 and we have another auspicious planetary alignment.

Sia became pregnant and it seemed the baby wanted to be born where there is the most love on the planet and said that would be at Sai Baba's Ashram. Sia and Virendra went to India to have the baby. Sweet Miriam was born and when she was around 7 months old they returned to the States - and you guessed it: more gems. And not only more gems - they brought me a gift. They made an essence in India from stones that a friend of Virendra's lent him. (They are VERY precious.) Therapeutic quality diamonds. 12 of them. The diamond essence was made in the sacred energy of Sai Baba at the Lakshmi Festival. (Sai Baba also came through with the Carnelian.)

There are so many excellent books on Gemstones and I encourage you to read them for more in-depth study, and especially to find out the physical qualities of the stones. Spirit told me that in regard to defining the Gemstones, the work is done. I don't need to reinvent the wheel. I only have to make and bottle and make available these essences that are made with super exquisite quality gemstones.

I had one daughter only, because I didn't think I could love another child as much as I loved (and adored) her. Then I had a granddaughter and when number two was coming I wondered if I could love her as much as number one. The happy answer is, of course, YES! I adore the flower essences. Then the gem essences came along to capture my attention. I find my ability to gloriously love is tremendously expanded, and I love them as much as the flowers and I love the Otter and the Chaska - the star essence - as well. Ah - what a great and expanded capacity of love that we have!

CHAKRAS

Through these energy wheels - these vortexes, located in our body, we draw energy from our environment. Until recently, they could not be detected by scientific instrumentation. Chakras operate like valves that channel the electric current of the universal life force into the body. They relate to the endocrine system. Chakras process energy - we take energy in and they send it to different organs. They are energy distributors and they link to higher spiritual energies. They transmit subtle energy into the body. They process both spiritual and emotional energy.

Here is some basic chakra information: You can extrapolate from here to help with determining essences to use. You can use the corresponding essences topically or orally.

1ST CHAKRA- ROOT

Location: Between the anus and genitals

Associated Color: **RED**

Gemstone: **RUBY**

Primary Issue: Survival, Physical Needs

Glandular Connection: Adrenals

Associated Body Parts: Bones, skeletal structure

Astrological Association: Capricorn

Associated Sense: Smell

2ND CHAKRA- SACRAL

Location: Lower abdomen between the navel and genitals

Associated Color: **ORANGE**

Gemstone: **CARNELIAN**

Primary Issue: Emotional Balance, Sexuality

Glandular Connection: Ovaries, testes

Associated Body Parts: Sex organs, bladder, prostate, womb

Astrological Association: Cancer, Scorpio

Associated Sense: Taste

◎3RD CHAKRA- SOLAR PLEXUS

Location: Between the navel and the base of the sternum
Associated Color: **YELLOW**
Gemstone: **CITRINE**
Primary Issue: Personal Power, Self-Will
Glandular Connection: Pancreas
Associated Body Parts: Digestive system, muscles
Astrological Association: Aries, Leo
Associated Sense: Sight

◎4TH CHAKRA- HEART

Location: Center of the chest
Associated Color: **GREEN**
Gemstone: **EMERALD**
Primary Issue: Love and Relationships
Glandular Connection: Thymus
Associated Body Parts: Heart and chest, lungs and circulation
Astrological Association: Libra, Taurus
Associated Sense: Touch

◎5TH CHAKRA - THROAT

Location: Centrally, at the base of the neck
Associated Color: **BLUE**
Gemstone: **BLUE SAPPHIRE**
Primary Issue: Communication, Self-expression
Glandular Connection: Thyroid, parathyroid
Associated Body Parts: Mouth, throat, ears
Astrological Association: Gemini, Virgo
Associated Sense: Sound/ Hearing

◎ 6TH CHAKRA - THIRD EYE

Location: Above and between eyebrows
Associated Color: **INDIGO**
Gemstone: **TRANSPARENT SODALITE (INDIGO)**
Primary Issue: Intuition, Wisdom
Glandular Connection: Pituitary
Associated Body Parts: Eyes, base of skull
Astrological Association: Sagittarius, Pisces
Associated Sense: 6th Sense

◎ 7TH CHAKRA - CROWN

Location: Top of head
Associated Color: **VIOLET**
Gemstone: **AMETHYST**
Primary Issue: Spirituality
Glandular Connection: Pineal
Associated Body Parts: Upper skull, cerebral cortex, skin
Astrological Association: Aquarius
Associated Sense: Beyond Self, in tune with the Sacred

These are the seven basic chakras. There are many more.

*Note- I mention one stone only for each chakra here- specifically the ones that we used to make our chakra essences. There are many other stones that work with the different chakras.

We made another new group of essences at the **SUMMER SOLSTICE OF 2001**, and this is the mail I sent out:

I trust you had a Happy 4th of July and Let Freedom Ring.

Yes- we do have some (28 so far) new spangly (my current favorite word) gemstone essences to announce to you. Yay! They were made with a huge amount of Angelic Love and on the day of maximum light- the Summer Solstice.

The evening before making them, I went to the Solstice Harmonic Renewal- a sound feast presented by the fabulous group called "Tingsha". The special blessing I received was Unreasonable Joy. How perfect! I love it! After connecting with Nature at the moment of the Solstice, I went to bed. I was awakened around 4:40 a.m. to the sound of the foghorn. I realized that I was awakened so I could feel the energies of the moment of the eclipse that was happening. Yummy! The fog cleared early and presented us with a gloriously beautiful day.

The group (in body and out) that appeared to help hold the energy for this mega-essence-making event was magnificent. About fifteen highly dedicated light workers showed up physically. (Thank you Angels!) I felt honored by the presence of so many embodied masters. Virendra called in all of the Guardians of the gemstones. Over-the-top high. I am still basking in the bliss. (By the way - I got news that my escrow on the downtown building closed during all of the essence making - which added to the radical delight, as a sense of solvency swept over me for the first time in years.)

So we made 28 new gemstone essences. Why so many, you might ask (as did I). I have in the past resisted making so many essences - and the resistance has been mundane. Storage, labels, brochures, etc. The rest of the process is such a Gift - bringing forth so much extraordinary awesome energy. Being brought the most perfect and exquisite gemstones to use from Virendra is a grand blessing - so I have chosen to say Yes - to be the Gemstone Essence Pharmacy and keep making them as he finds the wondrous stones. We have the vehicle to get them out to people.

As Virendra explains, we are multi-dimensional beings with a huge spectrum of light around us. Each gemstone has different qualities, and the subtle color changes within that gem provide even more specific attributes.

The vibrations are very pure - as the gemstones that are brought to us are of the highest quality and perfection. They are all rounded and thus radiate a gentle steady stable energy. They are the finest therapeutic gemstones that can be found. Certain physical characteristics and quality are required for a stone to be considered energetically therapeutic (there are specific physical parameters - standards of purity and quality).

The sphere has access to a great amount of life force. There is maximum healing energy available when Gemstones are fashioned into spheres... The sphere represents wholeness and infinite potential and is the safest way to use crystals.

Bliss and Blessings, Star

Crystals - Christ Alls- Crystal is the flower of the mineral world, that peak of perfection in matter.

I encourage you to read more about the Gemstones to get deeper insights - especially if you are looking to address a specific physical condition. Sometimes there are whole books on one Gemstone. I do my best not to mention very much about the physical uses in my literature...(the FDA prefers it that way...) In other countries they are used extensively for physical healing, and in Atlantis and Lemuria essences were used for tissue regeneration.

Roger, Star and Virendra

THE GEMMIES

CARRY THE COLOR RADIANCE OF THESE BEAUTIFUL THERAPEUTIC GEMSTONES.

TAKING THESE ESSENCES IS LIKE DRINKING COLORS.

☆ **AGATE - BLUE LACE** *(opaque white with light blue veins)*
Calming, flexibility, self-expression. Flight, air, movement, grace. Security in new situations. Strengthens and stimulates a positive attitude. Brings forth inner beauty. Contentment with work.

☆ **AGATE - WHITE** *(opaque)*
Mild, swanlike. Wholeness, equality, purity, innocence. Compassion. Smoothes out the edges. Allows for turning inwards and fully becoming present into the here and now. Gives a sense of wholeness and promotes a state of equality. Brings clarity to see that everything is as it is. Good for yoga.

☆ **AGATE - YELLOW**
Connected with the Nature Spirits. Relaxes solar plexus and eases the tensions within. Good while fasting and with any physical cleansing. Found to be a physical purifier and cleanser of the lymph system. Brings light into the cells and prepares the body for higher frequencies.

☆ **ALEXANDRITE** *(translucent green)*
Regenerative. Reinforces self-esteem. Augments one's ability to experience joy and appreciate the interconnectedness of all of nature. Creates a more balanced state. Eternity. The Universe is one and we are part of that Universe. Beyond life & death. Watchful - the spirit of all. Embrace wholeness. Unity in diversity. Opens the hara and the belly into spaceless space. Centering. Detached peace. Nervous system. Said to improve assimilation of protein.

☆ **AMAZONITE** *(opaque aqua-green)*
Self-confidence. Aligns physical and astral bodies. Brings clarity. Enhances communication concerning love. Project completion. Concentration. Endurance. Strengthens coping abilities. Fully experience all the things you love. Thymus.

☆ **AMETHYST** *(violet)* (part of the **Chakra** Collection)

My good buddy **St. Germain** graces the Amethyst essence with his energy and essence. He brings to us the Violet Ray of transmutation, alchemy, and transformation. There is mastery of thought. The crown chakra is opened to receive energy from higher chakras and to receive spiritual insight into highly refined aspects of higher potentials. There is divine love and inspiration. Useful in leadership positions. See the divine perfection in all things. It is a visionary essence.

☆ **AMETRINE** *(transparent lavender and yellow)*

Higher golden light frequencies of transformation. High frequency. Nourishes and balances the brain. Expand oneself with a clearing effect. Protective energy against lower frequencies. Lightheartedness. Opens and relaxes the solar plexus. Connects crown and solar plexus, bringing light into the body. Warming and energizing. Tension releaser. Creates a feeling of youthfulness.

☆ **APATITE - BLUE** *(transparent light blue)*

Related to service and development of humanitarian pursuits. Teaching. Awakens finer, inner self.

☆ **APATITE - BLUEGREEN** *(transparent)*

Creates calm. Clears the brain. Balances and connects mental, emotional and spiritual. Awakens psychic abilities. Suppresses hunger. Enhances creativity. Endocrine, adrenals, upper back and chest.

☆ **APATITE - GREEN** *(transparent light green)*

Stimulates intellect. Helps integrate emotional, intellectual and etheric bodies. Acceptance. Ability to love everybody and ability to accept love and love oneself.

☆ **APATITE - YELLOW** *(transparent)*

Stimulates intellect and humanitarianism. Integrates, balances, coordinates emotional, intellectual, physical and etheric bodies. Works on glands, meridians and organs. Suppresses hunger. Reflects the openness of our own heart. Light quotient builder.

☆ AQUAMARINE *(light transparent bluegreen)*

(part of the **Chakra** Collection)

Aquamarine opens the spiritual high heart, the thymus chakra, and quiets the mental body to become receptive to transmissions from higher realms. It has humanitarian qualities as well as serenity, peacefulness, balanced emotions and abounding patience. There is a strong connection to the dolphins. **Aquariel, the Archangel of clarity**, has infused this Aquamarine essence. It helps bring rhythm of breath, creating peaceful equality and lifting our perspective.

☆ AVENTURINE - BLUE

Activates energy flow in the body. Releases pressure or tightness within the head. Calming. Brings force of blue within the body. Respiratory system. Brings oxygen into the blood.

☆ AVENTURINE - DARK GREEN *(translucent dark green)*

Strength, physical healing, greater wellness, strengthens organs beginning with the weakest. (You may take this for a long time - as it goes from organ to organ and eventually strengthens the whole body.) Good with Emerald. Eyesight, creative visualization. Stabilizes heart. Soothes physical and emotional heart pain. Emotional security. Loves adventures.

☆ AVENTURINE - LIGHT GREEN

Protects the heart. Puts a wash of love around it. Emotional safety. A very gentle healer. Balance and align mental, physical, spiritual and emotional bodies. Ability to be light-hearted. Good when fasting. Lungs, heart, adrenal glands, muscular and urogenital systems.

☆ AVENTURINE - PEACH

Works with the heart. Inspires new ideas. Amplifies one's leadership qualities. Good communication. Encourages playful sexuality. Promotes gentle joyful pregnancy. Manifest new life or new art on earth plane. Fertility in all senses.

☆ AZURITE *(opaque blue)*

Stimulates pursuit of our heavenly self. Third eye and psychic development. Expanding into inner space of mind. Aligns both sides of the brain. Purifies and detoxifies the brain. Activates general expansion of consciousness. Good energizer. Calms nervousness. Natural healing abilities amplified.

☆ **BLOODSTONE** *(marbled opaque red, burnt orange, and dark green)*

Overall strengthener. Stimulates energy flow. Directs healing forces to area of disharmony to restore health. Purifier. Good in baths. Flow of earth energy. Psychic protection. Provides one with a grounding and centering energy in the heart. Fosters self-respect, trust, loyalty. Strengthens veins, fortifies blood. Lungs. Rashes.

☆ **CARNELIAN** *(orange)* (part of the **Chakra** Collection)

The Carnelian increases access to prana by clearing energy paths. It gives us motivation and vitality. **Shakti and Sai Baba** came to infuse their energy into this essence, which stimulates and awakens the creative force and helps us focus on our goals. It magnetizes harmonious thoughts. Carnelian enhances attunement with the inner self. It grounds energy into the physical. Can increase fertility on all levels.

☆ **CAT'S EYE - GREEN**

Works on the heart and solar plexus chakras. Responsibility. Amplifies luck (synchronicities). Enhances awareness and stimulates intuition. Improves eyes and vision. Great for nervous system. Clears energy fields. Shifts disappointment. Aligns and opens the heart.

☆ **CAT'S EYE - YELLOW**

Angelic connection. Helps us to align with our higher selves. Raises the vibration of our solar plexus. Promotes positive thinking. Aids in connection with the realm of the Masters.

☆ **CHALCEDONY - BLUE** *(translucent whitish blue)*

Encourages brotherhood and sisterhood among all. Clears the cobwebs of the past. Benevolence, good will, generosity, receptivity.

☆ **CHALCEDONY - YELLOW** *(translucent whitish yellow)*
Ceremonial uses. Increases mental stability. Aids positive discrimination.

☆ **CHAROITE** *(rich purple)*
A stone for the now times. Synthesis between heart and crown chakra. Links us to the source of inspiration. Grounds our spiritual self. Recognize oneness. Awakens gifts - especially of vision and visioning. Brings magic. Stimulates the ability to let go. Manifest future technology now. Encourages healthy hair growth. Eyes, heart, liver, pancreas.

☆ **CHRYSOCOLLA** *(bluegreen opaque)*
Base, navel and solar plexus chakras. Revitalizes and calms. Increases our capacity to love. Good for silence. Earth attuned. Helps us hear the Earth, and good for Earth healing. Treasure Mother Earth. Female well-being. Brings joy, certainty and peace. Inner strength, endurance. Good for purification. Pancreas, blood sugar, digestion, sinus, lungs.

☆ **CHRYSOPRASE** *(light green)*
Creates a feeling of calm, peace and harmony. Be happy. Ignites compassion. Heart chakra. Emotional balance. Trust in God/Goddess. Opens and relaxes tensions in the upper chest and around the heart. Loosens the grip of attachment, creating a "letting go." Deepens meditation. Teaches us to love ourselves so we will be able to love others.

☆ **CITRINE** *(transparent yellow)* (part of the **Chakra** Collection)
Master Jesus came to overlight this essence, to help us prepare for greater spirituality as the Citrine helps open our inner sight and hearing. The Citrine essence enhances concentration, clears old thought patterns, and is a bridge to access the Divine. It is useful for intellectual communication and balances the rational mind. It is about sovereignty, courage, confidence and self-esteem. The sunlight it represents is uplifting and helps us to recognize beauty and joy.

☆ CORAL - PINK

Stimulates sensitivity. A great emotional balancer. Activates heart chakra and enhances intuitive aspects of love. Heals and protects the emotional body. Helps to release toxins.

☆ CORAL - RED

Provides practicality. Balances material and spiritual. Helps us to become in harmony with the natural forces of the universe. Stimulates the metabolism and activates the thyroid. Increases blood circulation. Improves self- worth. Builds the physical powerhouse within.

☆ CORAL - WHITE

Opens and clears the crown chakra. Brings a sense of purity, health and wholeness. Brings forth the information needed to assist humanity.

☆ DIAMOND *(clear)*

This essence gives clarity with alignment to a higher purpose. It reminds us of our spiritual goals- and clears the mind. It helps us to see and feel the invisible. It also strengthens the physical eyes. It majorly amplifies light and thought. There is richness, self-satisfaction and healthy discrimination. It builds strength and stamina, stimulates unity and love, and gives courage and confidence. (Wow!) There is a brilliance of light - acting on many layers and levels. It fills the chakras with light. This stone holds the template of marriage in its matrix. It promotes harmony in marriage and relationships. Be emotionally satisfied. Use Diamond at the base of the spine to move the kundalini. Possibility of cleared sinus (clear-headed). Diamond is called the King of Crystals and symbolizes the Great Central Sun. It vibrates to the number 33. Diamond touches peoples hearts. The Diamond essence was made from 12 exceptional Diamonds. Each of them showed evenly the full color spectrum, which makes them highly therapeutic and the very best to use for this essence. It was made during the Lakshmi Festival (Goddess of Luck and Prosperity) in Poona, India, in the energy field of an enlightened Master. It is one of the birthstones for August - and Diamond is ruled by the signs of Leo and Taurus and Aries.

☆ **EMERALD** *(green)* (part of the **Chakra** Collection)

The Emerald activates our heart chakra, teaching us empathy and unconditional love, allowing us to experience an expansion of love energy. This essence, overlit by **Archangel Rafael** - the angel of healing - works very strongly in the physical field, so it is good for all physical healing. Emerald delivers grace, beauty, and balance, and aids in healing scars (at all levels). Emerald helps us to understand rhythms and patterns and cycles in Nature. It is also about fertility and prosperity. The Emerald assists all forms of communication through the heart, and healing with love. Emerald has been proclaimed for its prophetic capabilities as the gemstone of sight. It can strengthen memory, increase perception, and preserve love. Heart, liver, kidneys and pancreas.

☆ **FIRE OPAL** *(transparent orange to red)*

Mystery, variety, progress, change. Charisma. Helps us to reflect on the many facets of our life. Strengthens faith in our self. Very energetic. Protection around high energy. Physical endurance. Ability to operate powerfully in situations that require action.

☆ **FLUORITE - BLUE**

Brings inner peace. Calm energy. Stimulates communication skills and brings order to the mind. Activates throat chakra. Opens the body up for deep breathing. Brings an overall sense of clarity. Connects mind with guidance of Spirit - helps us to be our true self.

☆ **FLUORITE - GREEN**

Mint-like freshness. Transmutes negativity. Emotional balancer. Renews chakras. While Blue Fluorite works more on the energetic level, the Green Fluorite tends to work more on the physical levels.

☆ **FLUORITE - PURPLE RAINBOW**

Clarity. Helps clear blockages and congestion so our consciousness can expand. Heightens spiritual experiences. Connects mind to spirit instantly. Works on brain waves to open up to new energies descending to Earth. Sinuses. Relieves congestion.

☆ **FLUORITE - YELLOW**

Activates entire brain - light of higher intelligence. Clears attachments. Heals sub-personalities. Quiets voices. Stimulates and heals the powers of the mind. Improves access to mental grid and to the light body. Good for neuro-linguistic programming and mental re-programming. Think Immortality.

☆ **HELIODOR** *(transparent golden yellow)*

Great Central Sun. Helios and Vesta. Builds light. Expands light into cells. Improves communication. Assists in compassionate understanding. Good for delicate issues. Use to purify items (it beams golden white light). Great tool during meditation. Helps to connect and open crown chakra.

☆ **HESSONITE** *(transparent dark burnt orange)*

Improves self-esteem. Provides courage to continue / move forward in personal endeavors. Keeps conversations productive and positive.

☆ **HOWLITE** *(opaque white w/gray veins)*

Patience, discernment, ambition, action. Brings new ideas into clear focus and inspires us to action.

☆ **INDIGO - TRANSPARENT SODALITE** (part of the **Chakra** Collection)

Indigo addresses the inner vision, paranormal vision. As light comes through the third eye, dream your dream and have it come true. There is keenness of perception, enriched experiences of synchronicity. **Ascended Master Serapis Bey** infuses his energy into this essence. Indigo enhances intent, focus, telepathy, deep thought and clearing of the mind. There is clarity of purpose.

☆ **IOLITE** *(light and dark indigo)*

Third eye, crown, astral travel. Stimulation of visions. Acceptance of responsibility. Confidence in abilities. Excellent for leadership.

☆ **KYANITE** *(transparent deep blue)*

Activates third eye opening. Calming, good for the head. Connects us to our higher self, hear sounds of silence. Promotes relaxed awareness. Meditation. Body-mind connection. Uplifts mood. Show affection. Centeredness. Soothes skin. Links resources to gifts, integrates light body into mental body, promotes new ideas and new thinking. Good for telepathy with angels, animals and guides.

☆ **LAPIS LAZULI** *(opaque blue)*

Voice. Power of mind. Intuition. Memory. Releases and heals emotional wounds. Harmonizes the heart and mind. Quickens reflexes. Empowerment, clear choices. Enhances wisdom. Universal Truth. Keep positive outlook. Move into new empowering patterns. Good with Amethyst and Rose Quartz to mellow its effects.

☆ **LAVENDER** *(light lavender)*

Washes & expands. Borderless. Deep clearing. Uplifts perspective and promotes love of service. Clears the channeling column and chakra column. Helps to activate chakras above the crown.

☆ **LEPIDOLITE** *(light opaque purple)*

Opens us to universal light. Acceptance. Good during transitions. Facilitates astral travel. Enhances awareness of well-being. Help in business with communication, diplomacy, openness, honesty. Helps stabilize ley lines and tectonic plates. Aligns energies in gardening and agricultural activities. Trust in life and understand your life purpose. Smoothes skin. Wholeness. Relaxed mind.

☆ **MALACHITE** *(opaque dark green striated)*

Earth energy. Connects us to the Earth's energy flow and information of our evolution. Stabilizes weak points. Strengthens memory. Helps to detect toxins within the body.

☆ **MARBLE - WHITE**

Offers clarity in the state of meditation and offers access to peak states. Enhances common sense. Teacher of light and meditation. White silence. Eases and harmonizes brain. Nurturing qualities. Great for dream recall.

☆ **MOLDAVITE** *(transparent dark green)*

Zing. Galactic. Extraterrestrial telepathic qualities enhanced. Facilitates direct interdimensional access - move among the dimensions. Remember our origin - life on other planets. Be more comfortable on the earth. Look through the heart. Brotherhood, Sisterhood. Access galactic energies. Use on hands as well as internally. Honesty. Embrace change. Change of lifestyle, broader perspective. Find new answers. Initiation and acceleration. Asthma, toxin sensitivity, thymus, emotional sensitivity, epilepsy.

☆ **MOONSTONE** *(translucent white)*

Raises the vibration of the emotional body and activates it. Balancing and nourishing for emotions. Appreciation of stillness. At home in our heart. Creates an opening in the belly area. Works on the ovaries and breasts.

☆ **MOTHER OF PEARL** *(pearlescent)*

Heals the holes of disappointment. Heals what hasn't been healed due to lack of love or nourishment. Gives the feeling of being in the arms of a loving mother. Helps to soften and heal emotional traumas. Self-love and self-worth.

☆ **NEPHRITE** *(translucent lime green)*

Good for balancing male/female. Good to use with partner. Healing and rejuvenation.

☆ **OBSIDIAN - RAINBOW** *(black with purple, green, etc. sheen)*

Safety - in any situation. Brings gratification and joy to one's life. Perception of our own spirituality. Gratifying relationships. Ceremonies with Mother Earth. Stomach. Grounding.

☆ **OBSIDIAN - SNOWFLAKE** *(black with white/gray)*

Stone of purity and balance. Allows us to recognize unnecessary patterns. Promotes sensitivity to love and beauty. Great intestinal tract.

☆ OPAL - CLEAR

Clarifies and assists understanding our mission. Amplifies traits in order to take a closer look at them. Gives us the strength to overcome our lesser attributes. Helps to clear emotions and release emotional ties.

☆ OPALITE *(translucent bluish white)*

Helps us recognize our own creative qualities. Releases inhibitions. Clears the head - releases excess energy. Faithfulness and loyalty. Encourages intuition.

☆ PEARL - SOUL SHINE

Made from 12 exquisite quality undrilled South Sea pearls. Reflects and reminds us of our positive qualities. For self-reflection. Pearl will mirror our super inner beauty and pure light of the soul. It will also reflect to us our visions of the future. Helps enhance personal integrity, sincerity, innocence. Helps to provide clear channel for receiving the highest information. Softens behaviors, providing reflection. Pearl's luster will help us see our finest traits. It increases feelings of Love. Also good for calming hyperactive children. Digestion, soft organs. Childbirth, fertility. Rub on belly.

☆ PREHNITE *(translucent lemon yellow)*

For protection and for dreaming and remembering. Divine inspiration. Enhanced ability to predict. Promotes calmness.

☆ QUARTZ - CLEAR (part of the **Chakra** Collection)

The rainbow essence of Quartz brings light in and radiates it. It attracts life force and brightens and energizes the aura. It awakens the pure light of the soul. It is good for mental balance and facilitates positive thinking. Quartz is programmable, as well as having its many innate gifts. The beautiful clear Quartz spheres this essence was made from were programmed with all the love in the universe - which many feel right away when they take this essence. We radiate positive energy when we take the Quartz rainbow essence. It enhances rejuvenation and balances the etheric body. It brings the energy of the stars to the soul. Quartz is also excellent for earth healing. Use the drops directly on the earth. Quartz activates psychic gifts. This essence is great to use to enhance other essences and it is very powerful alone. It is also excellent with other modalities - especially homeopathy. **Archangel Metatron** overlights this essence. Clear Quartz brings in the light and radiates it along with all the love in the universe and enhances all of the essences. Put seven drops in a regular bottle of eye drops for quartz eye therapy, as it helps to bring in more light. Use it to amplify your prayers.

☆ QUARTZ - ROSE

Purification of emotional body. Self-love. All love. Confidence. Personal expression. Gentle. Use with Ruby to heal the emotions of the heart. Acceptance and forgiveness. Weight loss - lighten up. Grace, beauty, perfect weight, youthful body and heart. Self-esteem. Regenerates love love love. Endows us with appreciation. Listen to our feelings and create joy. Demonstrate love.

☆ RHODOCHROSITE *(opaque deep rose)*

Pushes change. Shifts patterns, cleanses, rebuilds. Creates healthy emotional patterns. Reprograms emotional body to receive joy. New responses to old habits, events - that are uplifting and harmonious. Self-confidence, inner freedom. Beyond imagination. Heals infection, (old) wounds, scars. Heals self-blame. Digestive problems, ulcers. Use with **ONE♥HEART** (orchid essence) to soften.

☆ RHODONITE *(opaque rose pink)*

Unconditional love. Energizes heart chakra. Morale booster. Promotes self-worth, self-confidence. Enables one to remain confident, dignified. Encourages generosity of spirit. Emotional harmony. Higher state of consciousness. Strengthens ears. Enhanced sensitivity to mantras.

☆ RUBY *(red)* (part of the **Chakra** Collection)

Ruby keeps the lower chakras open so energy can move up. It may activate kundalini (in a balanced manner). **Mother Mary** has infused her energy into this essence, which has a profound effect on the heart, strengthening the spiritual heart. Ruby is about mastery and love of self. Ruby teaches us and opens us to the infinite source of divine love. It raises the vibration of the physical body. Ruby gives us courage to express our highest potential. It energizes the physical being and emancipates creative energy devoted to our highest aspects. Ruby is the soul and heart connected - expressing love in action.

☆ **SAPPHIRE - BLUE** (part of the **Chakra** Collection)

Archangel Michael's energy comes into the Blue Sapphire with his blue shield of protection and blue sword of truth. Blue Sapphire addresses the throat chakra and is about communication and self-expression. It is about listening as well as speaking. There is mental discrimination, enlightened intuition, language mastery. We choose the thoughts we think. Blue Sapphire aligns our energy with our purpose and opens us to our spiritual nature.

☆ **SAPPHIRE - GREEN**

Calming, relaxing, rhythmic. Good for physical sight. Use in eye drops. Motivation. Encourages memory of dreams. Fidelity, loyalty. Provides impetus for material manifestation - through lightness. Eyes, ears, nose, throat.

☆ **SAPPHIRE - YELLOW** (part of the **Chakra** Collection)

The Yellow Sapphire that brings in the gold light from the halo above the head is about Cosmic Truth and love for others. For the wise counselor who brings warmth, nourishment, empathy and inspiration for one's brothers and sisters. The instinctive nature is of service. It is beautiful to share. Gold is a master teacher, teaching through grace so you can express your soul's beauty in words, thoughts and communications. Love radiates from Gold. The band of **Kumara Angels** infused this Yellow Sapphire essence. There is wisdom, exultation, illumination and Christ-like qualities.

☆ **SCAPOLITE** *(very light transparent yellow)*

Encourages independence. Provides impetus to change. Take the initiative. Promotes the stamina and clarity required to achieve goals. Eyes.

☆ SELENITE *(translucent white/clear)*

Expands awareness of our surroundings. Access possible future lives. Provides energy to promote justice during disputes. Gives strength to decisions. Use directly on the spinal column for alignment and flexibility with muscular structure. Lifespan extension. Advancement of mental powers. Clear, telepathic communication with like-minded people.

☆ SODALITE *(opaque dark blue)*

Great purifying agent. Super for healers to use. Activates the hand chakra. Enhances truthfulness in emotions. Provides direction of purpose with heart. Helps eliminate confusion.

☆ SPINEL - RED *(translucent deep red)*

Spicy, vital, good luck. Increases the positive aspects of one's personality. Rejuvenates. Assists in losing the sense of "I" while entering the realms of love. Dissolves borders and limitations around the heart.

☆ SPINEL - BLUE

Helpful in letting go of unnecessary things - in one's body, in one's space, in one's life.

☆ SPINEL - DARK PINK

Heart energy. Fosters devotion to loved ones. Strengthens positive aspects of one's personality. Encourages appropriate behavior.

☆ SPINEL - GREEN

Brings light in through crown chakra, aligns and stimulates heart chakra. Compassion, devotion, kindness. Brings light-heartedness, optimistic outlook. Helps in building the light quotient while bringing in energies for physical healing. Works on the gland system. Works also on inner / outer hearing and on the eyes. Good for stomach, liver, gall bladder and pancreas. Protects physical structure during Kundalini movement through the body.

☆ SPINEL - LIGHT PINK

Brings beauty and freshness to endeavors. Rejuvenating. Enhances appearance.

☆ SPINEL - ORANGE

Stimulates kundalini, fertility, and passion for love. Encourages further attempts at a difficult task. Delight in life. Stimulation of mental processes. Connect to the source of bliss.

☆ SPINEL - PURPLE

Immortality, spiritual development, assistance on path to enlightenment. Bridges the generation gap, assists in communication between all different ages. Protection while doing service.

☆ SPINEL - WHITE *(clear)*

Ammaji (the hugging Guru) carries this frequency. Clear and pure. Deep silence, pure emptiness. Helps to create a clear background on the mirror of mind, and amplifies attention given there to any issue or thoughtform held. Clears out tne vibrations of other gems within the bodies. Synthesis and connection of the energy of all chakras. Visions, mysticism. Furthers communication.

☆ SUGILITE - PURPLE

Lucid dreaming - integrates intuition and action. Spine and CSF (cerebral spinal fluid). Follow intuition. Opens, clears and balances Kundalini channels. Balances left and right hemispheres. Dyslexia, strokes, epilepsy.

☆ SUGILITE - PINK-PURPLE

Helps one to believe in oneself and to love the uniqueness. Spiritual love of all that is; facilitates the manifestation of this energy on the earth plane. Stimulates resonant love force-field which can be felt by others. Meditate with it. Creates a state of receptivity. Astonishing insights. Balances left and right brain. Pineal gland. Visions. Good with cranial adjustments.

☆ **TANZANITE** *(transparent purplish blue)*

Brain blast into love. Expands vision, inspires optimism, exposes eternal truths. Prepares us for the new times. Clears throat and lungs. Supports intense moments, helps to express eternal truths. Through the third eye we receive the inner command to go further. Follow your divine guidance and reap the rewards.

☆ **TEKTITE** *(translucent brown/black)*

Breath, grounding. Empty yourself. Clears blockages. Strengthens energy field. Promotes inner strength. Lower temperature (if needed). Diseases of no known origin. Balances feminine and masculine. Clears aura. Promotes safety and security. Connects to Pleiadian healers. Ganesh - Remover of Obstacles.

☆ **TOPAZ - BLUE**

Mental body cleanser and purifier. Psychic protection, mental balance. Harmonizes and aligns the body-mind. Opens for deeper, freer breathing. Enhances channeling abilities.

☆ **TOPAZ - IMPERIAL** *(transparent yellow to pink)*

Stimulates sense of taste. Love and joyfulness. Promotes the expression of ideas. Success in all endeavors. Individuality and creativity. Catalytic trigger for manifestation activities. Works with law of attraction. Helps in making choices, maintaining clear focus: confidence and trust in our decisions. Use with Amethyst to produce magic and for transmutation.

☆ **TOPAZ - WHITE** *(clear)* (part of the **Chakra** Collection)

Tap into the source of universal energy. The etheric body is rejuvenated and aligned with the physical body. White Topaz feeds the light body. It is a source of strength, and great to use on the meridians. **Kuan Yin** infused her energy into this magnificent White Topaz essence. Conscious connection and manifestation of wisdom: turn vision into realities. White Topaz is also about the reversal of aging.

☆ TOURMALINE - DARK BLUE

Activates the throat chakra and the third eye. Facilitates access to higher levels of intuition. Great for eyes and brain. Releases stress and tensions within the mind. Eases headaches.

☆ TOURMALINE - LIGHT BLUE

Assists us in relating to others in a loving manner. Brings true impressions. Great for upper part of head. Allows for relief of headaches.

☆ TOURMALINE - GREEN

Strengthens masculinity, while strengthening the connection to the heart energy.

☆ TOURMALINE - ORANGE

Stimulates energy centers of the body. Balances right and left brain. Stimulates navel chakra. Enhances sexuality, furthering of desire - with balanced emotions.

☆ TOURMALINE - PINK (part of the **Chakra** Collection)

Blessed by **Buddha** - the Zeal Point chakra, the ascension chakra, is opened. This chakra, located in the back of the head, at the base of the skull (the medulla oblongata), is also called the Mouth of God. The kundalini is assisted and is gentle and graceful. There is very strong protection associated with this essence. Good to use when traveling. Feel safe. It also strengthens the heart and hormones are addressed. It is good to have this chakra open when leaving the earth plane.

☆ TOURMALINE - PURPLE

Opens possibilities for channeling, clairvoyance and other psychic abilities. Dolphin connection. Past memory stimulation (Atlantis). The ultimate stone for the cerebellum.

☆ TOURMALINE - YELLOW

Illuminating. Stimulates the intellect. Inspiring. Strong on solar plexus, enhances personal power. Activates creativity and initiative.

☆ TSAVORITE *(green)*

Helps one to master one's personal issues: "know thyself." Take control of your destiny. Stimulates knowledge of inner self. Enhances sensitivity to our senses.

☆ TURQUOISE - BLUE

Valor. Spiritual attunement as well as grounding. Safety in travel. Protection from environmental pollutants. Improves meditation. Strengthening. Master Healer. Strengthens eyes.

☆ TURQUOISE - GREEN

Healer of Spirits. Provides soothing energy and a peaceful state of mind. Mental relaxation. Promotes spontaneity. Stimulates the initiation of romantic love and connectedness.

☆ UNAKITE *(burnt orange & olive green opaque)*

Facilitates re-birthing and release, promoting growth. Balances emotions and brings them to a higher state of spirituality. Personal power: Guardian of our own life.

PART FOUR

MORE INTERESTING STAR ESSENCE STUFF

❤ Otter Delight Essence ❤

from the Giant Amazon River Otter

Here is the story of the otterly divine Otter event …as we go into **Otter Space**

Giant Amazon River Otter

For the fourth day in a row I was up and out at 4 a.m. Being awake and meditating in bed is something I relish at 4 a.m. Up is one thing- out is another… And now this morning I am up at 3:45 in the Amazon jungle (with no electricity) in order to have breakfast (not my favorite time to eat) - to take a boat and a hike and another boat to possibly see- the Giant River Otters. I was choosing health that morning and waiting for my body to catch up with that choice- and feeling a bit cranky about sleep deprivation and angry with myself for judging myself, and for judging the judgment. Fortunately I had a full set of flower essences with me and I got myself into balance- choosing them by candlelight. I couldn't cope with my camera- and at the last moment I did throw my bathing suit into my bag, remembering something about the possibility of swimming- that there were Piranhas but that they didn't attack because they were very well fed. Oh, well, the suit didn't weigh much. I poured most of the water out of a Nalgene water bottle I had- to be as light as possible.

We hiked to the boat in the dark and took a lovely sunrise ride to another place where we got out to begin our hike to Tres Chimbadas Lake. I still did not have full appreciation for the day. We arrived at the catamaran and all got aboard the platform. We were quietly rowed along the lake. We were told that we will often get a glimpse of the otters and when they see us they will swim off. Well, that morning they came, and they stayed. We watched them play, love, cavort, and dive in and out of the water so outrageously gracefully for over 40 minutes.

When the family of 8 otter adults and 3 otter children swam

off, one of our group decided to dive into the water. She was followed by another and another. Even though I was high from the otterly delightful otter show, I was still feeling low and listless, from the sleep deprivation. When our whole group of 10 plus two of our Amazon River guides were in the water, I decided I would go in, too. What happened to me felt super-astonishing. I just was not expecting it. The moment I hit the water I felt wonderful - exuberant. I immediately went to high and vibrant. There was a hum in the water. I felt so HAPPY. I noticed everyone else did as well.

Then there was the loud voice. (I really thought everyone probably heard it the same as I did.) Otter Essence. I excitedly swam to our boat and asked Roger to get me the bottle I had in my bag (yay!) and filled it with the otter essence water. Several years ago I swam with Dolphins in Florida- and the water there had a hum. This was a similar - palpable - vibration. The Otter is a fabulous loving creature. They are champions bathed in love and abounding bliss. We immediately made a dosage bottle so we could continue to use it at different times throughout the trip, and each time we could feel its special gifts.

Otter Essence Gifts:

The Otter essence addresses the holy relationship we have with ourselves (that self-love stuff) which allows us to have abounding love of others. It is about having beautifully strong family bonds while remaining detached! Freeness of love. Complete trust. Joyously receptive. Otter is a representative of the Aquarian Age. There is play and there is an expression of joy in everyone's accomplishments. Unity of Spirit. We are aware of the Solar presence of our Christed selves.

Star bottling Otter Essence in the Amazon jungle for instant gratification.

★ Chaska Essence ★

Star Connection ☆ Cosmic Consciousness ☆ Labyrinth Essence

This brilliant essence connects us to the galactic matrix, and accelerates and assists us in communicating through the heart with our cosmic and galactic brothers and sisters. This celestial essence is the energy of the spectacular comet Hale-Bopp on the Full Moon Lunar Eclipse. We also called in the energy of the elements, the four directions and the Sun and the Moon. Leave the arena of manifest matter and soar in the cosmic ethers. Access dimensional doorways - through the heart - especially etheric temples of regenesis. This is a magnificent essence to use when walking labyrinths, and when connecting Heaven and Earth through the heart- as well as for intergalactic communication. Use Chaska to tune in to the ascended galactic beings of light. It is a good connector to the stars and to cosmic consciousness. Throat Chakra - I express.

Making the Star Essence - Chaska

The night we made the Hale-Bopp Chaska Essence we were in Peru, in the Sacred Valley of the Incas, at our land we call Chaska (which means star in Quechua). It was the night of a powerful Lunar eclipse and the night that the Hale-Bopp comet was closest to the planet Earth in South America. We had built a labyrinth on the land that day.

Kathy Doore, our friend and a labyrinth expert and enthusiast from the United States, had come to help us dowse for the perfect spot. We arrived at ChaskaLand in the afternoon. Kathy dowsed and we all got a sense of the placement of the labyrinth. After pulling away the weeds, we spotted an abandoned nest, with a heart-shaped rock. The spot felt just right. As you walk out of the labyrinth, you face the Urubamba River, and on the other side of the river is the mountain called PachaTusan- which means Anchor of the World. In 1972 or '73 there was a Kumbhamela held there, where holy men and women from all over the world gathered - to bring the Goddess Ray from Tibet to this sacred valley. They bathed in the Urubamba River, which runs right by our special piece of land.

After we finished the labyrinth, we walked it, and also ran it with the neighbor kids who had helped us build it. They also joined us in our ceremonies.

In the middle of our labyrinth we built a triple spiral altar - which created a triangle in the center. Some friends who do a lot of work with crystals (Kaysee and SuRay) had given us three large generator crystals to charge in Peru. We had charged them during our ceremonies at **Machu Picchu**, and they were now on the corners of the triangle in the middle of the triple spiral altar.

The sun was going down, and I heard a very clear message - put the bowl out. I had to hear this several times before I got that an essence was to be made in the middle of this energy vortex. The bowl of water went out at sunset and spent the night there. Our group was camping on the land that evening. Diamond and I stayed on our hexagonal platform that we had built there. We watched the bowl all night, during the eclipse, and while the Hale-Bopp comet passed through at its zenith, sending that Super Comet energy into the Earth. It was a spectacular evening - I didn't sleep a wink - the energy was so intense and rarefied and wonderful.

Other notes about the Chaska Essence

Sometimes there is an extraordinary downpouring of high-vibrational energy rays. Here in Santa Barbara it feels like we are engulfed in a cloud ship for days. (Some people think it is "just fog.") This has allowed a filter to be in place - so we can absorb even more of the special dispensations of energy that are raising our frequencies as fast as our bodies will allow. For those of us desiring to tune in to those ascended galactic beings of light, the Chaska Essence can assist. These are the beings that are assisting with our current transitions. The Chaska Essence has the Hale-Bopp Comet energy. This essence is a connection to the stars - and to cosmic consciousness.

The Chaska essence can also help put you in balance if you are feeling out-of-sorts from this energy download. For me sometimes it has felt like my sacrum was working overtime pumping the CSF (cerebral spinal fluid) - and the essence has eased the awareness in that area, as well as amplifying my connection to the stars. This is a reminder that we take essences for many reasons - sometimes because something is out of balance - and often to raise our consciousness. And, for **FUN**. *Let the good times roll!*

♥ Angel Spray ♥

Angel Play Angel Spray

Kelsea Rose Peace

How does it feel to be misted by an Angel?
When you need a lift from above-
Use Angel Spray with Love

The Story of Angel Rejuvenation Spray

The five ingredients from the material world in the Angel Rejuvenation Spray are: **distilled, activated sacred healing water, Frankincense, Lavender and Geranium essential oils, and the Eternal Youth Andean Orchid Flower Essence made from the Epidendrum Ibaguense Orchid.** We made the Epidendrum orchid essence at the sacred site of Wiñay Wayna. It is a few hours' hike from **Machu Picchu** on the Inca Trail in the rain forest/ cloud forest, at around 10,000 feet elevation. This particular orchid is also called the Wiñay Wayna orchid. Wiñay Wayna means Forever Young in Quechua.

After receiving the original information that the gifts of this essence are major qualities of rejuvenation, I kept hearing *get it on the skin*. A mister seemed like the obvious thing to do. Some people put all their essences in misters or atomizers. I had mixed flower essences in essential oil floral waters before and given them as gifts - so I started blending. Nothing. Absolutely nothing. I loved the idea of using Lavender - because it has a zillion healing qualities - and Lavender alone was the same old thing. Geranium had the uplifting and rejuvenating qualities that were great - and the smell just didn't please me. Finally - the 4 a.m. call. From a loud voice in my head I heard Lavender, Frankincense and Geranium. I actually got up and blended it up - and there you have it. Wow! The response has been so monumental that I am continuously gratified.

We know the angels are around all the time - and the Angel

Spray sometimes makes it easier to see them. They like its frequency. Thus it became Angel Rejuvenation Spray. It has multitudes of uses that continue to emerge.

Some of **Lavender's** qualities are: cleansing, uplifting, detoxifying, healing, and stimulates the immune system. **Frankincense** can be used to clear a room - the same as sage. It promotes healing as well as inviting relaxation and calm. **Geranium** is relaxing and soothing and works profoundly on the emotions (uplifting).

Healers use the Angel Spray to clear rooms between sessions, to balance and clear the energy. On your pillow it promotes restful sleep. It is especially nice when traveling, to spray in your hotel room and on your pillow. It is sweet evidence of angelic intervention.

I keep a bottle of Angel Spray in the car, and on my desk, in the bathroom, by my bed and in my purse. Children enjoy being misted before they go to bed, for a nice ritual, nice sleep and nice dreams.

SOME ANGEL SPRAY PRAISE:

What a wonderful addition to my practice. The Angel Rejuvenation is enjoyed by everybody. It clears the workspace quickly and lightly. – Michael

I love the Angel Rejuvenation. It has been such a blessing since I bought a case from you. It's assisted me greatly in my transition and healing. – Cory

Every time I spray myself with the Angel Mist a huge smile of joy fills up my whole essence. – Marcia

I gifted my mother with a bottle of the Angel Rejuvenation Spray... and when she sprayed me with it, the headache I'd had for more than a day disappeared instantaneously. – Johanna

The Angel Spray and the Angel Drops are Heaven on Earth! Purely divine products, like I've never ever experienced before. – Scott

Angel Spray – Knocked my socks off. I felt as though thousands of bliss-filled children's soap bubbles were emanating from all around me and then popping. What an amazingly sweet energy feeling it was. – Danielle

Angel Rejuvenation Spray truly lives up to its name. As you spray its beautiful fragrance over you, you can feel your vibrational frequency elevating. I highly recommend Angel Rejuvenation Spray to anyone who needs a natural lift or boost, and especially for those who are seeking clearer communications with heaven. – Doreen Virtue, PhD, author

◆ Crystal Clear Spray ◆

Made with the rose-colored salt from Maras, Peru, Frankincense, Lavender and Mint essential oils, and the flower essences Balance and Stability (Habenaria), Faith and Courage (Odontoglossum), Purification (Muña), Freedom/Libertad (Xylobium with 24 karat gold), and Be Nurtured (White Ceanothus). It is great for clearing crystals, and now we see that it deeply cleanses us as well. It leaves the aura radiating pure golden light. It is excellent for clearing energy in a room. This very powerful spray brings one in touch with their Light Body and prepares the way for the anchoring of one's higher self into the physical body.

Necessity- the Mother of Invention....

Crystal Clear was birthed out of a need. We had several friends around us working with therapeutic crystals and crystal necklaces. They were using the Angel Spray to cleanse their crystals, and the crystal necklaces they were repairing. The Frankincense has a fine clearing quality - and Lavender is cleansing; however, the energy would hop off the crystals and onto something else. As I was hearing this, I immediately heard - make a blend with **Faith and Courage** (Odontoglossum) to build a field of protection, and **Freedom/Libertad** (Xylobium with 24 karat Gold) to take the energy and transmute it (Freedom/Libertad acts very much as the violet flame) and **Muña** for purification. We consulted with friends who were using our essences for these situations. We were all getting the same information (I always enjoy that confirmation).

Taking crystals to the ocean to cleanse them is great - yet not always convenient. Our spray mist is made with the rose-colored salt from Maras, Peru, which carries an especially high vibration. We added the essential oils of Lavender for its cleansing qualities, Frankincense for its high vibration and clearing qualities, and Mint for its qualities of purification. In the end - after mixing all of these ingredients - I asked the crystals if there was anything else they wanted in it and immediately the answer came back: **Be Nurtured** (White Ceanothus). At first I thought this spray was just for crystals - and named it Crystal Clear - and it was for just that- clearing crystals. It still is. My next thought was that it would be great, if you didn't have time for a salt bath, to spray with this before a shower, and it would work nicely. It does. However, our friends who were using this - and the main motivators for creating this essence - discovered they actually like the feeling of this crystal salt spray on their bodies, and now we have all fallen in love with it as a mist for ourselves. It also brings the Light Body right into alignment. It seems to have some extraordinary qualities, just as the Angel Spray does - only different. Sometimes the Angel Spray is perfect - and other times you definitely want Crystal Clear. It is very powerful when sprayed in our energy field or on the skin. It clears energy immediately and coats us with a micro-layer of salt, which is very protective and cleansing. It can give new life to gemstones and crystals, and to us.

◆ ANGEL DROPS *to kiss and make it better* ◆

Made with *Star Essences* Balance and Stability (Habenaria), Freedom/Libertad (Xylobium with 24 karat gold), Be Nurtured (White Ceanothus), Purification (Muña), Sweet New Beginnings (Pink Jasmine), Nature Communion (Trichoceros Parviflorum) and the essential oils of Tea Tree and Lavender in a base of sacred activated healing water. I made this potion out of necessity because I had an itchy bite and my friend Diamond had blisters, and I had a desire to have something that would work for my granddaughters' miscellaneous boo-boos. These Wondrous Drops are useful for minor cuts, itches, burns, scrapes, bruises, and bites. Angel Drops promote healing of physical wounds on all levels. Great for kids and animals and they work for adults, too. The drops are remarkable (Angel Drops and a band-aid, and tears disappear). Massage into children's or baby's feet to bring them peacefulness and calm them. Massaging their feet is great anyway, and the drops are a superb addition to this ritual. It is relaxing for both the child and the parent - as the drops get absorbed into our hands as well as their feet. (This will work for grown-ups, too.) Put a few drops on their pillow to help promote sweet sleep.

◆ Rose-Colored Salt from Maras, Peru ◆

In the Vilcabamba- Sacred Valley

Salt (of the Earth) Worth its Salt!

Star at the Maras Salt Ponds

Maras is a town in the Sacred Valley of the Incas - located at an altitude of around 10,000 feet. This rose salt comes out from an ancient inner ocean through a small opening in the earth. From this opening, a stream of warm salty water flows out onto flat ponds. As the water evaporates, the salt remains and is gathered by the people of Maras. The salt is loaded onto donkeys and taken into the valley to trade. This has been going on for nearly 2,000 years. We get it directly hand-harvested- as it has been since around the time of Christ. The ponds are passed on from family to family. This rose salt has a very high vibration.

I have always been very fond of salt - and I was so happy to find the book, “Sea Salt’s Hidden Powers.” This book explains that, as I suspected, salt is very important to us. Not refined salt: true salt that still has its mineral content. Salt is also used in alchemy - and I was called to use the rose salt in the Super Immune Combination - on an energetic level. Later I was guided to use the salt in the Attention Combination - in a saturated solution - in order to add the chemistry of the salt as well as the energy of the salt. Crystal Clear Spray is also made with this salt.

It is noted that minerals are required for higher consciousness. These minerals are found naturally in salt and wild food. This is a mineral-rich salt, a gorgeous salt with an amazing and palpable energy. Most folks who see it, feel it, taste it are in awe.

I use it for everything - for eating as well as in sacred ceremonies. A few crystals every day may help bring back our cellular memory. Salt contains ancient DNA coding.

Salt is a symbol of Earth's light. Its beauty is that it can receive and hold etheric magnetism better than most substances. It can bring forth glorious spiritual love and beauty for an individual, whether involved in spiritual enlightenment or just in need of purification of the heart.

In the bath, this salt will provide a heart opening for anyone willing to make that lovely crossing into wholeness in heart and mind. One spoonful of rose salt added to one pound of regular salt, and (approximately) 22 gallons of water and 7-10 drops of iodine, make an awesome cleansing and purifying bath. Of course you will add flower essences to this - use a clean tub, and swirl the mixture in a figure eight. Experience the energetic boost given by this sublime element, the life-giving healing properties. Sea Salt (unprocessed!) is a product of Earth's internal fire element of transmutation. In alchemy it is a powerful element of transmutation. Consecrate your altar with it. Salt is crystallized fire.

mmmmmmm. I love good salt.

Combo World

We affectionately call the combinations of Star Flower and Gemstone Essences the Combos. They are a combination of several *Star Essences*, addressing some general issues. I have listed them here. You can see more about each combo by looking up each ingredient. If you have the concentrates you can make up these combinations, and vary them to your liking, as you make energy soup.

☆ Attention Formula ☆

Focused and Peaceful

Ingredients: Balance & Stability *(Habenaria)*, Be Nurtured *(White Ceanothus)*, Creation/Focus *(Jacaranda)*, Divine Child *(Ponthieva Montaña)*, Inocencia Coca *(Coca)*, Strength & Chi (*Fava*), 3 Corals - *(White, Red & Pink)*, Chrysoprase, Sugilite & Rose Salt

This essence has been reported to be of great value to children and adults diagnosed with ADD & ADHD. It assists one in staying attentive, focused, relaxed and peaceful. It can help improve concentration. The Peruvian rose salt and the 3 Corals help to balance minerals. The Fava has a connection to L. Dopamine. A note to parents of children taking medication (i.e. Ritalin): The essences will support change and eventually a balance may be achieved and medication reduced (with doctor's approval). Some children have been able to stop prescribed medication completely.

I have long had an interest in children being diagnosed with ADD, ADHD, etc. (all those initial things where Ritalin is prescribed). It just seems too strange, and very sad to me, that so many little kids would be on drugs. I have had some thoughts about this; why does this happen? Maybe their guides want to keep them distracted enough that they don't fill their minds with the incorrect information and programming from certain schools. I certainly could never concentrate in a history class. My attention would go anywhere else. Now I realize that it served me well not to be programmed with someone else's story.

It has seemed to me that there must be a way that flower essences can help balance out this situation without having to do the drug route. There are a lot of flower essences on the market. I suspect there are many that will help. With flower essences, it is very useful to look at the particular child and see what is happening. When I spoke to parents about why they chose drugs, they said their sanity was at stake. This is not a simple issue. However, a one-to-one path with a flower essence counselor treating the parent and the teachers, as well as the child, is a slow way to get to the huge number of children who are "riddled" with Ritalin. Even though I am sure the one-to-one is an effective method, I wanted a broader means to address the issue. I wanted something safe that folks can buy off the shelf. I was looking for a formula that could address a large-spectrum audience, for those who don't come into the range of one-to-one counseling. I have been asking Nature and Spirit to work with me to create a formula that will help these kids, whose symptoms show themselves in myriad ways, while the ultimate cause of the "affliction" is still not determined. Current research is pointing to the fact that rather than thinking linearly, many "A.D.D." folks are functioning more holographically. I love that.

I will share with you what has shown up so far. First of all, came the making of the Andean Orchid flower essence, Ponthieva Montaña, that we call "Divine Child." It is a beautiful, delicate, baby white flower, and it was shown to me by a 12-year-old boy. I was not wanting to be told what to do by this boy, so I asked in meditation if I should make it and what the essence would be good for. A big "A.D.D." flashed before me. Later that morning, I found out that Skip, the 12-year-old boy, had been diagnosed with A.D.D. He was not on his medication during his trip to Peru, and he did great. Divine Child is one of the ingredients in our Attention Formula. Another is the Fava essence, Strength and Chi.

Through divine guidance (and a surprise to me), I made a Fava flower essence. I was told in my meditation to research Fava. I looked in the library, and found a few interesting bits about how the beans were considered valuable in Peru, and had actually been used as offerings in ceremonies. Then I looked on the internet and found an article called "Fava Knows Best." It mentioned that Fava had a high concentration of L-Dopamine. A few days later, my friend mentioned that she had just come from the doctor because she possibly had A.D.D. I laughed and said jokingly, "Don't we all?" She told me that she actually had low amounts of L-Dopamine, a possible characteristic of A.D.D. Mmmm- interesting.

Through more synchronicities and magic, I was guided to become very interested in salt. Being a vegetarian can be dangerous if you don't get enough of the right salt, that still has its good minerals in it. I learned about Celtic Sea Salt. Then I learned about the rose-colored salt in Peru and I visited the salt ponds there. It is amazing salt. It is totally pure, nothing has been added and nothing has been taken away. It comes from an altitude of 10,000 feet in the Andes Mountains of Peru, in the Sacred Valley of the Incas, a couple of hours from **Machu Picchu**. This salt has a special frequency. I acquired some, and we have been using this special salt in a diluted, energetic form in our flower essence combination called Super Immune. Then I read somewhere that another characteristic that A.D.D.-diagnosed children have is a mineral deficiency, and not always the same mineral is deficient in every child. We make the Attention Formula with a super-saturated salt solution. Also included in the formula is Be Nurtured (White Ceanothus), Balance and Stability (Andean Orchid Habenaria) and Creation/ Focus (Jacaranda).

All of the reports I have gotten back have been very positive. I have had a mother stop me on the street to tell me how well it was working, and a great story from my escrow officer, who gave it to her boyfriend's son instead of Ritalin. She said that at first, the school was not liking the idea, but afterwards they were pleased and surprised with the results. There are many more success stories.

I doubt if there is any one thing that is the answer for everyone, and I do feel this may be the answer for many. It is well worth a try. Remember that it will taste salty. It is something you can administer yourself (four to seven drops on or under the tongue, or in water or juice); and if none of that works you can use it topically on the skin, or put it in shampoo and the bath. One very good way is to give it to your child to hold onto, to take by themselves, when they feel the need. It is very empowering for them. There are no side effects. As with all flower essences, the worst that can happen is NOTHING, which is very rare, and the most that can happen is miracles.

☆ Brilliant Student ☆

Studying ❤ Creativity ❤ Alertness

Ingredients: Ancient Wisdom *(Lycaste Longepetalia)*, Creation/ Focus *(Jacaranda)*, Faith & Courage *(Odontoglossum)*, I Remember *(Rosemary Officinalis)*, Inner Guru *(Purple Sage)*, Inocencia Coca *(Coca)*, My Passion *(Passion Flower)*, Kyanite, Purple Tourmaline

Stay focused, energized and awake, with acute concentration. This essence keeps your mind interested and the creativity and imagination flowing. It is revitalizing and refreshing. (It can also be useful when you are tired and driving a car). Boosts confidence for public speaking, test taking and presentations. Radiant inspiration. Access the part of you that knows the answers. Brilliance is divine.

☆ Celebration ☆

Sacred Ceremony

Ingredients: Anchoring Light *(Sobralia Dichotoma)*, Balance & Stability *(Habenaria)*, Dance *(Bougainvilla)*, Eternal Youth *(Epidendrum Ibaguense)*, One Heart *(Epidendrum Cuscoense)*, Otter Delight *(Giant River Otters)*, Pure Joy *(Orange Blossom)*, Clear Quartz

This Magic Elixir uplifts the spirit. It's a fun, wonderful happy birthday party essence - and perfect for weddings and ceremonies of all kinds, including full moon and new moon events. It's great when everyone takes this essence and plays in the same high frequency. It is also good for dance, Tai Chi, yoga and other forms of movement. Put it in party punches or take the drops directly in the mouth. Good in the bath (make your bath a celebration - a ceremony). Stellar and earthly at the same time.

☆ Emancipated Master ☆

Addresses Addictions

Ingredients: Balance & Stability (*Habenaria*), Emancipation (*Tobacco*), Freedom/Libertad (*Xylobium w/ 24K Gold*), Inocencia Coca (*Coca*), Sublime Chocolate (*Cacao*), Emerald

Use this essence for support to gain freedom from anything that has power over you. It helps you to change habits and release cravings gracefully. Remain peaceful, balanced and strong. Focus your intention on good health and be liberated.

☆ Exalted Earth ☆

Grounding ❤ Earth Healing
Environmental Sensitivity

Ingredients: Anchoring Light (*Sobralia Dichotoma*), Balance & Stability (*Habenaria*), Nature Communion (*Trichoceros Parviflorum*), Clear Quartz, Rainbow Obsidian

This essence is for the Earth and for environmentally sensitive folks. Great when doing ceremony with water, and for Earth healing. Soar along a rainbow. Make contact with the earth, trees, plants and animals, the elements, cycles, and the directions. Establish a partnership with Nature. Anoint yourself, each other and the Earth. Put a few drops in the water you use for your plants and your garden. This essence is also especially good to use on the Earth to release energies and entities that are stuck.

☆ Fforever Young ☆

Rejuvenation

Ingredients: Eternal Youth (*Epidendrum Ibaguense*), Freedom/ Libertad (*Xylobium w/24K Gold*), Alexandrite, Ametrine, White Topaz

This essence addresses the reversal of aging and promotes rejuvenation. Tap into universal energy. Regain your childlike, youthful qualities. Very good on the skin. Use in the bath (3-4 droppers full), and in all your body products (7 drops per ounce). Put it in your drinking water (7 drops per quart). This essence is known for its restorative properties, and for speeding recovery time.

☆ Glorious Menopause ☆

Graceful Change

Ingredients: Balance & Stability (*Habenaria*), Divine Goddess (*Masdevallia Veitchianna*), Freedom/Libertad (*Xylobium w/24K Gold*), Graceful Shift (*Fennel*), Master Teacher (*Chiri Sanango*), Strength & Chi (*Fava*), Sublime Chocolate (*Cacao*), Wild Feminine (*Wild Potato*), Moonstone, Pink Tourmaline

This essence can facilitate a fun, gentle, easy, graceful and empowering menopause. It creates a resonant field to play in. It balances metabolism and temperature, and is strengthening. This is a deeply profound, powerful time of life. Rejoice and acknowledge yourself!

☆ Graceful Passages ☆

Birth ❤ Rebirth ❤ Transitions

Ingredients: Balance & Stability (*Habenaria*), Divine Child (*Ponthieva Montaña*), Faith & Courage (*Odontoglossum*), Let Go & Trust (*Oregano*), One Heart (*Epidendrum Cuscoense*), Soul Family (*Blue Ceanothus*), Alexandrite, Clear Quartz, Pink Tourmaline

Harmony, inner peace, easy transition. Useful for parents to take prior to childbirth to get in touch with the soul of baby and good during the birthing process. 7 drops on or under the tongue repeated often, or in juice or water and sip throughout the day (good for mom and for dad, too). For a baby put 1 drop diluted with water in baby's mouth. Put in a spray bottle and spray the room (7 drops per ounce). Good for everyone involved to take the essence. Also especially great for hospice work, and conscious transitions. Puts one in alignment with soul collective, guides and teachers.

☆ Happy Kid ☆

Precious Child

Ingredients: Balance & Stability *(Habenaria)*, Be Nurtured *(White Ceanothus)*, Divine Child *(Ponthieva Montaña)*, Faith & Courage, *(Odontoglossum)*, Otter Delight *(Giant River Otters)*, Pure Joy *(Orange Blossom)*, Mother of Pearl, Preserved with Vegetable Glycerin

This nurturing essence, made especially for children and babies, is an all-around balancer and is great for all sorts of emergencies and upsets. Use topically (on pulse points, and/or on top of head) and orally - directly in the mouth or in water or juice. Children respond quickly to these essences. And they are totally safe to use.

☆ Happy Pet ☆

and Happy Wild Critters, Too

Ingredients: Balance & Stability *(Habenaria)*, Be Nurtured *(White Ceanothus)*, Faith & Courage *(Odontoglossum)*, Nature Communion *(Trichoceros parviflorum)*, Clear Quartz, Kyanite

Animals (wild and domestic) respond extremely well to vibrational essences. This combination has proven effective time and time again, for all kinds of pet upsets including moving, animal incidents and accidents, and transitions. Very good for when pets travel or make changes. Use this essence to speed the recovery process. Add the essence to their water or put it on their paws, or put it directly in their mouths or on their fur, or on your hands and pet them. Also available in spray.

☆ ILLUMINATION ☆

ANGELIC CONNECTION ❤ MEDITATION ❤ SPIRITUAL ELIXIR

Ingredients: Anchoring Light *(Sobralia Dichotoma)*, Divine Goddess *(Masdevallia Veitchianna)*, High Frequency *(Pleurothallis)*, Initiation of the HeartLight *(Pink Lotus)*, Gold+ Silver/White Chakra *(Sobralia Setigera)*, Heliodor, White Marble, White Topaz, Yellow Cat's Eye

This profound essence will expand you to very high states. It moves you through octaves, and assists with bringing light into you gently. Opens the heart & receptive qualities. Heightens intuition, vision. Avail yourself to cosmic energy. Take a pilgrimage to infinity and back. Great for meditation.

☆ LOVING THOUGHTS ☆

INFINITE PATIENCE

Ingredients: One Heart *(Epidendrum Cuzcoense)*, Initiation of the HeartLight *(Pink Lotus)*, Chrysoprase, Aquamarine, Rose Quartz, Yellow Fluorite

Remember we are always praying ~ A thought itself is a prayer. This essence expands us to a frequency that will help quiet the mind and think the thoughts that angels think. Our coping abilities are strengthened through an open heart. With intent, energy and action ~ our thoughts (prayers) are very powerful! Remember we are the divine creator through our thoughts, ideas, beliefs, attitudes and expectations. Remind yourself at any time to have only loving thoughts, and that EVERY situation offers an opportunity to send love. Folks on the freeway, ex-spouses, bless everyone, all the time.

☆ Magnificent Moontime ☆

I Am a Divine Goddess

Ingredients: Balance & Stability *(Habenaria)*, Divine Goddess *(Masdevallia Veitchianna)*, Freedom/Libertad *(Xylobium w/24K Gold)*, Full Moon *(Lavender)*, Nature Communion *(Trichoceros Parviflorum)*, Strength & Chi *(Fava)*, Sublime Chocolate *(Cacao)*, Bloodstone, Moonstone

Honor, enjoy and tune into your cycles and rhythms, with reverence and peace. Stay balanced during each period. Flow in a stream of love. Also especially useful for those few days before moontime begins.

☆ Man Alive ☆

A Vital, Virile Elixir

Ingredients: Balance & Stability *(Habenaria)*, Freedom/ Libertad *(Xylobium w/24K Gold)*, Male Strength *(Agave)*, Solar Power *(Sunflower)*, Strength & Chi *(Fava)*, Green Tourmaline, Malachite

A powerful and energetic tonic, this invigorating essence has been known to increase motivation and stamina, to increase sexual desire and to enhance virility and vitality. Capture the rapture. Have abounding excitement and enthusiasm. Dance into the night.

☆ Perfect Weight ☆

Radiant Body

Ingredients: Balance & Stability *(Habenaria)*, Freedom/ Libertad *(Xylobium w/24K Gold)*, Inocencia Coca *(Coca)*, Let Go & Trust *(Oregano)*, Master Teacher (*Chiri Sanango*), Sublime Chocolate *(Cacao)*, Sacred Union *(Maxillaria)*, Bluegreen Apatite, Yellow Apatite and Rose Quartz

This combination of essences supports a balanced appetite, balanced metabolism, confidence and self-love. It is easy to change habits. Feel free to let go of anything- especially thoughts that no longer serve you, and enjoy being in your beautiful body. Take this essence at least 4 times daily consistently, for a good period of time, so you can maintain this frequency.

☆ Prosperity Alchemy ☆

Open and Willing to Receive

Ingredients: Freedom/Libertad *(Xylobium w/24K Gold)*, I Am Generosity *(Chijchipa)*, I Am Gratitude *(Yuyu/Mustard)*, I Remember *(Rosemary Officinalis)*, Emerald

Use this essence consistently with intent, energy and action. Your desire, emotion and imagination directly affect your prosperity consciousness. This essence helps propel you into that frequency. Affirm your generosity and gratitude. Gratitude ignites hidden sources of energy and light, lifting you to new levels of joy and peace. A grateful heart is the most powerful force in the universe. Prosperity is natural, and lavish abundance is our nature. There is infinite abounding wealth. Financial well-being comes with ease. Abundance is constantly flowing from source. You are wildly optimistic and let good fortune leap all over you. This essence is a treasure! Expect abundance and wealth from unexpected sources.

☆ Quintessential Balance ☆

Peace ❤ Emergency Essence

Ingredients: Balance & Stability *(Habenaria)*, Faith & Courage *(Odontoglossum)*, Clear Quartz

We have taken our broad spectrum anti-stress, stabilizing essence, Balance & Stability, and added Faith & Courage and Clear Quartz to amplify the effects with universal love. Works like MAGIC. The "rescue remedy" for the new millennium. Use whenever you are off-center, for balancing. Good for everyone, kids, pets, plants, adults and anyone else that you can think of - like teenagers. If you can't decide what essence to take, then take this one. Works quickly! Use as often as needed. Put 7 drops in a glass of water and sip it during acute situations. Keep it everywhere.

Good to have in your medicine cabinet, your desk, your purse (if you carry one) and the car. If you only have one essence, have this one.

☆ Radiant Sensuality ☆

Love ❤ Charm

Ingredients: Freedom/Libertad *(Xylobium w/24K Gold)*, Let Go & Trust *(Oregano)*, Male Strength *(Agave)*, Mango Paradise *(Mango)*, My Passion *(Passion Flower)*, Open Mind/Future Vision *(Mugwort)*, Sacred Union *(Maxillaria)*, Wild Feminine *(Solanum Diploide)*, Otter Delight, Carnelian, Ruby

A magical Star Flower & Gemstone Essence blend that encourages you to be the love that you desire. Take this ecstatic synergistic combination to enhance your romantic mood. It covers a beautiful range of sexual vitality and sensuality. Marvelous for drawing your beloved to you and especially pleasurable to take with your beloved. Be creative, enjoy a flower essence cocktail. Put four droppers full in your tub. Immerse yourself in the essence of the essence. Cherish yourself, cherish each other.

☆ Shield of Light ☆

Safe and Protected

Ingredients: Balance & Stability *(Habenaria)*, Faith & Courage *(Odontoglossum)*, Freedom/Libertad *(Xylobium w/24K Gold)*, Gold + Silver/White *(Sobralia Setigera)*, Magic Healer *(Plantain)*, Blue Sapphire

Creates a vibrational frequency around you so nothing disruptive can enter your field. Valuable essence for healers. Great to use when working with and around computers. Useful for traveling in big cities, and around high-tension wires and airports. It is especially valuable to use (for patient and visitor) in hospitals. Feel confident and safe. Archangel Michael overlights this essence. Also use this essence on the perimeters of your house, yard, office, etc. (inside and out) to build a shield of light.

☆ Soul Purpose ☆

Dreams

Ingredients: Ancient Wisdom *(Lycaste Longepetalia)*, Inner Guru *(Purple Sage)*, Open Mind/Future Vision *(Mugwort)*, Blue Sapphire, Indigo, White Marble

Take this essence when you have questions regarding direction, and regarding divine will. Your dreams and curiosity will help determine your direction. This essence assists choice making and helps discover the goal that is contained in each step. You become tuned into life's current and allow your spiritual source to flow through. Live in love with life. Ask yourself what contributions you have for the world and listen for the answers. In discovering your purpose, pay attention to your feelings- they are signs. Be an artist of the sacred and have your life be a work of art. Vibrate in unison with the universe. Have clarity, and make clear choices. Physical healing often comes about when you discover your soul path, so it is important to find what makes your ♥ and soul sing. This essence helps you direct and remember your dreams. Go for your wildest, most dazzling ones!

☆ Super Immune ☆

Wellness ♥ Purification

Ingredients: Balance & Stability *(Habenaria)*, Faith & Courage *(Odontoglossum)*, Freedom/Libertad *(Xylobium w/24K Gold)*, Magic Healer *(Plantain)*, Master Teacher *(Chiri Sanango)*, Purification *(Muña)*, Strength & Chi *(Fava)*, Emerald, 3 Corals *(White, Red & Pink)*, Green Aventurine, Yellow Agate, Rose Salt

A combination of flower and gemstone essences and the powerful rose-colored salt from the Sacred Valley of the Incas in Peru. When dealing with any physical healing, this essence is very good for strengthening the immune system via the electrical system, allowing the body to concentrate full-time on the physical - thus speeding up recovery time dramatically. Take the drops when you feel a first symptom. The body says thank you - every time you take it. It is useful for radiation exposure and protection on any level: diagnostic, therapeutic, accidental or employment-related. Good before and during a cleanse. It is a valuable adjunct to any therapeutic modality; it will enhance and accelerate your healing. Super Immune is also available in spray.

☆ Travel Solution ☆

Airplanes ❤ Altitude

Ingredients: Balance & Stability *(Habenaria)*, Deep Breath *(Eucalyptus)*, Faith & Courage *(Odontoglossum)*, Graceful Shift *(Fennel)*, Inocencia Coca *(Coca)*, Purification *(Muña)*, Pink Tourmaline

Helps you to adapt to the changes that take place while traveling. This super balancing essence also helps with altitude and jet lag, and assists with flying trepidation. It protects you from electromagnetic radiation and strengthens coping abilities. It is helpful to start taking a day or 2 before you leave, and continue during your journey as necessary.

PART FIVE

Reference

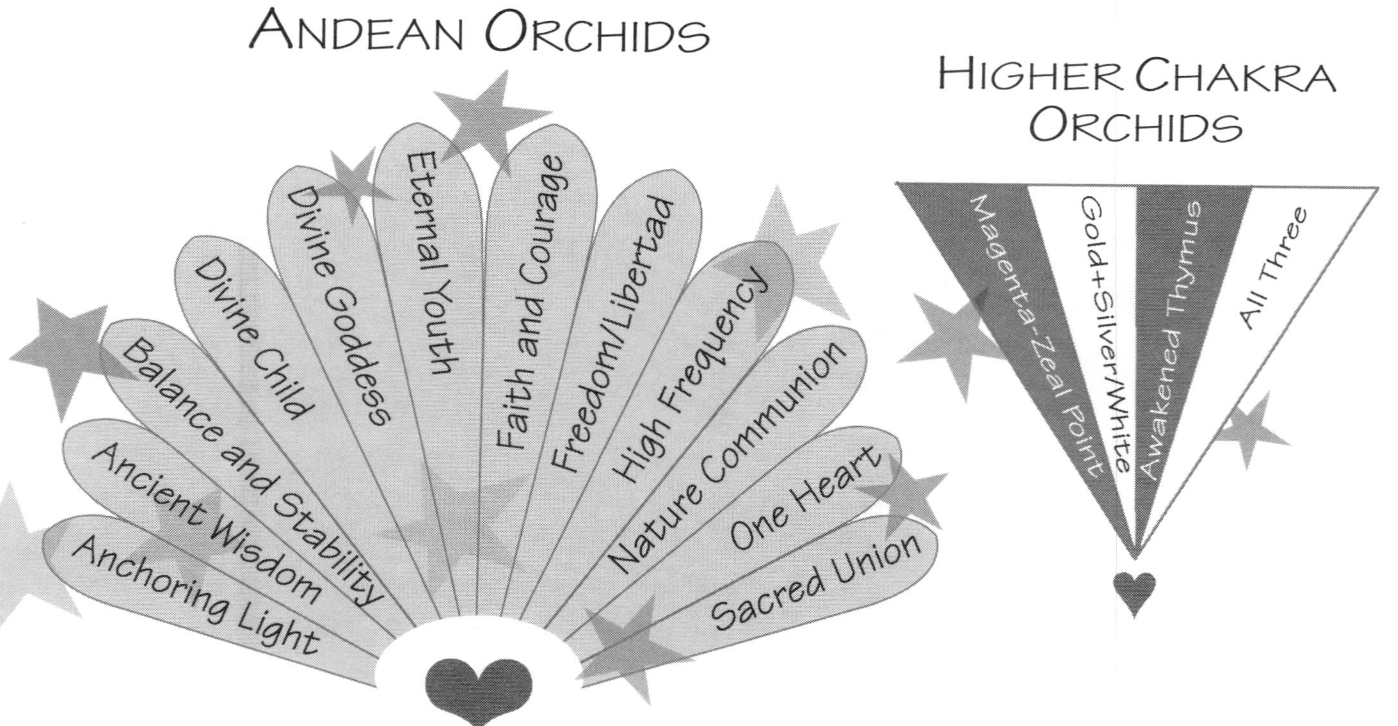
Andean Orchids
Anchoring Light
Ancient Wisdom
Balance and Stability
Divine Child
Divine Goddess
Eternal Youth
Faith and Courage
Freedom/Libertad
High Frequency
Nature Communion
One Heart
Sacred Union
Higher Chakra Orchids
Magenta-Zeal Point
Gold+Silver/White
Awakened Thymus
All Three

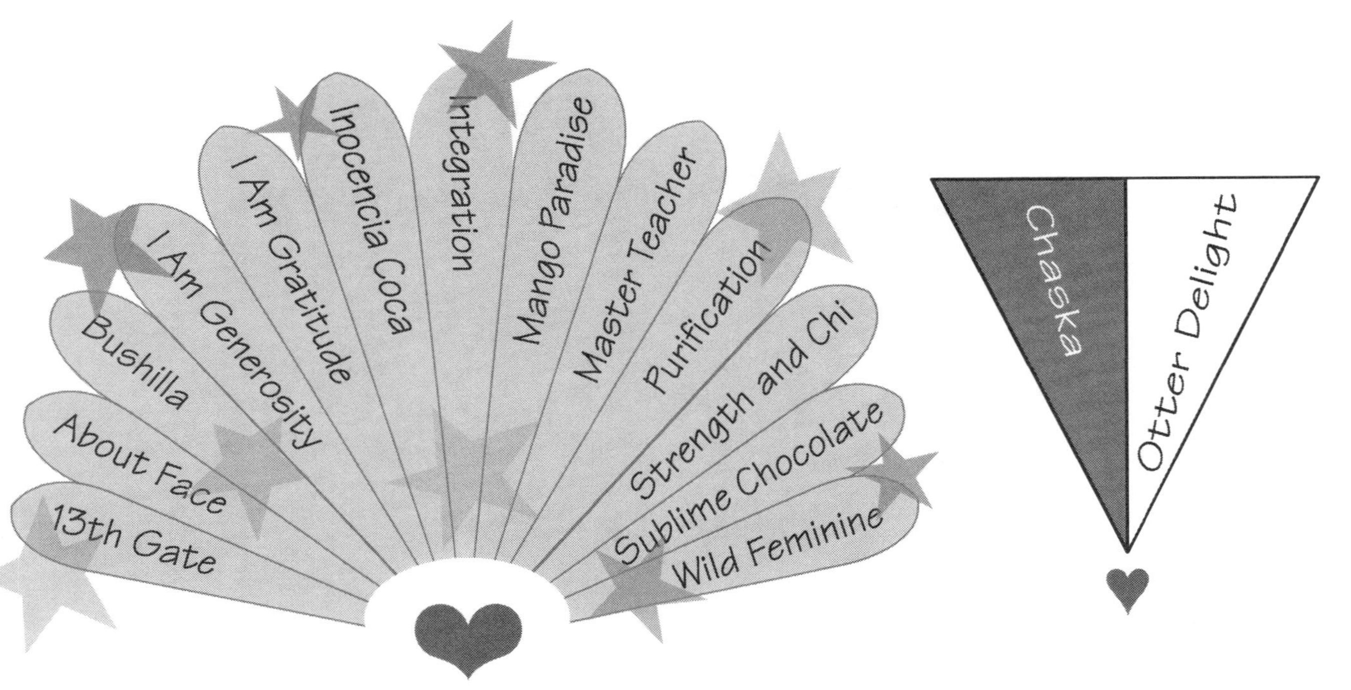
Peruvian Flowers
13th Gate
About Face
Bushilla
I Am Generosity
I Am Gratitude
Inocencia Coca
Integration
Mango Paradise
Master Teacher
Purification
Strength and Chi
Sublime Chocolate
Wild Feminine
Chaska
Otter Delight
Pendulum Charts

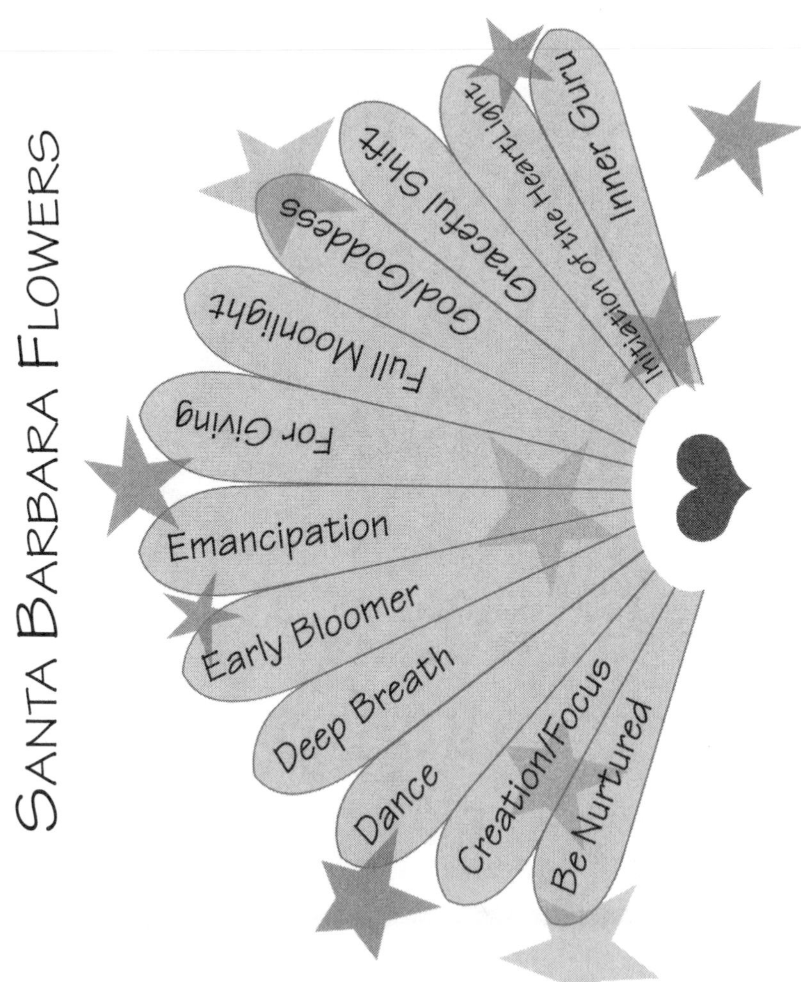
Santa Barbara Flowers
Be Nurtured
Creation/Focus
Dance
Deep Breath
Early Bloomer
Emancipation
For Giving
Full Moonlight
God/Goddess
Graceful Shift
Initiation of the Heart Light
Inner Guru

Santa Barbara Flowers

Pendulum Charts

Gemstone Chakra Essences

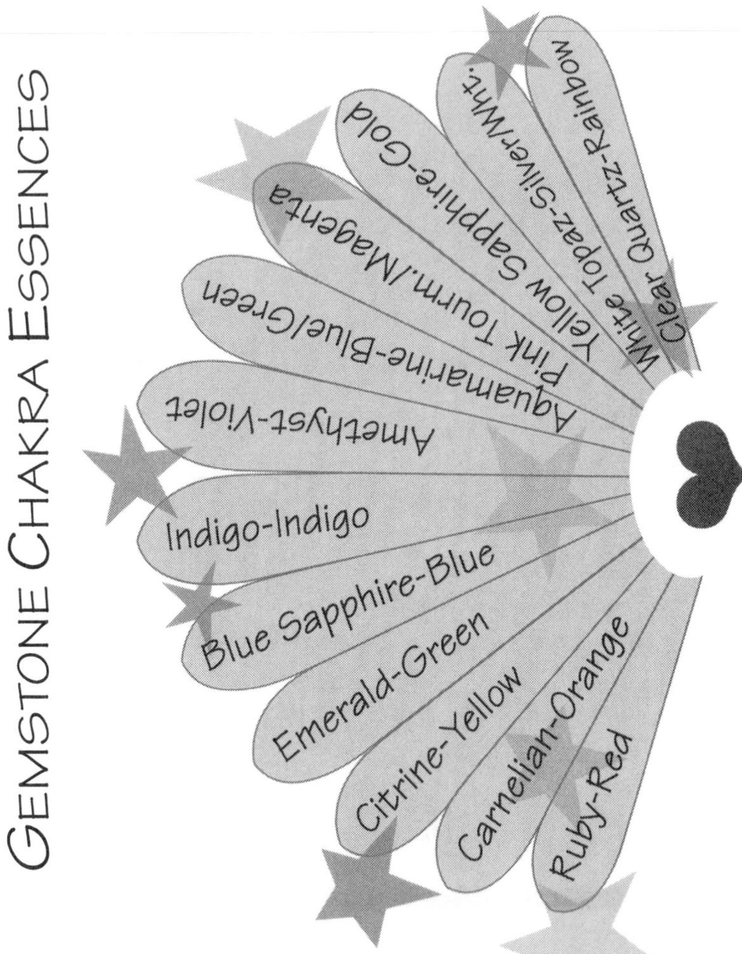

Gemmies 1

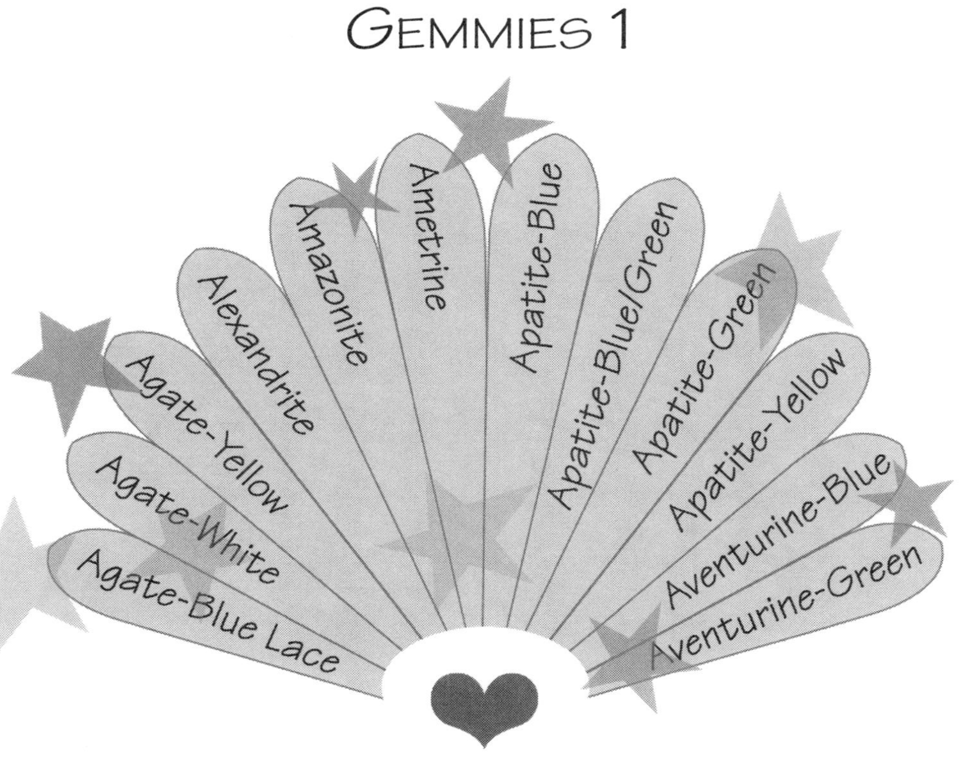

PENDULUM CHARTS

Gemmies 2

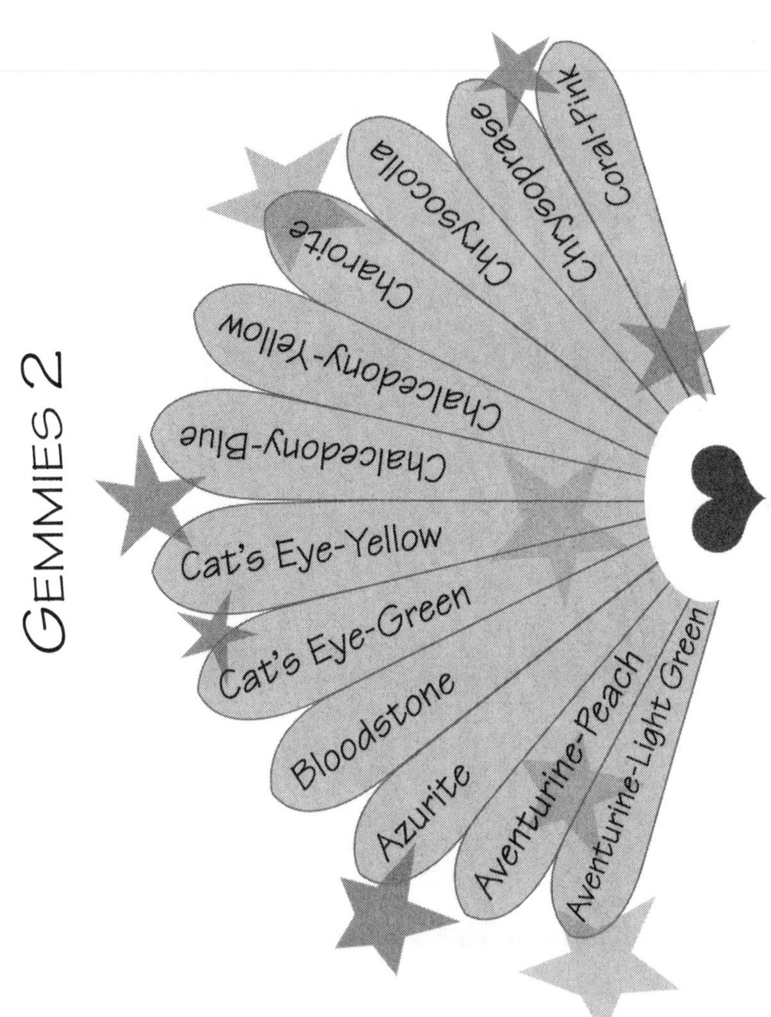
Aventurine-Light Green
Aventurine-Peach
Azurite
Bloodstone
Cat's Eye-Green
Cat's Eye-Yellow
Chalcedony-Blue
Chalcedony-Yellow
Charoite
Chrysocolla
Chrysoprase
Coral-Pink

GEMMIES 3

PENDULUM CHARTS

Gemmies 4

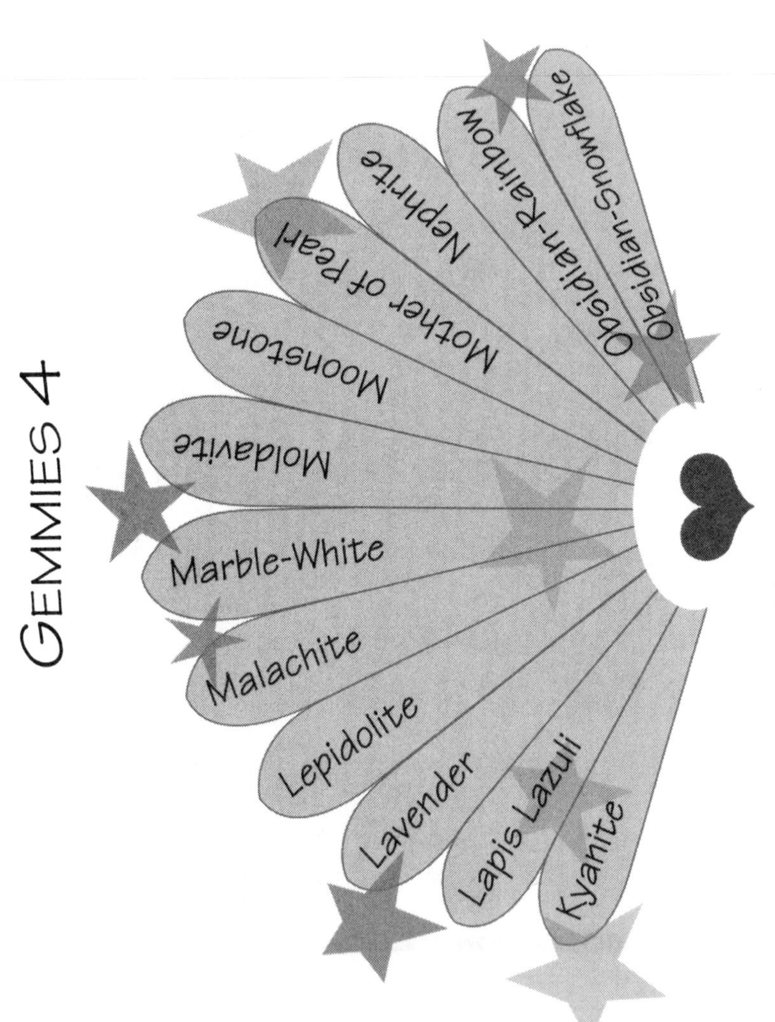
Obsidian-Snowflake
Obsidian-Rainbow
Nephrite
Mother of Pearl
Moonstone
Moldavite
Marble-White
Malachite
Lepidolite
Lavender
Lapis Lazuli
Kyanite

Gemmies 5

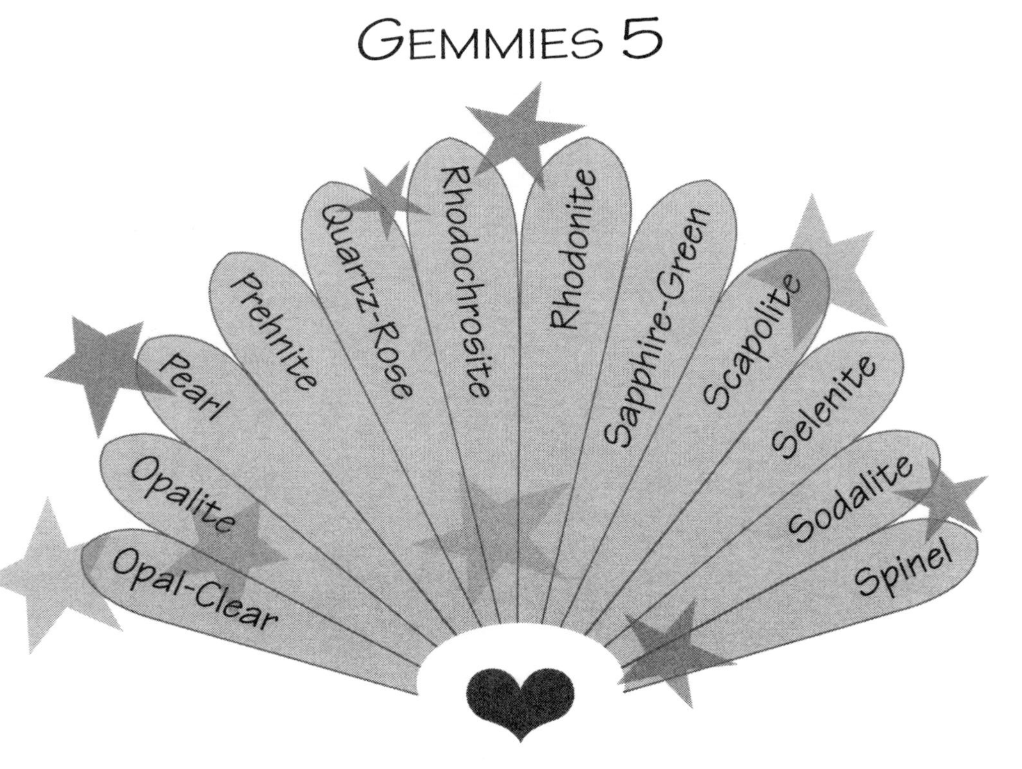
Opal-Clear
Opalite
Pearl
Prehnite
Quartz-Rose
Rhodochrosite
Rhodonite
Sapphire-Green
Scapolite
Selenite
Sodalite
Spinel

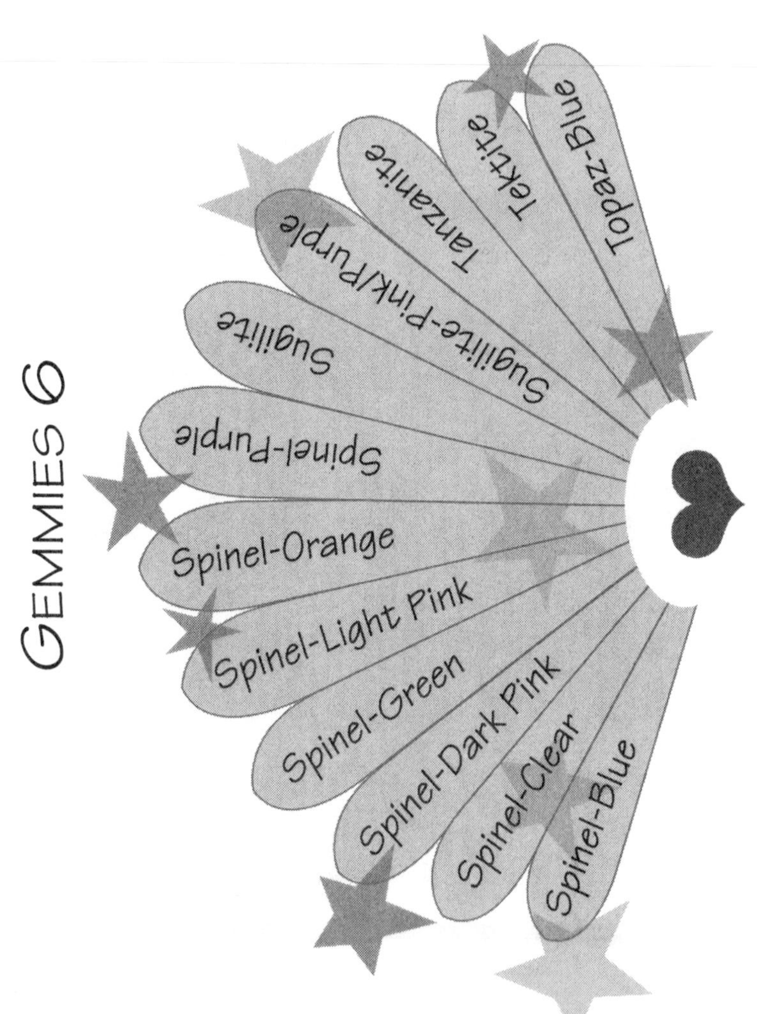
GEMMIES 6
Topaz-Blue
Tektite
Tanzanite
Sugilite-Pink/Purple
Sugilite
Spinel-Purple
Spinel-Orange
Spinel-Light Pink
Spinel-Green
Spinel-Dark Pink
Spinel-Clear
Spinel-Blue

GEMMIES 7

Topaz-Imperial
Tourmaline-Dark Blue
Tourmaline-Light Blue
Tourmaline-Green
Tourmaline-Orange
Tourmaline-Purple
Tourmaline-Yellow
Tsavorite
Turquoise-Blue
Turquoise-Green
Unakite

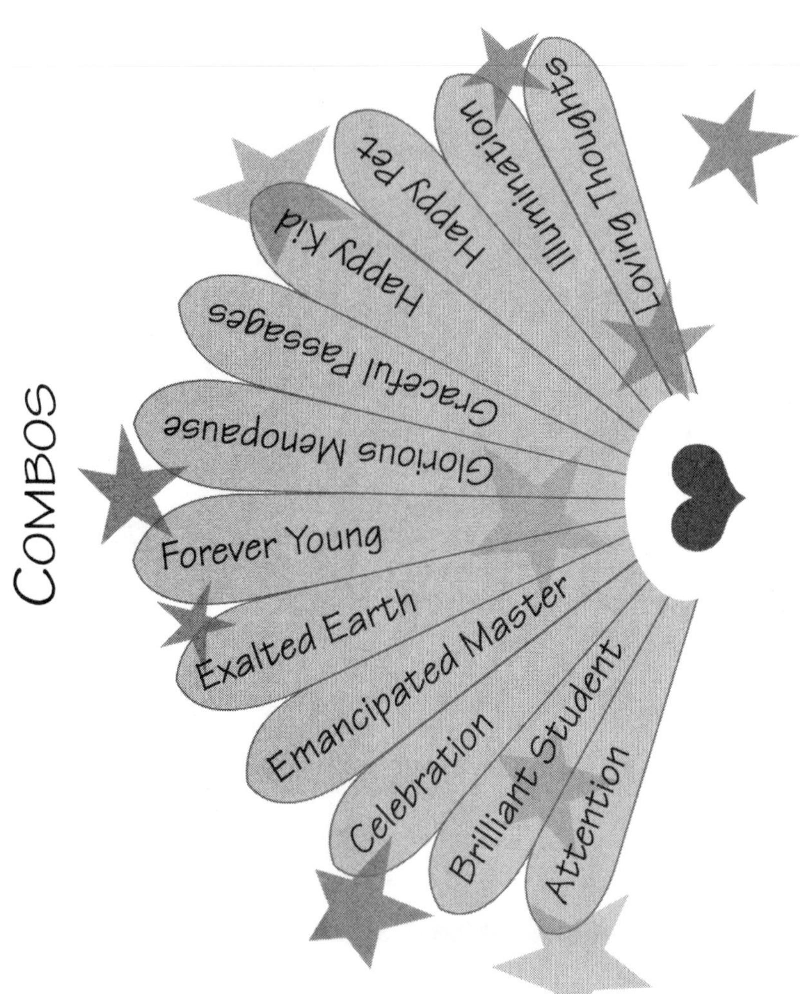
COMBOS
Loving Thoughts
Illumination
Happy Pet
Happy Kid
Graceful Passages
Glorious Menopause
Forever Young
Exalted Earth
Emancipated Master
Celebration
Brilliant Student
Attention

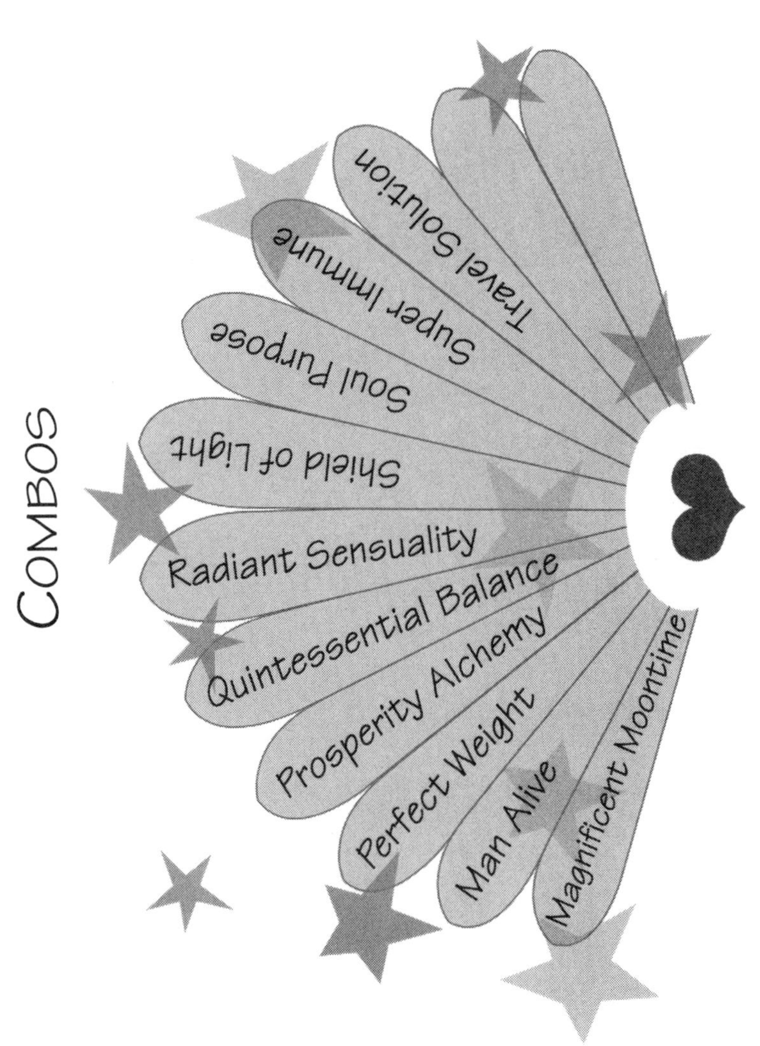
COMBOS
Travel Solution
Super Immune
Soul Purpose
Shield of Light
Radiant Sensuality
Quintessential Balance
Prosperity Alchemy
Perfect Weight
Man Alive
Magnificent Moontime

PENDULUM CHARTS

Translation of Bach Essences to Star Essences

When speaking in Mexico it came to my attention that nearly 100 percent of the floral therapists began with the Bach essences. Here in the States that is not always true. Some of you started right off with Star essences. I am often asked which Star Essences could be used in place of the Bach essences. I have made a list converting Bach to Star. The StarBachs.

Pattern of Imbalance

Bach Essence-Virtues and gifts of the essence

Star Essences

Other Star Essences to consider

Hides worries behind brave face, avoids conflict. Addictive behavior to anesthetize feelings.

Agrimony- Honesty of emotions. Address addictive behaviors. Good self-esteem, self-worth and self-acceptance. Peace.

Emancipation, Divine Goddess, Citrine, Sodalite

Inocencia Coca, Be Nurtured, Solar Power, Freedom/Libertad, Balance and Stability

Apprehension for no known reason. Fear of the unknown. Vague anxiety. Subconscious fear.

Aspen- Courage to face the unknown. Believe in one's self and love one's uniqueness. Feel safe. Inner strength from the spiritual world.

About Face, Faith and Courage, Pink/Purple Sugilite

Inner Guru, Light Navigator, Otter Delight, Citrine, Pink Tourmaline

Critical, intolerant and judgmental of others.

Beech- Tolerance and unconditional love. See good and beauty in all things.

One Heart, Emerald

ForGiving, I am Gratitude, Initiation of the HeartLight, Freedom, Pearl

Weak-willed, exploited, imposed upon.
Centaury- Service to others and oneself, through inner strength. Healthy recognition of one's own needs. Encourages appropriate behavior.
BE NURTURED, FREEDOM/LIBERTAD, YELLOW SAPPHIRE, DARK PINK SPINEL
Ruby, Male Strength

Self-doubt - distrust of one's own intuition.
Cerato- For confidence and trust in one's own inner knowing.
INNER GURU, ANCIENT WISDOM, IOLITE
I Remember, Imperial Topaz

Fear of losing control, irrational thoughts, resistance to inner guidance.
Cherry Plum- Mental composure, inner peace, rational thinking.
LET GO AND TRUST, CHRYSOPRASE
Balance and Stability, Graceful Shift, God/Goddess Unity

Failure to learn from life and experience
Chestnut Bud- Wisdom. Learn from our experiences.
MASTER TEACHER, ANCIENT WISDOM
I Remember, 13th Gate, Charoite, Tanzanite

Over-concern for others. Self-pity. Demanding. Needy.
Chicory- Universal unconditional love. Appropriate Giving and Receiving.
ONE HEART, FORGIVING
Freedom/Libertad, Be Nurtured, High Frequency,
I am Generosity, Otter Delight, Pink/Purple Sugilite

Absent-minded. Dreamy/drowsy. Live in future.
Clematis- Grounded. Live in present. Open and clear mind.
ANCHORING LIGHT, TEKTITE
Nature Communion, Integration, My Passion,
Deep Breath, Creation/Focus, Carnelian

Feeling unclean. Self-disgust. Need for detoxification.
Crabapple- Cleansing, detoxification. Sense of inner purity.
PURIFICATION, MAGIC HEALER, YELLOW AGATE
Eternal Youth, Rhodochrosite

Overwhelmed by responsibility. Perfectionist ways.
Elm- Realistic idealism. Strength to perform.
BALANCE AND STABILITY, SOLAR POWER, FAITH AND COURAGE, FIRE OPAL
Zania, Pure Joy, Master Teacher, Bloodstone, Green Aventurine

Despondency, self-doubt, discouragement, melancholy.
Gentian- Confidence, joyfully creating our own reality. Inspired optimism.
ABOUT FACE, FAITH AND COURAGE, TANZANITE
Pure Joy, Let Go and Trust, I am Gratitude, Mother of Pearl.

Self-absorbed, self-centered, over-talkative, lonesome.
Heather- Fosters devotion to loved ones, and to self. Unconditional love.
BE NURTURED, ONE HEART, DARK PINK SPINEL
Soul Family, Hessonite

Envy, jealousy, suspicion, anger, revenge.
Holly- For open and loving acceptance of others, compassion, tolerance, universal love.
ONE HEART, ROSE QUARTZ, CHRYSOPRASE
ForGiving, Initiation of the HeartLight, God/Goddess Unity, Nephrite, Dark Pink Spinel, Chrysoprase

Living in the past. Homesickness.
Honeysuckle- Being fully in the present moment.
ETERNAL YOUTH, MANGO PARADISE, WHITE AGATE
Pure Joy, Zania, About Face, Sweet New Beginnings

Fatigue, weariness, inability to cope, insufficient energy for daily life.
Hornbeam- Strength, energy, vitality, stamina.
ETERNAL YOUTH, STRENGTH AND CHI, INOCENCIA COCA, FIRE OPAL
Balance and Stability, Male Strength, My Passion, Green Aventurine, Sugilite

Impatience, irritability, tension, intolerance.
Impatiens- Abounding patience. Seeing the perfection of the process.
GOLD + SILVER/WHITE CHAKRA, DEEP BREATH, AQUAMARINE
Freedom/Libertad, One Heart, Balance and Stability, Howlite

Lack of confidence, projecting failure. Immobilized.
Larch- Confidence, spontaneity, success.
WILD FEMININE, FAITH AND COURAGE, HESSONITE
My Passion, Dance, About Face, Amazonite, Howlite

Timid, shy, nervous. Fear of known things.
Mimulus- Faith and courage to face life's challenges. Self-confidence and freedom.
FAITH AND COURAGE, FREEDOM/LIBERTAD, DIAMOND
Balance and Stability, Let Go and Trust, Male Strength, Solar Power, Dance, Mango Paradise

Melancholy, gloom, despair for no apparent reason.
Mustard- For cheerfulness and mental fortitude- finding joy in life- faith to go forward.
I AM GRATITUDE, FAITH AND COURAGE, ANCHORING LIGHT (Note: When you are the light - there can be no shadow), **HESSONITE**
Pure Joy, Chaska, Rainbow Obsidian

Struggle, iron-willed, inflexible, over-striving beyond limits.
Oak- Surrender and feel safe and supported. Flexibility.
LET GO AND TRUST, SACRED UNION, BLUE LACE AGATE
I am Generosity, Blue Aventurine

Mental and physical exhaustion.
Olive- Regeneration, stamina, revitalization- tapping into our inner source.
ETERNAL YOUTH, STRENGTH AND CHI, INOCENCIA COCA, ALEXANDRITE
My Passion, Sweet New Beginnings, Emerald, Green Aventurine

Self-critical. Guilt complex. Self-blame.

Pine- Self-acceptance, forgiveness, responsibility (ability to respond). Healthy emotional patterns and self-confidence.

FORGIVING, DIVINE GODDESS, RHODOCHROSITE, GREEN CAT'S EYE

Master Teacher, About Face, Freedom/Libertad, One Heart, Rose Quartz, Mother of Pearl

Obsessed with others' problems. Projecting angst. Worry.

Red Chestnut- Recognize our greater identity and speak our own truth. Inner sensitivity, inner connection with others and positive thinking.

ZEAL POINT CHAKRA, FREEDOM/LIBERTAD, YELLOW CAT'S EYE

Let Go and Trust, Be Nurtured, Otter Delight

Terror, panic. Sudden alarm. Hysteria.

Rock Rose- Transcendence. Courage, valor, fortitude. Self-reliance.

BALANCE AND STABILITY

Integration, Bushilla, Faith and Courage, Deep Breath, Ametrine, Snowflake Obsidian

Rigid. Self-denial. Extreme self-discipline. Structure.

Rock Water- Broad outlook. Balanced discipline with ourselves - Flexibility, spontaneity and receptivity.

ANCIENT WISDOM, AWAKENED THYMUS, SNOWFLAKE OBSIDIAN

Chaska, Orange Spinel

Uncertainty, vacillation, instability.

Scleranthus- For certainty and inner knowing, and ability to make clear decisions. Achieving a balance point in all areas of our lives.

BALANCE AND STABILITY, TEKTITE

Strength and Chi, Sublime Chocolate, Inner Guru, Male Strength, Solar Power, Creation/Focus

Shock and trauma, past and present.

Star of Bethlehem- Inner peace and soothing healing qualities.

HIGH FREQUENCY, MOTHER OF PEARL

Balance and Stability, Be Nurtured, Initiation of the HeartLight, Green Fluorite

Anguish, desolation, despair. Dark night of the soul.
Sweet Chestnut- Deep courage. Trusting the spiritual world, peaceful transformation, conscious evolution. Light night of the soul. Moving beyond boundaries.
FAITH AND COURAGE, I AM GRATITUDE, PURPLE RAINBOW FLUORITE
Nature Communion, Divine Goddess, Graceful Shift, High Frequency

Fervent enthusiasm, fanatical.
Vervain- Balance, moderation, grounded idealism, universal will.
BALANCE AND STABILITY, SACRED UNION, OPAL
Dance, Freedom/Libertad, Yellow Cat's Eye, Moldavite

Dominating, arrogant, inflexible, demanding.
Vine- Loving, flexible, tolerant, wise teacher, leader. Selfless service.
MASTER TEACHER, ONE HEART, GOD/GODDESS UNITY, YELLOW SAPPHIRE
One Heart, Be Nurtured, Initiation of the HeartLight, Marble

Overly influenced by outside forces. Bound by old thought patterns.
Walnut- Freedom to follow our own unique direction, break out of boxes, clearly hear our own inner voice.
FREEDOM, INNER GURU, PREHNITE, PURPLE SPINEL
Emancipation, Open Mind/Future Vision, Faith and Courage, Lepidolite, Blue Topaz, Alexandrite

Distant, self-reliant, aloof, alone.
Water Violet- Connectedness, social communion, sharing one's gifts with others.
SOUL FAMILY, OTTER DELIGHT, BLUE CHALCEDONY
Initiation of the HeartLight, I am Generosity, Mango, Blue Apatite, Yellow Chalcedony, God/Goddess Unity

Unwanted, unnecessary, repetitive thoughts. Mental chatter.
White Chestnut- Peaceful, serene, positive thoughts. Clarity and inner calm. Quiet mind. Creative, intuitive faculties.
GOLD + SILVER/WHITE CHAKRA, YELLOW FLUORITE
Freedom, Inner Guru, Balance and Stability, Faith and Courage, Ametrine

Lack of direction or commitment. Unfulfilled. Seeking purpose.
Wild Oak- Definite and purposeful life direction.
Right Livelihood.
ANCIENT WISDOM, MALACHITE
I Remember, Inner Guru, Open Mind/Future Vision, My Passion, Creation/Focus, Inner Guru, Lepidolite, Diamond

Resignation. Apathy. Lack of Hope. Giving up on life.
Wild Rose- Positive and involved. Vitality, spirit of joy and adventure. Creative power.
ETERNAL YOUTH, MANGO PARADISE, FIRE OPAL
Strength and Chi, Balance and Stability, Pure Joy, My Passion, Dance, Nature Communion, I am Gratitude, Howlite

Resentment, bitterness, dissatisfied. A victim.
Willow- Accept responsibility - Create a positive reality.
I AM GRATITUDE, MY PASSION, GOLD + SILVER / WHITE CHAKRA
Divine Goddess, ForGiving, Sweet New Beginnings, Rose Quartz

Emergency, Trauma, Accidents, Emotional upsets, panic, disorientation
Rescue Remedy- restores peace, balance, inner calm.
BALANCE AND STABILITY

Information compiled from:
Julian and Martine Barnard - *The Healing Herbs of Edward Bach*
Richard Katz and Patricia Kaminsky FES
Qualities of the Bach Flower Essences, by Suzanne Garden
Yona, Kisha and Jem, our illustrious office staff,
SuRay Raycraft- Star Essence Master Teacher, and numerous other practitioners
An ongoing project/work in progress, subject to additions and changes...
Star Riparetti- 2003

Flower Names - Alphabetical

Peruvian and Santa Barbara Flowers

Acacia	For Giving – Santa Barbara
Agave	Male Strength – Santa Barbara
Banana Flowers	God/Goddess Unity – Santa Barbara
Bougainvilla	Dance – Santa Barbara
Bushilla	Bushilla – Peru
Cacao	Sublime Chocolate – Peru
Cantu	13th Gate – Peru
Ceanothus, Blue	Soul Family – Santa Barbara
Ceanothus, White	Be Nurtured – Santa Barbara
Chijchipa	I Am Generosity – Peru
Chiri Sanango	Master Teacher – Peru
Coca	Inocencia Coca – Peru
Dandelion (Peru)	About Face – Peru
Eucalyptus	Deep Breath – Santa Barbara
Fava	Strength and Chi – Peru
Fennel	Graceful Shift – Santa Barbara
Jacaranda	Creation/Focus – Santa Barbara
Jasmine, Pink	Sweet New Beginnings – Santa Barbara
Lavender	Full Moon – Santa Barbara
Lotus, Pink	Initiation of the HeartLight – Santa Barbara
Mango	Mango Paradise – Peru
Mugwort	Open Mind/Future Vision – Santa Barbara
Muña *(Andean Mint)*	Purification – Peru
Mustard, Peruvian *(Yuyu)*	I Am Gratitude – Peru
Mutuy	Integration – Peru
Orange Blossom	Pure Joy – Santa Barbara
Oregano	Let Go and Trust – Santa Barbara

Oxalis	Early Bloomer – Santa Barbara
Passion Flower	My Passion – Santa Barbara
Pepper Tree, California	Light Navigator – Santa Barbara
Plantain	Magic Healer – Santa Barbara
Potato, Wild	Wild Feminine – Peru
Rosemary	I Remember – Santa Barbara
Sage, Purple	Inner Guru – Santa Barbara
Sunflower	Solar Power – Santa Barbara
Tobacco Flower	Emancipation – Santa Barbara
Zinnia	Zania – Santa Barbara

Andean Orchids

Epidendrum Cuscoense	One Heart
Epidendrum F. Guillemi	Zeal Point-Magenta – (Higher Chakra Trilogy)
Epidendrum Ibaguense	Eternal Youth
Erythrodes	Awakened Thymus –(Higher Chakra Trilogy)
Habenaria	Balance & Stability
Lycaste Longepetalia	Ancient Wisdom
Masdevallia Veitchianna	Divine Goddess
Maxillaria	Sacred Union
Odontoglossum	Faith & Courage
Pleurothallis	High Frequency
Ponthieva Montana	Divine Child
Sobralia Dichotoma	Anchoring Light
Sobralia Setigera	Gold + Silver / White – (Higher Chakra Trilogy)
Trichoceros Parviflorum	Nature Communion
Xylobium W/24K Gold	Freedom/Libertad

Gem Essences

* indicates Chakra Essences

Agate - Blue Lace
Agate - White
Agate - Yellow
Alexandrite (crystals)
Amazonite
Amethyst*
Ametrine
Apatite - Blue
Apatite - Bluegreen
Apatite - Green
Apatite - Yellow
Aquamarine*
Aventurine - Blue
Aventurine - Green
Aventurine - Light Green
Aventurine - Peach
Azurite
Bloodstone
Carnelian*
Cat's Eye - Green (Chrysoberyl)
Cat's Eye - Yellow (Chrysoberyl)
Chalcedony - Blue
Chalcedony - Yellow
Charoite
Chrysocolla
Chrysoprase
Citrine*
Coral - Red
Coral - Pink
Coral - White
Diamond
Emerald*
Fire Opal
Fluorite - Blue
Fluorite - Green
Fluorite - Purple Rainbow
Fluorite - Yellow
Heliodor
Hessonite
Howlite
Indigo*
Iolite
Kyanite
Lapis Lazuli
Lavender
Lepidolite
Malachite
Marble - White
Moldavite
Moonstone
Mother of Pearl
Nephrite
Obsidian - Rainbow
Obsidian - Snowflake
Opal - Clear
Opalite

Pearl
Prehnite
Quartz* (Clear)
Quartz - Rose
Rhodochrosite
Rhodonite
Ruby*
Sapphire - Blue*
Sapphire - Green
Sapphire - Yellow*
Scapolite
Selenite
Sodalite
Spinel - Red
Spinel - Blue
Spinel - Clear
Spinel - Dark Pink
Spinel - Green
Spinel - Light Pink
Spinel - Orange
Spinel - Purple
Sugilite - Purple
Sugilite - Pink/purple
Tanzanite
Tektite
Topaz - Blue
Topaz - Imperial
Topaz - White*
Tourmaline - Dark Blue
Tourmaline - Green
Tourmaline - Light Blue
Tourmaline - Orange
Tourmaline - Pink*
Tourmaline - Purple
Tourmaline - Yellow
Tsavorite
Turquoise - Blue
Turquoise - Green
Unakite

Bibliography
Books and People I've Received Inspiration From

A Guide to the Bach Flower Remedies, by Julian Barnard - C.W. Daniels 1979

Applied Kinesiology, Volume I: Basic Procedures for Muscle Testing, by David S. Walther

(The) Awakening: Eternal Youth, Vibrant Health, Radiant Beauty, by Patricia Cota Robles - New Age Study of Humanity's Purpose 1993

Before... The Missing Records of Creation, the War in Orion, Lemuria and Atlantis, as told by the Master Merlin and Received by Bob Fickes - The Fulfillment Foundation 2001

Behaving as if the God in All Life Mattered, by Machaelle Small Wright - Perelandra 1983

(The) Book of Chakra Healing, by Liz Simpson - Gaia Books Limited 1999

(The) Christ Diet, by Charles J. Hunt III - Heartquake Publishing 1992

Co-Creative Science, by Machaelle Small Wright - Perelandra 1997

Colourpuncture: A New Medicine of Light, by Jack Allanach - Element Books, 1997

Conscious Eating, by Gabriel Cousens, M.D. - Vision Books International 1992

Crystal Enlightenment, by Katrina Raphael - Aurora Press 1985

11:11 Inside the Doorway, by Solara - Star-Bourne Unlimited 1993

Energy Medicine, by Donna Eden - Jeremy P. Tarcher/Putnam 1998

Essene Gospel of Peace, translated by Edmond Bordeaus Szekely 1937

Flower Essences: Reordering our Understanding and Approach to Illness and Health, by Machaelle Small Wright - Perelandra 1997

Flowers That Heal, by Patricia Kaminsky - Newleaf 1998

Flower Essences and Vibrational Healing, by Gurudas -Cassandra Press 1983

Gem Elixirs and Vibrational Healing, by Gurudas - Cassandra Press 1989

Gemisphere Luminary, by Michael Katz - Gemisphere 1994

(The) Gnosis and the Law, by Tellis S. Papastavro -Balkow Printing Co. 1972

Heal Thyself, by Edward Bach, M.D. - Keats Publishing 1931

Heal Your Body, by Elizabeth Hay, Hay House 1988

(The) Healer Within, by Dr. Roger Jahnke - Harper 1997

Healing Mudras: Yoga for Your Hands, by Sabrina Mesco - Ballantine 2000

(The) Healing Tones of Crystal Bowls, by Renee Brodie - Aroma Art Ltd. 1996

Heart of the Christos, by Barbara Hand Clow - Bear & Co. 1989

How to Heal with Color, by Ted Andrews - Llewellyn Publications 1992

How to Live Large on a Small Planet, by Solara - Star-Bourne Unlimited 1996

Letter to Earth: Who We Are Becoming...What We Need to Know, by Elia Wise - Harmony Books 2000

(The) Little Book of Pendulum Magic, by D.J. Conway - the Crossing Press

Love is in the Earth, by Melody - Earth-Love Publishing House 1991

Messages From Water, by Masaru Emoto - pub. HADO Kyoikusha Japan 1999

Paracelsus: His Mystical and Medical Philosophy, by Manly P. Hall

(The) Pleiadean Agenda, by Barbara Hand Clow - Bear & Co. 1965

Seasalt's Hidden Powers, by Jacques de Langre, Ph.D. - Happiness Press 1994

Seventeen Ways to Eat a Mango, by Joshua Kadison

Soul Bodies, by Chris Griscom - Light Institute Press 1996

Stone Power, by Dorothee L. Mella - Warner Books 1986

Stones Alive, by Twintrees - Treehouse Press 1999

(The) Sunfood Diet Success System, by David Wolfe - Maul Bros. Pub. 1999

Unveiled Mysteries (Original), by Godfre Ray King - St. Germain Press 1982

Vibrational Medicine: New Choices for Healing Ourselves, by Richard Gerber, M.D. - Bear and Co. 1988

Vibrational Medicine For the 21st Century, by Richard Gerber, M.D. - HarperCollins 2000

You Can Heal Your Life, by Louise Hay - Hay House, 1984

Your Body Doesn't Lie, by Dr. George Goodheart - Warner Books 1979

Your Time is at Hand, by Patricia Cota Robles - New Age Study of Humanity's Purpose 1992

People and Websites to Know:

Conscious Languaging: the Mastery of Language, by Robert Tennyson Stevens - Copyright, Mastery Systems Corp. 2001

Mastery Systems - 1000 Howard Gap Rd., Hendersonville, NC 28792
(828) 698-7800 fax (828) 698-7888
emastery@aol.com www.masterysystems.com

Stephen Longfellow Fiske - www.fiskemusic.com
"Earth Anthem" from self-titled tape.

Solara's Website www.nvisible.com A vast, wondrous website where the Invisible is made visible. The latest information on the 11:11, Solara, being Real and living our Love during this powerful time of transformation.

Swami Beyondananda: www.wakeuplaughing.com

Patricia Cota Robles - New Age Study of Humanity's Purpose -
(520) 885-7909 P.O. Box 41883, Tucson, Ariz. 85717
(She has an awesome newsletter which I highly recommend - called "Take Charge of Your Life.")

PattiCR@aol.com www.1spirit.com/eraofpeace - Era of Peace

A website with sacred geometry information:
www.soulinvitation.com/indexdw.html

Tools for Transformation - www.tools4transformation.net - Virendra and Sia
(our Gemstone connection)

Messages From Water www.wellnessgoods.com/message.asp
Excerpts & photos from the book

Pamela Oslie: www.auracolors.com

Lucky Sweeney, Astrologer - 3905 State St., Suite 7, Santa Barbara, CA 93105 (805) 884-1531 coachlucky@aol.com

Peace Pole Project - Danielle Sato, 3554 Chama Ave., Las Vegas, NV 89121 (702) 736-0902 dksato@msn.com

Dr. Margarita Carman, D.C. - 1319 Garden St., San Luis Obispo, CA 93401 (805) 541-5736 drmargaret@juno.com

Tim Tupper, D.C. - 1911 De La Vina St., Ste. D, Santa Barbara, CA 93101 (805) 687-7733

Oceanna (Artist) (805) 331-1331

INDEX

H

I

N

O

P

Q

R

S

W

X

Y

Z

An Addendum: Whale Time

3/03

Just as this book is ready to go to the printer, a new essence is created - and it wants to be in the book, even though it won't get a page number... I amO excited. Through a series of magic and miracles, I was on a boat returning from a fantastic three-day trip with seven awesome women, including my daughter, to Santa Cruz Island. As soon as I heard about the trip, the **WHALE** started coming into my consciousness. Just in case, I packed a bucket and a bottle.

We had a glorious weekend on the island communing with Nature- and on Sunday, they even opened up the chapel on the island for us so we could say some prayers there for world peace. The energy in the chapel was super-powerful - and I went right out into a deep meditation. I remained partially in that altered state for the rest of the afternoon. Our return home was a perfect day for making the essence, as I was in a wonderful, connected, relaxed, meditative state.

On the boat I had my bucket and rope and bottle ready. With the Sun in Pisces, it would be a great time to be surrounded by water. As divine perfection would have it - we saw one awesome **WHALE**. The captain described him as an old guy who had really been around. He was pretty far away when he was first spotted, and I was wondering how we would ever get close enough for us to get the water right around him that I wanted to get. The captain was surprised at the behavior of the **WHALE**. It came way out of the water and opened its mouth. The captain was saying, wow - the **WHALE** smiled at us. Then somehow, quite perfectly, we were on the right side of the boat at the perfect moment (oh how usual) to get water right from the whale's footprint- after it dove down. We dipped the bucket into the footprint and got the whale water. I got SO excited. I know the **WHALE** presented a gift.

Going home on the freeway, I saw a sign saying "milagro" (miracle in Spanish), then shortly after, there was a BILLBOARD - advertising - a **Celebration of WHALES**. I love it! I do love getting confirmation signs. They are continuing to come. **I AM SO GRATEFUL !!!!**

WHALES are record keepers for all eternity. There are treaties around the world to protect them- signed by hundreds of countries- even ones that have no water. Humanity knows, on a deep cellular level, that the **WHALES** carry a vast amount of knowledge. They are the record keepers of the Earth.

Some very important knowledge that they carry is the knowledge of how to change the past.

This essence, this gift from the grandfather Gray Whale passing through the Santa Barbara Channel, has many levels of attributes. One very important one is to help us to **RECREATE OUR PAST.** To make PEACE in our own hearts, and in the heart of the planet, it will be much easier if we change history- and we can. We, being the microcosm of the macrocosm, must have **PEACE AND HARMONY IN OUR OWN HEARTS** in order to have **PEACE AND HARMONY ON THE PLANET**.

Begin to remember your past differently- you can remember a happy marriage, a happy childhood, etc. From there begin to remember happy peaceful harmonious times for others and for the planet- REGARDLESS of what you may have been taught to remember in the past.

The **WHALE TIME** essence can support you in this activity.

Another quality of the **WHALE ESSENCE** is to teach us how to save ourselves from extinction (the whales have brought themselves back from the brink of extinction, twice).

The **WHALE** can teach us to listen. Interestingly- I picked up a shell on the beach that was calling me. It was shaped like an ear. It was telling me to listen. This essence will assist our hearing.

The **WHALE ESSENCE** will help us to know the destiny that is coded in our DNA- this helps us to know the significance of our life. And it is a navigation tool.

The whales (as well as the dolphins) know how to work with the new children on Earth. The indigo children. The crystal children. The children that are here to help guide us into our golden future. They bring the potential for **PEACE AND HARMONY** on our planet. This essence will support and promote our connection with these children. It will also support the children in their work, their missions.

I'm sure that is only the beginning of the attributes and gifts of this essence, as with all of the essences. Dive deeper.

A Whale Tale. What a nice conclusion for this book. And we know it's only the beginning. There are no previews for the coming attractions.

WHERE TO GET THE *Star Essences* and **Rose Colored Maras Salt** and **Gonzalo prints** and the Star Pocket Oracle, and find out about trips to **PERU** and *Star Essence* **Certification Courses:**

Star Essence

312 W. Yanonali Street

Santa Barbara, California 93101

e-mail bliss@staressence.com

www.staressence.com

Phone/fax (805) 965-1619

Toll-free (888) 277-4955

Please contact us. We would love to send you a catalog.

We also send out an e-mail newsletter every month or so. If you would like the up-to-the-minute news, e-mail us your e-mail address. We send one out by regular post every year or two, maybe. For that, give us your mailing address.

We would love to hear from you, with your questions, comments, praise, testimonials and things of that nature.

Bliss and Blessings